The *The* **MIGRATION** *of* **BIRDS**

The MIGRATION of BIRDS

Seasons on the Wing

Janice M. Hughes

FIREFLY BOOKS

To my husband Ron and my daughter Eliana,
who lighten my journey from the first word to the last.

A FIREFLY BOOK

Published by Firefly Books Ltd. 2009

First printing

Publisher Cataloging-in-Publication Data (U.S.)
Hughes, Janice M.
The migration of birds : seasons on the wing / Janice M. Hughes.
[208] p. : col. photos. ; cm.
Includes bibliographical references and index.
Summary: An all-encompassing look at the science and phenomenon of bird migration, featuring species from around the world. Topics examined include history, evolution, anatomy, flight, technique and current issues.
ISBN-13: 978-1-55407-432-7
ISBN-10: 1-55407-432-0
1. Birds — Migration. I. Title.
598.1568 dc22   QL698.9.H84 2009

Library and Archives Canada Cataloguing in Publication
Hughes, Janice M. (Janice Maryan), 1958-
The migration of birds : seasons on the wing / Janice M. Hughes.
Includes bibliographical references and index.
ISBN-13: 978-1-55407-432-7
ISBN-10: 1-55407-432-0
1. Birds—Migration. I. Title.
QL698.9 H83 2009   598.156'8   C2009-900778-9

Published in the United States by
Firefly Books (U.S.) Inc.
P.O. Box 1338, Ellicott Station
Buffalo, New York 14205

Published in Canada by
Firefly Books Ltd.
66 Leek Crescent
Richmond Hill, Ontario L4B 1H1

Interior design and maps: Kathe Gray Design
Cover design: Erin R. Holmes / Soplari Design
Illustrations: Wendy Schroder, except pages 59 and 108 by Kathe Gray

PHOTO, PAGES 2–3: Many sandhill cranes (*Grus canadensis*) migrate thousands of miles from arctic and subarctic breeding grounds in Alaska, Siberia and western Canada to winter on the playa lakes of the southwestern United States and northern Mexico.

PHOTO, PAGE 4: Tundra swans (*Cygnus columbianus*) were once called "whistling swans" because of the sound made by their slow, powerful wingbeats.

PHOTO, PAGE 194: Wetland habitats are among those most critically imperiled by global climate change, yet they are essential roosting and feeding locations for countless migratory birds.

Printed in China

The publisher gratefully acknowledges the financial support for our publishing program by the Government of Canada through the Book Publishing Industry Development Program.

CONTENTS

INTRODUCTION

Bird migration is the world's only true unifying natural phenomenon, stitching the continents together in a way that even the great weather systems fail to do.

SCOTT WEIDENSAUL

Animals move from place to place. In fact, old school text books herald mobility as a singular defining feature of animals, one that consistently sets them apart from our other earthly colleagues, the plants. Although branches may sway in the breeze and twigs may turn toward the sun or stretch out tiny tendrils to grasp a support, we do not consider plants to be mobile. Plants colonize the reaches of our planet only through dispersal, by sending the next generation farther afield than the previous one. Animals, on the other hand, move regularly to find food or mates, to escape from predators or to find a sanctuary for rest or shelter. Sometimes animals move for apparently no reason at all.

Certainly not all animal movement is migration. So where do we set the boundaries of our definition? We will find that they encompass both direction and purpose. And for the animals that do migrate, that purpose is so deeply entrenched in their being that it has allowed evolution to mold every aspect of their anatomy, physiology, ecology and behavior.

About 97 percent of the world's elegant terns (*Sterna elegans*) breed in dense colonies on Isla Rasa in the Sea of Cortez, then migrate south along the western coast of South America to spend the winter.

Animal migration entails a two-way journey between places that differ significantly in the resources they offer. There must be a distinct advantage to the voyage, because costs are undoubtedly incurred in getting there. Moreover, migration usually occurs in a fixed direction and is associated with a predictable cycle. We are most familiar with seasonal migration, a widespread phenomenon marked by an exodus of animals in autumn. What comes to mind most readily in this regard is latitudinal migration. As the seasons change, many Northern Hemisphere animals travel south; likewise, those in the Southern Hemisphere may journey north. But migration can also occur longitudinally or vertically, particularly among creatures in the world's oceans, and altitudinally, as animals move up and down mountainsides to take advantage of diverse resources at different elevations. Patchy resources may have causes other than climate, and animals migrate for those reasons as well.

Many thousands of animal species migrate. Among them are insects, fishes, frogs, reptiles, birds and mammals—representatives of every class of vertebrate, and many invertebrates as well. But birds stand out among them as the very essence of migration. Why? Because among all these creatures, only birds exhibit such a striking union of two characteristics: flight and endothermy, or "warm-bloodedness."

Studies of animals that migrate on foot, by swimming or on the wing clearly demonstrate that these modes of travel differ considerably in speed and energy consumption. Flight may be energetically expensive, but it can yield the fastest speed over land. In addition, flight allows passage over barriers that may restrict the movements of other animals. Walking, on the other hand, may consume less energy than flight but it sacrifices speed, and thus distance.

Among terrestrial mammals, woodland caribou (*Rangifer tarandus*), which migrate seasonally about 800 miles (1,300 km) between their forested winter home and spring calving areas on the tundra, travel the farthest. Endothermic animals like caribou are able to sustain a moderate pace because they can maintain the high rate of metabolism needed to fuel their activities. Terrestrial ectothermic, or "cold-blooded," animals such as frogs and snakes, on the other hand, barely migrate at all. Ectotherms use their environment to raise their body temperature enough to pursue their daily routines; their greatest sacrifice is endurance. This primary limitation-by-design restricts the lowly striped whipsnake (*Masticophis taeniatus*) to migratory journeys of no more than about 2.5 miles (4 km). The European pool frog (*Rana lessonae*) fares slightly better by hopping; its migratory voyage between overwintering sites and breeding ponds measures an extremely dangerous

Although flight is an energetically expensive means of locomotion, particularly for large birds such as Canada geese (*Branta canadensis*), it yields the fastest speed over ground, thus making it ideal for long-distance travel.

9 miles (15 km). This is in no way intended to malign ectothermy, nor to imply that endothermy is an inherently better strategy. After all, ectotherms have certain advantages: some hibernating toads can exist quite comfortably without food for three years or more.

Endothermy is the preferred metabolic mode for migration on land, but it may not be so critical under water. Indeed, gray whales (*Eschrichtius robustus*)—which are endothermic mammals, of course—travel about 5,100 miles (8,200 km) between their rich northern feeding waters and their calving grounds off the coast of Mexico's Baja California peninsula. However, female loggerhead sea turtles (*Caretta caretta*), which are ectothermic reptiles, migrate farther—some 7,150 miles (11,500 km)—as they return to their traditional sandy beaches every two to four years to lay their eggs. Even a few fish species, such as the European eel (*Anguilla anguilla*) and bluefin tuna (*Thunnus thynnus*), are capable of migrations of many thousands of miles over an extended period of time. Unlike terrestrial animals, of course, aquatic animals are suspended in a buoyant medium, which makes swimming quite cost-effective. But speed is still a major consideration for most species.

Time is of the essence in migration. The journey itself serves only to move the animal from one place to another, where it will linger until a change in the environment stimulates a return trip. A voyage that takes too much of a species' annual cycle is not practical unless the travel is no more

In Antarctica, emperor penguins walk 60 miles (100 km) or more across the ice between their inland breeding colonies and their ocean feeding grounds.

hazardous than the destination, and this is rarely the case. Consequently, swimming and walking are usually too slow for most species to feasibly make round trips of 6,000 miles (10,000 km) or more. And most of those longer trips, including the reproductive migrations of sea turtles, are not accomplished every calendar year. Speed of travel is key, and this, of course, brings up the issue of flight.

Under favorable conditions, flight can be very swift—perhaps 10 to 20 times or more faster than swimming or walking. For example, a 600-mile (1,000 km) journey that would take a large flying bird only a single day would require about 40 days for a swimming penguin to complete. A small terrestrial mammal would need most of the winter to make such a long voyage. Considering the distances birds cover over ground, flight is truly the most effective mode. The ruddy turnstone (*Arenaria interpres*), a small shorebird, can fly about 125 miles (200 km) on a single gram of fat. Emperor penguins (*Aptenodytes forsteri*), which walk across the ice on the first leg of their journey from breeding grounds to feeding grounds, use about 1,500 times as much energy to cover the same distance. That is why long-distance migration is most pervasive among the volant, or flying, animals—birds, bats and insects.

Among these species, birds triumph in their migratory feats. They are indeed the experts of long-distance travel. Perhaps this is because avian flight is not merely a strategy pasted onto the anatomy of a terrestrial creature. Birds are the very epitome of flight. Over the past 150 million years, every system in their bodies has been honed to increase lift and reduce drag, to maximize power and minimize weight. Their flapping wings drive them headlong through the slipstream, fueled by turbocharged respiratory and cardiovascular systems designed to deliver oxygen to their muscles at amazingly high rates. Even waste products are so swiftly removed from their bodies that birds do not suffer the muscle pain that haunts human athletes. Many species can beat their wings continuously for days without rest; for these travelers, the length of their journey is limited only by the size of our planet.

Birds also possess innate knowledge of where they are and where they are going—the ability to chart a course and navigate the route to its end. They have an undeniable sense of home and an unrelenting desire to return there. Passed down through evolutionary time from ancestral lineages, these tools have allowed birds to expand their distribution, reclaim lost populations and exploit a bounty of resources in faraway places. Almost 10,000 species strong, birds are second only to fishes in species numbers, and their innovations have ensured their success among the vertebrate classes.

Purportedly about 4,000 species of birds migrate, with songbirds, waterfowl, waders and shorebirds in the majority. The true number is difficult to tabulate, however, given the dynamic process of evolution. For sure, there are many long-distance migrants within the class Aves. There are also additional species whose transitory seasonal movements are hinting at the origins of migration; and there are others in the process of losing the behavior. Within some species, migrant and sedentary individuals coexist in a variegated tapestry of cost and benefit. These arrays of behaviors are only superficially confusing; indeed, such intermediate conditions are often the most enlightening as to how avian migration evolved in the first place.

Thomas Alerstam, a noted ornithologist, said that migration is the "central ecological factor, the heart, in the life of birds." Perhaps this is so, for there are many reasons why birds migrate, and many explanations for their astonishing abilities and feats of endurance. Some of the mysteries will be revealed among the pages of this book, but for now, perhaps it is enough to say that that birds travel because they must, they go because they wish to, and they journey because they can.

CHAPTER 1

BIRD MIGRATION
through HUMAN HISTORY

And there went forth a wind from the Lord, and brought
quails from the sea, and let them fall about the camp.

NUMBERS 11:31

Since the dawn of human understanding, we must have noted the seasonal passage of birds. It would be foolish to suggest that the earliest humans did not notice the great congregations of flocks at dawn or the silence of the forest in late autumn. And as our dependency on birds for their meat and feathers grew through the ages, we undoubtedly marked the places and times where their generous resources could be harvested. The first recorded acknowledgment of our interest in migratory birds appeared a mere five millennia ago, in the paintings and bas-relief carvings of the ancient Egyptians. These magnificent works clearly depicted flocks of ducks and geese, featuring a few migratory species such as greater white-fronted geese (*Anser albifrons*) and red-breasted geese (*Branta ruficollis*). The seasonal abundance of these species marked a time of plenty, and their images—which commonly adorned the tombs of nobles—were thought to guarantee a bountiful supply of food in the afterlife.

The Scriptures likewise overflow with references to migratory birds: "Doth the hawk fly by Thy wisdom and stretch her wings toward the south?" (Job 39:26); "The stork in the heavens knoweth her appointed

A tomb painting dating from about 1400 BCE shows Egyptian accountant Nebamun hunting migratory birds in the Nile River's fertile marshes.

time; and the turtledove, and the crane, and the swallow, observe the time of their coming" (Jeremiah 8:7). The immense flights of quails described in Numbers 11:31–32 and Exodus 16:13, which twice saved the Israelites from starvation in the wilderness, were undoubtedly flocks of *Coturnix coturnix* traveling between their nesting grounds in eastern Europe and western Asia and their winter homes in Africa. The Israelites made little effort to explain these "miracles" they had witnessed, save to be thankful for their bounty.

The Greek philosopher Aristotle (384–22 BCE), a student of Plato and teacher of Alexander the Great, may have been the first person to give the seasonal movements of birds due consideration. Among Aristotle's greatest works is his 10-volume *History of Animals,* in which he arranges and classifies more than 500 species of animals — including humans — in a hierarchical *scala naturae* ("ladder of life") based on their innate complexity and other aspects of their development and functional morphology, or form. Venerable avian biologist Erwin Stresemann later proclaimed, "Aristotle raised ornithology to the rank of a science." Indeed, the *History of Animals* contains references to about 140 species of birds, and the author's deep interest in their behavior and physiology ensured that migration is duly discussed.

Aristotle likens avian migration to human behavior. He notes that wealthier people often change their place of residence seasonally to pursue comfort in more equitable climes, and so do cranes, pelicans, swans, geese, doves and quails. He even knew where some of these species went: his descriptions of cranes migrating from the steppes of Scythia (near the Black Sea) to marshes at the headwaters of the Nile River undoubtedly refer to the seasonal movements of Eurasian cranes (*Grus grus*). He also recounts cases of altitudinal migration, in which species migrate downslope in winter to warmer elevations near sea level, and then retreat to higher in the mountains with the coming of spring.

Aristotle was also the first to write that birds appear to be fatter before they migrate south in autumn, and "in better trim" when they arrive back on the breeding grounds the following spring. Though expressed in simpler terms, this statement reflects a fact of avian flight metabolism: migratory birds typically weigh less at the end of their journey because they have burned their body fat as fuel. How unfortunate that this particular observation was disregarded by naturalists for two millennia.

Despite these insights, Aristotle was also responsible for two more-or-less outrageous explanations for the seasonal movements of birds from his Greek homeland. Regrettably, these scientific errors persisted through the centuries, repeated by numerous other authors perhaps because of the respect he had garnered from his many other contributions to classical knowledge. For

Aristotle postulated that summering common redstarts (shown here) transmuted into similarly plumaged European robins in winter.

example, Aristotle was a devoted proponent of the theory of transmutation: the belief that one species was capable of changing into another. He noted that groups of similarly sized birds seemed to disappear and then reappear almost at once. It was obvious to him that redstarts (*Phoenicurus phoenicurus*), which are ubiquitous breeding birds in Greece, became robins (*Erithacus rubecula*) in winter (robins are well-known winter visitors in that country). Likewise, summer garden warblers (*Sylvia borin*) changed into winter black-caps (*S. atricapilla*).

Aristotle's beliefs in this regard were only strengthened when he observed these birds in mid-"transformation"—when their plumage coloration displayed the attributes of both species. He was likely seeing the summering birds in the midst of prebasic molt: when many species trade their bright nuptial plumage for more somber winter colors. Aristotle's "transmuting" species could also have been misidentified because of similarities in their actions or songs. It was perhaps only when we began to travel more widely and saw these species in their other seasonal homes that we realized transmutation was not the most likely explanation for their disappearance from the north.

Incredible as it sounds, bird-to-bird transformation was considerably more logical than another transmutation hypothesis that persisted through the Middle Ages. Following Aristotle's lead, some authors maintained that barnacle geese (*Branta leucopsis*) spent the summer months as gooseneck barnacles (*Pollicipes polymerus*)—crustaceans that adhere to rocks, shipping piers and flotsam in intertidal waters. Barnacle geese breed on arctic islands of the North Atlantic and are seen in the United Kingdom and northern Europe only in winter. According to myth, these birds did not build nests or lay eggs in summer. On the contrary, they were spawned by trees overhanging the water's edge, where they dangled from the branches by the tips of their bills.

A woodcut print dating from 1552 depicts barnacle geese spawning from trees overhanging the sea. According to the legend, these birds wintered in the guise of gooseneck barnacles attached to rocks and piers.

Once sufficiently grown, they would fall from the trees; those that flew free or landed safely on flotsam survived, while the rest were ripe for the taking by hungry observers.

In his 1186 publication *Topographia Hibernicae,* the Welsh monk Giraldus Cambrensis vividly described his observations as he "witnessed" the autumn transformation of barnacle to goose while he was traveling in Ireland.

> . . . they hang down by their beaks as if they were seaweed attached to the timber, and are surrounded by shells in order to grow more freely. Having thus in the process of time been clothed with a strong coat of feathers, they either fall into the water or fly freely away into the air . . . I have frequently seen, with my own eyes, more than a thousand of these small birds, hanging down on the sea-shore from one piece of timber, enclosed in their shells and already formed.

The origin of this myth may have two explanations. First, these geese—being winter visitors—were never seen in summer, so it was reasonable to assume that they spent the off-season as something else. People with vivid imaginations would have no difficulty envisioning the black-and-white stalked barnacles as tiny, similarly colored geese. Second, the notion that barnacle geese were "born of the sea"—and perhaps spent some time in barnacle form later in life—allowed them to be classified as fish, not fowl. Thus it was acceptable to eat them during the fasting season of Lent, when consumption of animal flesh was otherwise prohibited. (Beavers were likewise categorized as fish in medieval Germany because of their aquatic tendencies and the shape of their tail.) Surely to the dismay of many Roman Catholics, the controversy was settled in 1215 when Pope Innocent III declared that barnacle geese are birds, regardless of their origins, and forbade his people to eat them during Lent. However, it would be five centuries more before scholars agreed that barnacle geese come into the world in the usual way.

It seems that Aristotle must also be credited with another migration fable, one that grew to have a life of its own and was surprisingly difficult to shake from scholarly literature for more than 20 centuries. This myth concerns swallows, small insectivorous songbirds that fly rapidly on swept-back wings. In Greece, five swallow species (family Hirundinidae)—all migratory—spend the nonbreeding season in the Middle East, Africa or southern Asia. Of course, Aristotle had never been to those locales to see them there, so he, and many great thinkers who came after him, determined that swallows must hibernate, spending their winter in a torpid (inactive) state hidden in crevices or holes in hollow trees. He claimed that naked swallows—for some unknown reason they had lost all their feathers—were frequently seen holed up for the winter.

Aristotle also suggested that kites might hibernate through the winter, and noted that they had been observed flying out from similar hiding places in spring. Kites are small to medium-sized, long-winged diurnal birds of prey that typically favor open grassland and woodland habitats; Greece is home to three species. Despite more reasonable explanations for his observations, Aristotle's theory took hold. British ornithologist Chris Mead suggests that Aristotle's denuded swallows could have been common swift (*Apus apus*) nestlings, which are about the same size as swallows, are featherless, and reside in crevices, hollows or holes. He adds that black kites (*Milvus migrans*), a migratory species that summers in Greece, sometimes seek shelter in cavities in early spring if the weather is still cool when they arrive on the breeding grounds. They typically leave their roosts around noon, once the day has warmed up. Nevertheless, the "hibernating swallow" legend would persist for millennia, while other classical intellects considered more troublesome species; in this case, the wicked cranes.

Gaius Plinius Secundus (23–79 CE), also known as Pliny the Elder, was a scholar, encyclopedist, military commander and legal advocate during the reign of the infamous (and incendiary) Roman emperor Nero. Pliny may also have been the most influential classical Roman author of natural history. His most famed work, the 37-volume *Historia naturalis* (*Natural History*), was published in 77 CE, about four centuries after the works of Aristotle. Pliny the Elder has since been criticized for simply retelling the tales of earlier authors, and for his preference for filling his volumes with descriptions of the curious and anomalous.

Indeed, Pliny does discuss much of what Aristotle wrote regarding bird migration. He also supplies additional information on the seasonal movements of storks—noting that they stage in flocks at predictable locations before departure—geese, blackbirds, thrushes, starlings and other species. He describes how some songbirds adopt different-colored plumage for winter, and that their songs often become less melodious then. Pliny the Elder's particular interest in the bizarre is well demonstrated in his writings. Within the chapters of *Historia naturalis* are vivid descriptions of cannibalistic migratory swans, nocturnal quails that alight on ships and send them to the bottom of the ocean, and a raven that learned to talk with such eloquence that it would greet Emperor Tiberius and his relatives Germanicus and Drusus by name.

Among Pliny's most unusual stories is a retelling of a tale of crane migration that may have originated in the *Iliad,* one of two epic poems from eighth-century BCE Greece that are traditionally attributed to Homer. The *Iliad* describes a few weeks in the final year of the Trojan War, which was waged between Troy and Sparta somewhere deep in Greek mythological time. In his poem, Homer likened the advancing Trojan army to a flight of shrieking cranes being driven south by the cold rains of oncoming winter. Apparently the cranes would continue their flight "off to the world's end, bringing death and doom to the Pygmy-men as they open fierce battle at dawn." Thus, according to both Homer and Pliny the Elder, Eurasian cranes spend their winter in the south waging war on the locals.

Pliny paints an extraordinary picture of "pygmies" fighting the cranes: in solidarity they march down to meet them heroically at the seashore, mounted on the backs of rams and nanny-goats and armed with arrows. However, the cranes are well prepared for battle; it is said that they are in great accord with one another, having appointed a leader, with others stationed in the rear to shout orders ahead—thus the purported derivation of the Latin verb *congruere,* "to agree" or "to coincide," from *grus,* meaning "crane." Pliny the Elder also explains that crane sentries hold a stone in their uplifted claw all night, so if drowsiness overtakes them, the stone will drop and alert others standing nearby. And so, at the very ends of the earth, the battle continues for three months every year. It is only by devouring the eggs and chicks of the enemy that the pygmies are able to survive the terrible avian onslaught.

Some authorities believe that this mythical war predates the writings of Homer and is derived from writings of the ancient Egyptians; others cite Asian or Arab sources. According to historian Alex Scobie of Victoria University in Wellington, New Zealand, similar versions of this fable occur in the oral traditions of four North American First Nations: the Cherokee, Nisga'a, Comox and Nisqually peoples. All tell of a host of men who are small in stature, fearful as they await the dreaded arrival of invasive flocks of large birds—the Cherokee fable specifically mentions cranes. Unfortunately

Many cultures recount legends of diminutive armies battling hordes of large migratory birds as illustrated in this 1555 woodcut of mythical dwarves fighting cranes in northern Sweden.

these four tales were not recorded until well into the 19th and early 20th centuries, so it is impossible to determine whether they were transmitted to the indigenous peoples by European settlers. Alternatively, the stories may have arrived when the first North Americans brought them over the Bering land bridge from central Asia, which would make them very ancient indeed.

Classical scholars had little else to say about bird migration, except perhaps to point out a few of Aristotle's errors. Marcus Tullius Cicero (106–43 BCE), for example, noted that birds flying in V-formation change position periodically as the lead bird falls back in the ranks. Aristotle had maintained that their position was fixed, based on hierarchical importance in the flock. Cicero erroneously embellished his descriptions by adding that tired birds rest their heads on the backs of individuals flying just ahead of them. Unfortunately, interest in such seemingly trivial matters as geese and their natural history vanished as the Middle Ages dawned in about the fifth century. Aristotle's writings, as well as the works of other classical thinkers, were plunged into oblivion, and all went quiet in the study of avian migration for more than 700 years.

The discipline of bird studies awoke once more with the fortunate appearance of history's first true ornithologist: Holy Roman Emperor Frederick II Hohenstaufen (1194–1250), king of Germany, Italy, Burgundy and Sicily, and also of Cyprus and Jerusalem for a brief time. Unlike his contemporaries, who continued to conform to the religious strictures of the Middle Ages, Frederick was an individualist, a "thinker" in the classical sense. He was apparently highly skeptical of many Christian beliefs and took some pride in mocking them publicly, often to the point of scandal. Frederick also

Written by King Frederick II Hohenstaufen between 1244 and 1250, *De arte venandi cum avibus* (*On the Art of Hunting with Birds*) is a notable ornithological text lavishly decorated with gold and silver.

spoke nine languages and was literate in seven. He was a patron of the arts and science, dispatching letters of enquiry to the world's scholars that posed difficult questions about mathematics, physics and philosophy. In 1224 he founded the University of Naples, one of the first chartered state institutions of higher education in Europe. Despite his overt opposition to the foundations of medieval culture, Frederick's peers bestowed upon him the title *Stupor Mundi* ("Wonder of the World") in honor of his accomplishments.

King Frederick was exceedingly interested in falconry, a noble pursuit that had apparently been brought to Sicily — where he lived most of his life — with the western migration of Saracens into Europe earlier in the medieval period. Frederick possessed a keen naturalist's eye, and he studied both his birds of prey and their quarry with great zeal. One tale recounts that the Mongolian ruler Genghis Khan sent a letter to Frederick requesting his "surrender"; the king replied facetiously that he would do so only if bestowed with the honor of being the Khan's premier falconer. Sometime between 1244 and 1250, King Frederick wrote *De arte venandi cum avibus* (*On the Art of Hunting with Birds*), now considered to be the first book devoted entirely to ornithology. This work was based on 30 years of the author's experiences with birds of prey and contains detailed guidelines on the care, training and use of hunting falcons that are still valid today. In addition, this lavishly decorated book includes writings on avian anatomy, feeding ecology, behavior, reproduction and flight.

Frederick's interest in bird migration was substantial. His book includes discussions of the types of birds that migrate and where to find them, why they migrate, where they go and when, even where they stop along the way. In general he attributed birds' seasonal movements to oncoming inclement weather and resulting shortages of food, but he was careful to note that differing tolerances of these conditions led to varying migratory strategies. For example, hardier species often traveled shorter distances, and species with particular food preferences might have to migrate farther in order to find them in abundance. He adds that tropical birds, not facing these challenges, do not migrate. Frederick also describes weather systems that affect avian migration, and how birds choose favorable winds for their passage.

Among the royal ornithologist's most noteworthy entries are passages that describe premigratory staging: "As summer wanes and winter approaches, both young and adults leave their breeding grounds and gather with their own kind…waiting, feeding, and preparing, for a day favorable to their long journey"; stopover sites: "Localities in which returning birds interrupt their journey are selected to meet specific needs"; and natal philopatry and territoriality: "The destination of most returning birds is their birthplace in the north. Furthermore, on their return to nest and brood, each species usually selects a region it occupied the previous year." He notes the urgency of spring migration—"Many birds take more time for their outward migration than for the return journey, when the vernal impulse to breed drives them on"—and adds that birds that migrate long distances must start their nests with great haste so their young are hardy enough to migrate south the following autumn.

It has been said that Frederick II spanned the gap between medieval and modern culture. His life, his beliefs and his *De arte venandi cum avibus* undoubtedly demonstrate this. Unlike those of his predecessors—and of the many scholars who came after him—Frederick's works did not descend into fanciful rhetoric, nor did they embrace folklore or whimsy. He acknowledged the classical teachings of scholars such as Aristotle, but was not burdened by their legacy. He searched for truth in natural processes and strived to explain his observations through rational consideration. How unfortunate that many of Frederick's accomplishments passed into obscurity after his death in 1250, his reputation a victim of the ecclesiastical regimes that would dominate Europe for a few hundred years more.

From a historical perspective, it is remarkable that Frederick II never considered the celebrated hibernating swallow. That pervasive hypothesis is entirely absent from his writings, despite his knowledge of Aristotle's *History of Animals*. Nevertheless, swallow hibernation had gained a firm foothold — with further embellishment, of course — during the years that passed since Aristotle. In the mid-16th century Olaus Magnus (1490–1557), Archbishop of Uppsala in Sweden, published *Historia de gentibus septentrionalis et natura* (*A Description of the Northern Peoples*). By then Aristotle's theories regarding swallows had become "fact," at least in the minds of most learned naturalists of the time.

In his book, Olaus describes in detail how the birds pass their winter beneath the waters of the sea, at the bottoms of lakes or immersed under the ice. As evidence, he cites that "in northern waters, fishermen oftentimes by chance draw up in their nets an abundance of Swallows, hanging together like a conglomerate mass." He commends experienced anglers who take their catch of fish but leave the birds to their chilly repose. These wise men knew that if the swallows were captured and taken to a warm place to thaw, they would wake up abruptly, fly around the room briefly and then perish. But how did the swallows get under the ice? Olaus provides a mechanism: they assemble in great numbers — perched toe to toe, bill to bill and wing to wing — in the reeds near the shore in autumn, and gradually sink beneath the water. *Historia de gentibus* contains a woodblock print from 1555, the year the book was published, that depicts two fishermen hoisting a net full of swallows from the bottom of a lake — readers could want no more evidence than that. This tome contains another illustration of note — one that shows a battalion of dwarves astride goats facing off against a flock of wicked cranes.

A handful of scholars opposed the hibernating-swallow hypothesis, which by this time had expanded to include a host of other avian species including storks, herons and parakeets. John Ray (1627–1705) was one such scholar. Ray was an English naturalist — sometimes referred to as the father of English natural history — who worked for a decade beside his student and patron Francis Willughby, an ornithologist and ichthyologist (expert on fishes) of

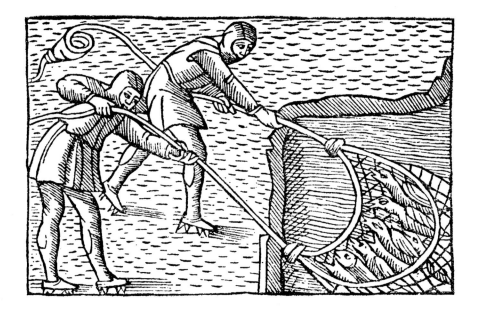

A 1555 woodcut from Olaus Magnus's *Description of the Northern Peoples* shows fishermen retrieving a net full of hibernating swallows from beneath a frozen lake.

some note. Upon Willughby's death in 1672, Ray continued to compile and edit their copious notes, publishing *The Ornithology of Francis Willughby of Middleton in the County of Warwick* in 1678. Among the pages of this book can be seen glimpses of modern ornithology. Ray and Willughby devised a means of classifying birds based on their anatomy — for example, bill and foot structure, body size — rather than on their "function," as had been done previously. Moreover, the authors refuse to entertain the notion of hibernating swallows: "To us it seems more probable that they fly away to hot countries, viz. Egypt, Aethiopia, etc. than that they lie in water under the ice." They also argue stridently and at length against the presumed association between barnacle geese and gooseneck barnacles, a belief that still persisted widely. Ray was generally suspicious of any accounts of apparent transmutation and spontaneous generation.

A few other contemporary naturalists were beginning to see the light regarding the seasonal movements of birds. For example, Baron Ferdinand von Pernau (1660–1731), perhaps the forerunner of modern behavioral ecology, suggested that the instinct to migrate was somehow predetermined by a "hidden drive at the right time" and was in no way either serendipitous or directly imposed by cold weather or acute hunger. This was all true, but were these arguments sufficient to quell the ridiculous? Perhaps not. Even amid these glimmers of light, a bizarre hypothesis emerged that for a time swayed reason and cast a shadow of doubt even over the ever-present hibernation explanation for the seasonal disappearance of birds. The title of the anonymous pamphlet was *An Essay Toward the Probable Solution of this Question: Whence come the Stork and the Turtledove, the Crane, and the Swallow, when they*

Know and Observe the Appointed Time of their Coming or Where the Birds do probably make their Recess and Abode which are absent from our Climate at some certain Times and Seasons of the Year. The "probable solution" explained that migratory birds flew to the moon, and that was where they spent their winter.

Heralded as the earliest English treatise on migration, this mysterious 50-page essay appeared in 1703 and was subsequently reprinted more than once in somewhat edited versions. The author was presented simply as "a Person of Learning and Piety" being published by the bookseller Samuel Crouch, "at the Corner of Pope's-Head-Alley, over against the Royal-Exchange." The work was originally attributed to the Honourable Francis Roberts, a 17th-century scholar who sat in the parliaments of Charles II and William III. (Roberts may also have been the first person to use the light-year as a measure of astronomical distances.) In 1928, however, ornithological bibliophile Sir Hugh S. Gladstone presented new evidence to the readers of *British Birds* as to the author of this notable piece. An 1811 version, published as *An Enquiry into the Physical and Literal Sense of that Scripture: Jeremiah VIII:7,* began with the inscription "Written by an eminent Professor, for the Use of his Scholars" and finished with the salutation "Your friend, C.M." According to Gladstone, "C.M." was Charles Morton (1627–98), a Puritan educator who emigrated to America in 1685 and later became vice president of Harvard University. Morton was also the author of a system of physics outlined in *Compendium Physicae,* a scholarly text used by both Harvard and Yale universities for almost five decades.

Morton's hypothesis about bird migration was certainly written while he resided in England. Unlike many of his contemporaries, he did not believe the popular notion that swallows hibernated underwater or in the mud below the seafloor. Rightly enough, he stated that these environs would be too cold for the birds in winter, that they would be unable to breathe once submerged, and finally, upon awakening, their feathers would be so ruined that they could not free themselves from their watery beds. But he could offer no other earthly explanation for their seasonal disappearance. Therefore, since birds neither hibernated in winter nor went anywhere they could be seen in sufficient numbers, they must fly to the moon. Morton did not come to this conclusion without due consideration. He reasoned that birds of passage could cover greater distances than other animals, such as fishes, because they were capable of flight. He also noted that travelers moving above the earth's surface would be less affected by gravitational forces and, since the thinner air would provide less resistance to movement, all the actions of a bird's wing would be translated into effortless forward motion; he concluded that the passage would be "swift and easy." Morton also assumed that the moon resembled the description suggested by the as-

tronomer Nicolaus Copernicus: composed of both dry land and water and enshrouded in a tolerable atmosphere.

Morton calculated a moon-bound voyage of about 60 days at flight speeds of approximately 125 miles (200 km) per hour. Energy to endure the flight would be supplied by the birds' onboard fat reserves. Fortunately for the travel-weary migrants, the last leg of their journey would be assisted by the gravitational pull of the moon. The two-month period had the added convenience of orienting the moon in more or less the same position relative to earth as at the time of departure (two lunar cycles having been completed). This allowed the birds the shortest possible straight-line journey between the two points.

Of course, Morton never considered the mechanics of lift-generating airfoils that require the structure to pass through substances such as air or water, which possess some inherent viscosity; nor did he acknowledge space as a vacuum bereft of breathable air. Nonetheless, given the scientific knowledge of his day, he had constructed a seemingly sound hypothesis to explain the phenomenon of avian migration. And, like many other Enlightenment thinkers, Morton got some things right, such as body fat being the source of in-flight fuel. As "modern" humans, we are often quick to criticize earlier beliefs, being reluctant to admit that scientific theory is built brick by brick; we stand on the shoulders of those who came before us. But perhaps it would be wise to concede that many "smarty-pants" 21st-century scientists will be ripe for ridicule in a hundred years or so. Morton's treatise on bird migration eventually fell into oblivion after it failed to convince the mainstream ornithological community, and once again, swallows hibernated beneath the water.

The next chapter in the migration saga was written by none other than the eminent Swedish botanist and zoologist Carolus Linnaeus (né Carl von Linné, 1707–78). He formalized the modern system of taxonomy and the concept of species, and is considered by some historians to be a founding father of ecological thought. Linnaeus certainly had no problem accepting the idea that birds migrated. Indeed, he published an extensive dissertation on the topic of Sweden's migratory birds called *Migrationes Avium (Bird Migration)* in 1757. In it he describes several significant migratory routes as well as stopover sites in southern Europe, along the shores of the Mediterranean Sea, and near Istanbul. He also contributes suggestions about wintering areas farther south in Africa.

For some reason, however, Linnaeus was convinced that swallows were not among these winged travelers. At the University of Uppsala, where he lectured, swallow hibernation was never questioned. For one thing, eyewitness accounts continued to pour in from learned people across Europe, although most of their "observations" were based entirely on hearsay evidence. Moreover, Linnaeus's beliefs were backed up wholeheartedly by some of the best minds in the business, including renowned French naturalists Georges Cuvier (1769–1832) and Georges-Louis Leclerc, Comte du Buffon (1707–88). Both believed the tales that swallows were being drawn up in huge torpid masses from beneath the ice.

In the concluding words of *Migrationes Avium,* Linnaeus proclaimed that "it would demand great effort, diligence and time by future generations spread over the world to solve the riddles of bird migration." Very true, and this being the Age of Enlightenment, when reason should triumph over folklore, empirical study of swallow hibernation began — at the cost of many poor swallows' lives. Among the principal investigators was British naturalist Gilbert White (1720–93). White adored swallows, and 20 years of letters to his scholarly colleagues express troubled thoughts about their winter behavior. He repeatedly paid schoolboys to look for hibernating swallows, but to no avail. The Comte du Buffon shut his swallows up in icehouses to see if they could be forced into hibernation. What he found was that birds that remained in the cold the longest died, and could not be revived even when exposed to the sun's warming rays. Other researchers covered hapless swallows with mud or submerged them in buckets of water. Of course, no one could induce spontaneous torpor in the experimental subjects, and the studies usually resulted in avian tragedy.

Although a compelling case was being made in favor of swallows' migrating, the old myths were not so easily abandoned. Devotees of the hibernating swallows theory lashed out viciously at those who sought the truth. Among their most rabid was Daines Barrington (1727–1800), an English lawyer, naturalist and fellow of the Royal Society. Barrington published a decidedly antimigration 61-page letter in the *Philosophical Transactions of the Royal Society* in 1772. He argued that Buffon's experiments were flawed for several reasons: it was too early in the year for the swallows to become torpid, or the birds had died because he did not feed them. He also chastised Buffon and others for their apparent inability to distinguish swallows from other types of birds. Michel Adanson, a French naturalist of some repute, returned from a trip to Senegal claiming to have observed European swallows there in late autumn. Barrington dismissed his observations by suggesting that Adanson was utterly unfamiliar with the swallows of Africa — hence, he could not have seen what he saw when he saw it.

Barrington's case in favor of swallow hibernation — and against any birds' migrating over large bodies of water — was based entirely on circumstantial evidence. For example, he reports one swallow captured by sailors far from shore that was "as wet as if it had just emerged from the bottom of the sea." In one paragraph he comments that swallows are rarely seen while submerged in the mud because it is their custom to remain hidden from predators and curious humans. Six pages later he adds that hibernating swallows are never reported by "common labourers, who have the best chance of finding torpid birds, [and] have scarcely any of them a doubt with regard to this point," because they are seen so often that such observations are not noteworthy. Perhaps Barrington's most compelling evidence to support swallow hibernation — at least in his own mind — was the "dignified testimony of Sigismond, King of Poland," who, under oath to Cardinal Gianfrancesco Commendon, declared that he had frequently seen swallows in the mud at the bottom of lakes. Despite the absurdity of Barrington's statements, his substantial letter coalesced a diverse band of followers — including Swedish botanist Pehr Kalm, Mexican scholar Francisco Saverio Clavigero, American historian Jeremy Belknap and Vermont naturalist Samuel Williams — and the controversy raged on into the 19th century.

The fundamental problem with the hibernating swallows issue was summed up by astronomer and naturalist Thomas Forster (1789–1860) at age 19, in his first publication, *Observations on the Brunal Retreat of the Swallow*. He writes that many previous authors "gave credit to the fabulous assertions of others, without examining into the truth of them." Forster's comments were timely, for they reflected the beginning of what eminent American ornithologist Donald Farner later called the "Period of Observation," a century of bird study in which accurate reports and reasonable implications began to emerge, despite being hampered by incorrect assumptions and preconceived ideas.

A contributor to the early days of this ornithological revolution was none other than famed artist, hunter and naturalist John James Audubon

A popular myth suggests that small birds such as ruby-throated hummingbirds — as depicted in this 1825 painting by John James Audubon — migrate by riding on the backs of geese and cranes.

(1785–1851). After emigrating from France in 1803, Audubon traveled extensively in the wilds of America with his gun and his paint box in search of birds to illustrate. He is best known for *Birds of America,* a substantial assemblage of hand-colored life-sized prints of his bird paintings, published between 1827 and 1838. Still touted as one of the greatest natural history books, a pristine copy of *Birds of America* sold at auction for almost $9 million in 2000, making it (as of 2007) the world's most expensive illustrated book. Despite his apparently true-to-nature representations of the birds—quite unlike the two-dimensional renditions by contemporaries such as Alexander Wilson—Audubon typically shot his subjects first and then fixed them into lifelike poses with wires before painting them.

Audubon kept detailed journals of his encounters with avian wildlife. Not long after his arrival in the United States, while living on the banks of Perkiomen Creek near Philadelphia, Audubon found a nest of eastern phoebes (*Sayornis phoebe*) in a cave. Just before the chicks fledged, he tied light silver threads around their legs to identify them if he encountered them later. When the phoebes returned to the creek the following year, he was pleased to find that the same individuals, still wearing their little rings, were now tending their own nests in the vicinity. Thus Audubon may have become the first North American bird-bander. Furthermore, his journal entries are among the first substantiated reports of migrating birds returning to their birthplace — known as natal philopatry — to breed as adults.

John James Audubon was not without his own legends. One describes how he shot a goose and, retrieving the dead bird, discovered a dazed hummingbird lying on the ground nearby. As the story goes, Audubon apparently assumed that the smaller bird had been migrating south by riding on the back of the larger, and had been knocked off when the goose plummeted from the sky. Whether Audubon actually said this remains unknown; however, the myth that small birds — which seem physically unequal to the rigors of migration — hitchhike on larger species has endured in both legend and academic literature for millennia. In northern Europe, cranes and owls were thought to transport corncrakes (*Crex crex*) and goldcrests (*Regulus regulus*). Farther south, many people believed that the small birds staging along the Mediterranean Sea were waiting for their ride to Africa. Several nations indigenous to North America, including the Crow and Cree peoples, tell stories of sandhill and whooping cranes carrying smaller birds such as hummingbirds.

Maybe humans simply cannot fathom the miraculous abilities of so-called lesser beings. Perhaps the idea of something as exquisitely fragile as a ruby-throated hummingbird (*Archilochus colubris*) navigating the Gulf of Mexico in one nonstop flight seems as ludicrous as hibernating swallows. Whatever the reason, we must admit that they can do something that we cannot. It has been estimated that the annual migration loop of the rufous hummingbird (*Selasphorus rufus*) measures 49 million of its own body-lengths, a feat equivalent to a human traveling more than 50,000 miles (80,000 km) — an awe-inspiring notion to say the least.

Likewise, the myths about swallows may have been easier to believe than the science behind the reality, and perhaps the power of consensus also gave these legends such persistence. Cornell University ornithologist Elsa Guerdrum Allen wrote in 1951, "Small wonder it is that the belief in the hibernation of swallows has so long endured, when persons of education and acumen would affix their names to such tales." Even the eminent 19th-century ornithologist Elliot Coues (1842–99), co-founder of the American Ornithologists' Union, could scarcely ignore the issue. In his 1878 book *Birds of the Colorado Valley*, Coues lists 182 publications dating back to 1630 that accept the possibility of swallow hibernation. Although Coues did not sanction the notion himself — he believed that insectivorous birds such as swallows needed to follow their food south once it failed in the northern winter—he was troubled by the sheer volume of supporting documentation. He writes, "I cannot consider the evidence as inadmissible, and must admit that the alleged facts are as well attested, according to ordinary rules of evidence, as any in ornithology." He adds eloquently that his readers have been presented with sufficient information to make up their own minds. Some myths die hard, even among well-respected ornithologists. Nevertheless, as the 19th century drew to a close, few ornithologists (if any) still upheld the notion of swallow hibernation. Swallows were by then assumed to migrate south in the autumn, and the case appeared to be more or less closed...well, maybe.

Twentieth-century bird study dawned in an age of scientific experimentation, which included numerous investigations of avian physiology and adaptation. Ornithologists soon discovered that many birds—such as chickadees, roadrunners, swallows and swifts—are able to lower their body temperature, becoming torpid, as a strategy to reduce cold stress and energy requirements on cold winter nights. These species became known as nocturnal hibernators. The Andean hillstar hummingbird (*Oreotrochilus estella*), which thrives at elevations between 12,500 and 14,000 feet (3,800–4,300 m), is an expert at nocturnal hibernation. Hummingbirds need to eat often to supply the substantial energy required for their hovering flight, but they cannot feed at night. So to stay alive, the hillstar seeks a safe roost in a cave, where it remains overnight in a state of torpor for seven to ten hours. Studies have demonstrated that these diminutive birds can drop their body temperature—normally about 105°F (40.5°C)—to about 40° to 50°F (5°–7°C). At morning's first light, they rev up their metabolic motors to reheat and leave their refuge in search of nectar-bearing flowers. Could these birds overwinter in such a state?

The Hopi peoples of the southern United States are familiar with a species they call *hölchko,* "the sleeping one." The name describes the common poorwill (*Phalaenoptilus nuttallii*), a short-tailed grayish nightjar (family Caprimulgidae) related to the whip-poor-will (*Caprimulgus vociferus*) that emits a haunting call at twilight. The Hopi name is disarmingly accurate: in December 1946, during a routine survey of avifauna in the Chuckwalla Mountains in southeastern California's Colorado Desert, Riverside College professor Edmund C. Jaeger found one such poorwill nestled comfortably in a rock crevice while sleeping peacefully through the cold winter. He returned to the location annually to find that the bird did likewise, using the same crevice year after year for its winter repose.

It was discovered that, unlike nocturnal hibernators such as hummingbirds, the poorwill enters an extended state of torpor by profoundly slowing its metabolic rate and drastically dropping its body temperature. It can easily maintain this state for several weeks when the weather is cold and its preferred insect prey is not active. Under laboratory conditions, poorwills

In 1946, Riverside College professor Edmund C. Jaeger discovered a common poorwill hibernating through the winter among the rocks in California's Chuckwalla Mountains.

deprived of food routinely enter torpor; in the wild, they rely on it. Another related species, the lesser nighthawk (*Chordeiles acutipennis*), survived 100 days of torpor in captivity on only 0.3 ounce (10 g) of body fat. And recent experiments indicate that the freckled-nightjar (*Caprimulgus tristigma*) of Africa is physiologically able to enter profound torpor, although hibernation has not yet been observed in the wild. Maybe Aristotle was not quite so foolish after all—perhaps he just got the species wrong.

With the dawn of the new age of ornithology, one door labeled "swallow hibernation" shut tight while another one—best described as "other possibilities"—opened. The second half of the 19th century saw migratory routes established for many bird species. A virtual explosion of collecting and cataloguing for the world's museums was carried out by such prominent scientists as Alfred Russel Wallace, Phillip L. Sclater and Spencer Fullerton Baird. The first international ornithological congress was held in Vienna in 1884; its primary mandate was to coordinate the world's experts in a cohesive attempt to map the migrations of birds. At the turn of the 20th century, bird-banding methods introduced by Danish schoolmaster Hans Mortensen ushered in a new discipline that would individually label 120 million birds in Europe, and more than 200 million worldwide, by the year 2000. Radar, radio telemetry and satellite tracking eventually showed us precisely where these birds go when they leave us in autumn.

But has the mystique of bird migration been overcome by millennia of controversy, discussion, persuasion and scientific investigation? As long as we still marvel at geese winging south with the falling leaves of summer, we know that it has not.

Chinese Cranes
A final oasis

There are places on this earth where large numbers of migratory birds stop to feed, rest and socialize. These sites, sometimes designated "important bird areas," are known for the great profusion of migratory birds that may be found there, either in transit or as winter residents.

There are places on this earth where large numbers of migratory birds stop to feed, rest and socialize. As critically important as their ultimate destinations are, through the generations these locations have become traditional waypoints where necessary resources can be found in abundance. Without them, most birds would be unable to reach the end of their journey. Sometimes the same oasis in a sea of inhospitable habitat is the final stopping place for other species. These birds may seek the same key resources, but rather than passing through on the way to some other destination, they linger through the winter. These sites, sometimes designated "important bird areas," are known for the great profusion of migratory birds that may be found there, either in transit or as winter residents.

Among the world's hit list of significant bird areas are the Mediterranean wetlands, the Iberian peninsula, the Gulf of Mexico barrier islands and the cloud forests of Costa Rica. In Asia, Lake Poyang in China's Jiangxi province is

near the top of the scroll. The largest freshwater lake in China, Lake Poyang is fed by the Gan and Xiu rivers, which flow from the lower reaches of the Yangtze (Chang Jiang) River through a narrow channel. The local climate is warm and moist, with sufficient rain and sunshine to balance the needs of many bird species. The lake itself is relatively shallow—the average depth is about 25 feet (8 m)—with a sandy bottom and abundant wetlands and mudflats that provide a wealth of feeding and resting opportunities. Nearly one million birds use Lake Poyang as a temporary residence for some part of their annual cycle.

Among this myriad of migratory birds are four species of cranes (family Gruidae). Cranes by nature flock to places such as Lake Poyang. Their life history favors feeding head down as they stroll through shallow water, searching with their long bills among the aquatic sedges for roots and tubers, small frogs, insects and crustaceans. They also seek the safety of small offshore islands and mudflats at night so they may roost in peace, undisturbed by predators. Eurasian, or common, cranes (*Grus grus*), the most numerous of the four species, funnel down from their nesting sites in Eurasia's northern bogs to winter in eastern China. Although Eurasian cranes, at perhaps 250,000 individuals strong, are not globally threatened, these Lake Poyang cranes comprise part of a central Siberian and northern Chinese breeding population that may number fewer than 5,000 birds.

Among the Poyang crane species officially considered vulnerable to extinction are hooded cranes (*G. monacha*) and white-naped cranes (*G. vipio*). Both species breed from

Ninety-eight percent of the world's Siberian cranes pass their winter days on China's Lake Poyang, where they interact socially and feed head-down among the submerged vegetation.

southeastern Russia south to northern China, many in shallow wetlands along the Amur River, which separates the two countries. Their populations are declining steadily and may now number only about 9,000 and 5,000 individuals respectively. These birds can also be found on the shores of Lake Poyang in winter; white-naped cranes resting there represent about 60 percent of that species' world population. Of greatest concern, however, is the elegant Siberian crane (*G. leucogeranus*). Although this statuesque pure white bird is only the third-rarest crane species—ranking behind whooping (*G. americana*) and red-crowned (*G. japonensis*) cranes— it bears the label "critically endangered," a designation that predicts a 50 percent chance of extinction within 10 years. The Siberian crane has achieved this rank because an estimated 98 percent of its total population (about 3,000 individuals) winter on a single wetland on the shores of Lake Poyang. Such a scenario is ripe for environmental catastrophe.

Once a paradise for countless migrating and wintering birds, Lake Poyang is a safe haven no longer. Ravaged by urbanization, intensive agriculture and overpopulation, Lake Poyang has been reduced considerably in size by large-scale land reclamation projects. In addition, industrial pollution from metal, chemical and paper manufacturers and pesticides in agricultural runoff have poisoned the water. So turbid is the lake now that fish breeding grounds and migration routes have been destroyed, and the elusive finless lake porpoise (*Neomeris phocaenoides*) teeters on the brink of extinction. Most recently, sand dredging is systematically collapsing the lake ecosystem. In the past decade this practice has become a principal player in local economic development. The sandy substrate beneath the waters of Lake Poyang is considered high-quality construction material, and large dredging ships can swallow hundreds of thousands of tons per day—a shipload sells for about 100,000 yuan (roughly $13,000). During high-water season in autumn, more than 200 such ships line up along the center of the lake, mining sand and undermining the lacustrine (lake-related) ecology of the entire region.

More than 700 years ago, Lake Poyang was the site of a fierce 37-day battle between Ming and Han naval forces for control of southern China. The encounter, often heralded as the largest in naval history, has been cited as contributing to the fall of the Yuan dynasty, the subsequent rise of the Ming dynasty and the unification of China. In some ways a battle is still being fought on the waters of Lake Poyang. Five wildlife protection zones have been established since 1970 for regions of the lake, its shoreline and watershed, but enforcement has been lax or nonexistent. As recently as April 2008, a temporary ban on sand mining in the lake was implemented until authorities could further assess the situation. However, official statements suggest that mining will resume in designated areas, according to the outcome of their analysis. Real estate is booming in China, and the demand for building materials continues to increase as local and national economies burgeon. It remains to be seen if there can be a place for the Siberian crane, and Lake Poyang's other migratory bird species, amid all this frenzy.

Phalaropes
Breeding roles turned upside down

Within the avian world, it is typical for the male of the species to be the showy one. Unlike most birds, female phalaropes are the fancy ones, and when it comes to breeding, females take the lead.

Within the avian world, it is typical for the male of the species to be the showy one. Usually he has the fancy plumage, the gaudy displays and the belligerent attitude. With these trappings comes a suite of responsibilities: males defend their nests and mates against predators or potential rivals; they advertise their territory with loud song and antagonistic behavior; and they solicit the attention of females by flaunting colorful adornments. The females of the species, on the other hand, often wear more somber plumage. This is because females usually take on the larger share of duties surrounding childcare, such as incubating eggs and feeding nestlings, and under these circumstances it is better not

to be seen. And since females do most of the choosing when it comes to mate selection, they have no need for fancy dress.

Numerous familiar migratory garden songbirds display this form of sexual dimorphism—for example, Baltimore orioles (*Icterus galbula*), common redstarts (*Phoenicurus phoenicurus*) and grey wagtails (*Motacilla cinerea*)—as do most ducks, hummingbirds, pheasants, tanagers, birds of paradise, manakins, widow birds and many others. Based on their appearance, we can anticipate the role that each gender of these birds plays in life. And pronounced sexual dimorphism can have implications for migration. Red-winged blackbirds (*Agelaius phoeniceus*), for example, exhibit dimorphism not only in their plumage but also in the phenology (timing) of their seasonal movements. The glossy black males travel in "boys only" flocks, arriving on the nesting grounds days, even weeks, before their dusky brown females arrive. During the interim, the males establish their prospective breeding territories by singing loudly from elevated perches among the cattails and chasing off any intruders. By the time the females arrive, the males have established their relative positions in the community and the selection process can begin.

A handful of bird species do something entirely different, and among them are the phalaropes (*Phalaropus* species). Phalaropes are a three-species subfamily of slender-necked shorebirds (family Scolopacidae) that are most closely related to the sandpipers, in particular, shanks and tattlers (*Tringa* species). Phalaropes are well known for their unique foraging technique:

Unlike most avian species, the female red-necked phalarope exhibits brighter-colored plumage than does the male, a characteristic known as reverse sexual dimorphism.

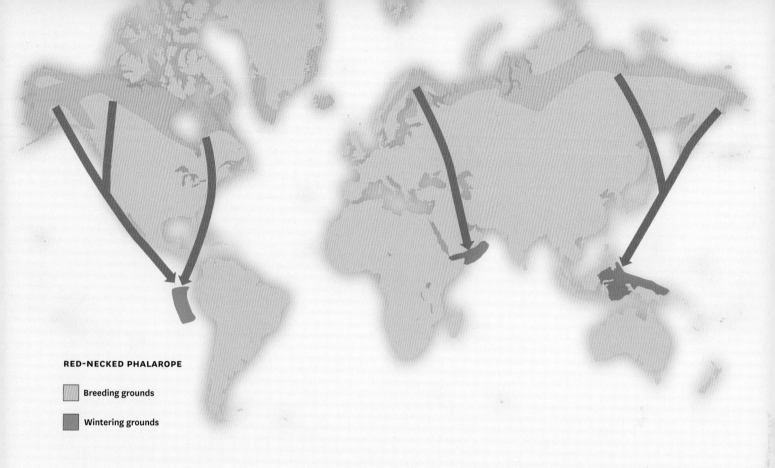

RED-NECKED PHALAROPE

Breeding grounds

Wintering grounds

they swim rapidly in a circle, forming a whirlpool-like vortex that sucks food up to the water's surface, where they can grab it conveniently with their bill. These birds are also noteworthy for their plumage, which exhibits what is known as reverse sexual dimorphism. Unlike most birds, female phalaropes are the fancy ones. The red-necked phalarope (*P. lobatus*) is a prime example. This long-distance migrant typically breeds near lakes and bogs on the Eurasian and North American tundra; it is also a localized breeder in the British Isles as far south as western Ireland. Red-necked phalaropes winter offshore in the warm waters of the Arabian Sea and the Pacific Ocean near the Philippines, New Guinea and western South America.

When it comes to breeding, female phalaropes take the lead. They arrive on the nesting grounds a few days before the males in order to stake out a spot, competing violently for the best vantage point. Although this species is rarely territorial in the strictest sense, early

arrival guarantees the best pickings among the males as they trickle into the breeding area over one or two weeks. Once the males arrive, the competition begins in earnest. Females fly rapidly over the water, striking at each other fiercely with their wings and bills to get access to preferred males. Even after pairing, aggressive females continue to antagonize potential rivals; occasionally the most dominant females will secure more than one male as her mate. Violence usually subsides as nest building begins. Predictably, the male phalarope gathers bits of vegetation from the ground and the female provides no assistance; she lays four olive-green eggs in the makeshift nest and then departs. While he is left to incubate the eggs and care for the chicks, she is already winging her way south to balmier climes.

Considerable scientific research has been undertaken to explain why phalaropes exhibit this unusual breeding behavior. Studies of hormones associated with breeding indicate that female phalaropes

have higher levels of the male hormone testosterone than do males of their species, thus accounting for their more dominant behavior and showier plumage. But why did reverse sexual dimorphism evolve in the first place? Ornithologists suggest that one benefit may be increased longevity among females. Nesting is a very dangerous time for attending parents, particularly where predator densities are high. Because the total number of young birds recruited into a population annually is limited by the females' ability to produce eggs, high female survivability is good for the species in the long run. Furthermore, when a female can attract more than one mate (this is called polyandry), she will be able to lay more eggs in multiple nests tended simultaneously by different males. As for early departure from the breeding grounds, overwintering survival among red-necked phalaropes appears to be high. Thus, it makes perfect sense why this unique breeding behavior evolved; perhaps the greater mystery lies in why it did not evolve more often.

CHAPTER 2

The *FIVE* Ws
of AVIAN MIGRATION

The most beautiful thing we can experience is the
mysterious. It is the source of all true art and science.

ALBERT EINSTEIN

E volutionary biologists know that even the most perplexing scientific riddles are little more than complex whodunits, and that includes the origins of bird migration. Finding the answer to the age-old question of how avian migration came into being—and the seasonal movements of other species, for that matter—can be as well served by Rudyard Kipling's dictum of the five Ws as any good detective story. In this case the *who* and *what* merely state the obvious. However, an examination into *when, where* and *why* should do more to solve the mystery.

Most nocturnal migrants begin their night's journey almost simultaneously, about half an hour after sunset.

T o discover when birds began to migrate, we must delve deep into the ancient past of the class Aves, which had its origins some time during the Mesozoic era, when dinosaurs walked the earth. Ornithologist Thomas Alerstam of the University of Lund in Sweden, an expert in migration ecology, suggests that "bird migration has no doubt existed for as long as birds have been present on earth, for more than 100 million years." This is surely true, for paleontological evidence supports the notion that even the primeval toothed seabird *Hesperornis* may have been migratory.

The hesperorniforms lived about 80 million years ago, during the late Cretaceous period, in what is now North America and northern Europe. Like today's penguins, they were flightless; however, some fossil reconstructions suggest that these ancient birds' legs were positioned so far back on their body that they would be unable to stand upright like their modern counterparts. Its ungainly locomotion would have restricted the terrestrial activities of *Hesperornis* to nesting, although some biologists do not rule out the possibility that it could have been ovoviviparous. This fascinating reproductive strategy, in which the female incubates and hatches her eggs internally and subsequently gives birth to live young, is relatively common in reptiles, but so far it has not been described in birds. *Hesperornis* was primarily aquatic, so its migratory journeys—like those of penguins—would have been accomplished by swimming.

The most extensive fossil remains of hesperorniforms are found in North America. During the late Cretaceous period, this continent was divided in the middle by a great inland sea that stretched from the Gulf of Mexico to the Arctic Circle. *Hesperornis* lived in this warm, shallow subtropical sea, fishing and diving for shellfish like a giant grebe; also like grebes, *Hesperornis* would have propelled itself through the water by kicking its powerful feet and legs. Numerous fossils of adult birds have been found in Manitoba, Alberta, Saskatchewan, Montana, South Dakota, Nebraska, Wyoming and Kansas; however, the remains of their juveniles and subadults are almost entirely restricted to Cretaceous fossil strata in Alaska and the Northwest Territories. Does this suggest that *Hesperornis* wintered in the south and swam north in spring to breed on the shores of arctic seas? If so, its seasonal movements mirrored those of a myriad of seabirds living today.

Luis M. Chiappe, curator of vertebrate paleontology at the Natural History Museum of Los Angeles County, suggests that migratory behavior may have been practiced by some volant (flying) Cretaceous birds as well. Among them were the Enantiornithes, called "opposite birds" because of the unique development of their leg bones. Some enantiornithines lived low in the Southern Hemisphere, where the climate, even during the balmy Cretaceous period, likely resembled that of the American Midwest today. Birds at these polar latitudes would have to endure long, dark winters; certainly a more profitable strategy would be to migrate north when the weather turned chilly.

Fossil evidence implies that bird migration was widespread by the late Eocene epoch, about 40 million years ago, a time when most modern bird orders were becoming enormously diversified in number and type. The Eocene was also a period when many of the world's biomes were becoming cooler and drier; plant communities were gradually changing from tropical to more temperate species. The consistently warm, languid climates that had lingered at higher latitudes throughout the Cretaceous period were becoming more seasonal, thus favoring the movements of birds.

Phylogenetic analyses, which reconstruct evolutionary relationships between species, indicate that in many avian groups migratory behavior evolved independently countless times. This is not surprising, since some of the attributes required for migration predate birds themselves; for example, navigational systems based on a geomagnetic compass are commonly found among amphibians and reptiles. It seems that the patterns of migration and the places that birds visit during their annual cycle form the most fluid components in the evolution of this behavior, the parts of their seasonal movements that change through the generations. Migration as an ecological option, however, may be more ancient than flight itself. So in response to our original query—when did birds begin to migrate?—maybe they always have.

The patterns of avian migration—the *where* in our equation—have only recently been revealed. What began as simple banding experiments with little hope of recapturing the marked individuals has burgeoned into a science rich in technology. The global movements of birds are now tracked and plotted using radar imaging, satellite telemetry, genetic analyses and feather isotope chemistry. These tools have the power to explain not only where birds go when they migrate, but also differences in migratory tendencies among populations, subpopulations, genders and even individuals. To understand how and why migration evolved, we must indeed examine the effects of seasonal movements—their costs and benefits throughout the annual cycle—on units as small as a single bird.

Radar tracking had its origins in "moon watching"—literally counting migratory birds as they passed in front of a full moon. This technique was first introduced in 1951 by George Lowery at Louisiana State University in Baton Rouge. Using complex calculations involving the moon's size, distance from the observer and position in the sky; the time it takes for the flock to pass across the moon's disc; and the number of bird silhouettes and their position relative to the horizontal plane, it is possible to estimate the intensity of a migration event and the birds' general direction of travel. Moon watching attained epic proportions in October 1952 when a major cold front was providing southbound migrants with a brisk tailwind. In three Canadian provinces and forty-five U.S. states, 1,391 students, birdwatchers

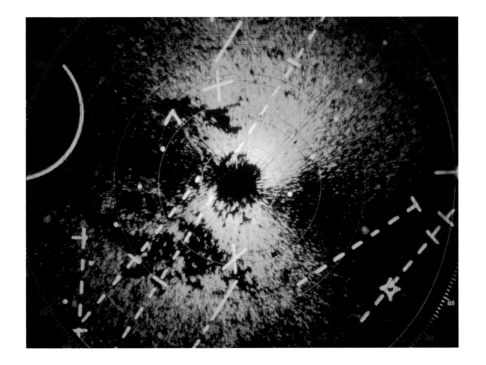

Approximately two million migrating songbirds appear as a large green "cloud" on radar screens at a South Carolina airport. Clemson University studies use these data to determine flight speed and direction and to predict population trends.

OPPOSITE Radar tracking had its origins in "moon watching" — literally, counting migratory birds as they pass in front of a full moon.

and astronomers in 265 places watched the skies for four consecutive nights. What the observers found was astonishing: at some locations, up to 50,000 birds passed over per kilometer (0.6 mile) of storm front every hour. Many millions of birds were obviously on the move. The data collected revealed both general geographic migratory patterns and also how these trajectories could be affected by passing weather systems.

Within a decade of this incident, radar technology—first developed during the Second World War to detect advancing enemy aircraft (the word is short for "radio detection and ranging")—was being used to track migratory birds. Early radar ornithologists included Ernst Sutter in Europe, David Lack in the United Kingdom, and William Drury and Ian Nisbet in the United States. Radar transmitters function by emitting radio waves that reflect off objects to produce an echo back to a receiver. The nature of the echo can provide information about the object's range, altitude, direction and speed. Migrant birds—initially called "angels" by radar operators—appear on radar viewing screens because the water in their blood and body tissues reflects radio waves. Tracking radar projects a very narrow-wave beam skyward, and its echo signatures can reveal elements such as wing-beat patterns that can be used to identify the "angel" by its general taxonomic group.

The advent of Doppler radar provided a new generation of data on avian migration patterns. Doppler radar stations send out pulses of microwaves, which can better determine an object's radial velocity—its speed and direction of movement relative to the tracking station. In the United States,

158 high-resolution Doppler radar stations comprise the NEXRAD weather surveillance network, which has helped save countless human lives through precise early detection of severe meteorological events such as thunderstorms, tornadoes and hurricanes. Since 1990, Sidney Gauthreaux and his colleagues and students at the Clemson University Radar Ornithology Laboratory (CUROL) in South Carolina have been using the NEXRAD system to track migratory birds. To these experts, migrants first appear as massive "clouds" that virtually explode into existence on the radar screens as the birds take flight almost simultaneously about half an hour after sunset. Waves of migrants, perhaps millions of individuals strong and spanning hundreds of square miles, can be tracked as they move across many parts of their journey. CUROL has recorded the direction and flight speed of migrants crossing the Gulf of Mexico, as well as their points and times of departure and landfall. It has also been able to quantify trends in numbers of migrating birds from year to year, studies that have recently revealed alarming declines.

In 2000 the Cornell University Lab of Ornithology — which boasts an impressive tradition of birdsong study — began a joint pilot project with CUROL to better identify the species that were forming these migrating "clouds." Doppler radar can easily detect the difference between warblers, waterfowl, shorebirds and birds of prey by their distinctive flight movements. By adding sound-recording equipment calibrated to analyze the short, high-pitched call notes characteristic of migrating birds in flight, researchers were able to identify many of these darkness-cloaked migrants by species.

But is it possible to plot specific links between migrating birds in terms of their place of origin and their ultimate destination? In other words, do the members of a species or a population that breeds in a certain area all winter together in one section of their nonbreeding distribution, or do they disperse more widely as they travel south? Researchers found that this distributional *where,* which has important conservation implications, could be determined by examining characteristic signatures in the birds' feather chemistry and genetic "fingerprints" that develop among closely related individuals over evolutionary time.

The black-throated blue warbler (*Dendroica caerulescens*) is a stable breeder throughout much of its eastern North American distribution, except among its southernmost populations in Georgia and West Virginia, which have been declining precipitously for three decades. Very little was known about precisely which part of the wintering range these imperiled birds used in the off-season. Could their decline be explained by something that was occurring over winter? Attempts to track individual birds between summer and

winter had failed, so researchers at Dartmouth College in Hanover, New Hampshire, and the Smithsonian Institution in Washington, DC, decided to identify geographic groups of black-throated blue warblers by a chemical "signature" embedded in their feathers.

The ratios of two isotopes of carbon (carbon-12 and carbon-13) change with latitude, and plants and animals in a particular environment will reflect this ratio in the body tissues that grow while they are living there. This happens right up the food chain: plants initially incorporate these isotopes, which are then passed on to herbivorous insects. Insect-eating birds such as warblers acquire their isotope ratio in the same manner, and this chemical fingerprint is fixed in the keratin of feathers that grow during their autumn prebasic molt, just before migrating south. The Dartmouth–Smithsonian study analyzed carbon ratios in the feathers of more than 700 warblers, representing every corner of their breeding distribution as well as wintering populations on the Caribbean islands of Puerto Rico, Jamaica, Cuba and Hispaniola. The results were devastatingly clear: much of the declining population wintered in Haiti, on the western half of Hispaniola. Once it was a richly vegetated tropical paradise; now less than 2 percent of Haiti's forests remain, the rest laid waste by unsound agricultural practices and unbridled human population growth. The wintering warblers simply had nowhere left to live.

Researchers used feather chemistry to determine that some black-throated blue warbler populations were declining as a result of rampant loss of forest habitat on their wintering grounds in Haiti.

Shorebirds, such as these semipalmated sandpipers (*Calidris pusilla*), are excellent candidates for migration studies, in part because of their habit of congregating in immense flocks at key feeding locations, including the Bay of Fundy and Delaware Bay on North America's Atlantic coast.

The advent of molecular genetics toward the end of the 20th century provided migration ecologists—avian and otherwise—with another powerful tool to "type" specific populations, enabling them to assign individuals to particular locales throughout their year. Merely banding birds has proved considerably less effective in this regard. Despite the extraordinary efforts of bird-banders around the world, only about 1 to 2 percent of all banded non-game birds are ever recaptured, and without recapture data it is virtually impossible to reconstruct migrants' seasonal movements. Genetic population markers, on the other hand, can apply to an entire population or species. All life on our planet possesses a genetic code, and retrieving information from a bird's genes is often as simple as extracting a drop of blood.

Studies of this kind have typically focused on migratory shorebirds such as knots, sandpipers, dunlins and dowitchers. Many shorebirds occur in geographically distinct breeding populations, and their long migratory journeys often separate these cohorts by large distances. These characteristics favor the evolution of specific genetic markers within subgroups of a species that might be different enough to tell them apart. When biological populations are physically separated from one another, they are unable to interbreed, so their genetic codes evolve a distinct "flavor." Also, the environment where the population lives will stimulate additional adaptive modifications through natural selection. In evolutionary biology textbooks this is known as allopatric speciation. The more genetically distinct one population is from another, the more likely a researcher is to find a useful marker to distinguish them.

Shorebirds have also been an appropriate focus for these studies because many species face critical conservation challenges. Their lengthy migration corridors usually feature long nonstop legs punctuated by a few essential stopover sites; the ecological integrity of these way stations is crucial to the success of the voyage. Survival in winter is also vital: nonbreeding habitats, particularly those in coastal or estuarine (river-mouth) areas, may be facing loss and degradation from human activities. Hence, knowing where shorebirds go, and the route they take between their breeding and wintering grounds, is essential before comprehensive conservation intervention can be carried out.

Molecular geneticists began searching the genomes of shorebirds for suitable molecular markers in the 1980s. Many studies demonstrated the usefulness of randomly amplified polymorphic DNA, also known as RAPD. RAPDS are precisely what their name implies: random pieces of genetic material (DNA) whose presence or absence is revealed, or amplified, during molecular analysis of blood or tissue. They are *polymorphic* because they can vary with genetic differences between individuals. The power of RAPDS in this type of work is that they are random. The researcher first designs a primer, which is a short piece of simulated DNA sequence designed to ferret out and replicate any chunk of authentic DNA that resembles it. If that sequence is present on a gene, it will amplify.

DNA is merely an extended chain of simple molecular units called nucleotides; their specific order contains a blueprint for development and continuation of life in a particular biological entity. Because RAPD primers seek out random pieces of DNA, the researcher need not know precise details of the experimental species' genetic makeup. Despite the recent intense focus on unraveling the genetic mysteries of life on earth, it took hundreds of molecular geneticists 13 years to map the DNA of a single species—ourselves. Intimate knowledge of avian DNA across all 10,000 species is still generations away. In the meantime, RAPDS have proved useful in separating shorebird breeding populations and also in linking individuals captured in winter with a known breeding site. Travel corridors, staging areas and stopover sites have likewise been mapped for some species.

Advances in molecular genetics since the 1980s led to the development of other polymorphic molecular markers, such as short tandem repeats (STRS), which could often provide better resolution among populations than RAPDS and could even be used to distinguish between individuals within a population. Unlike RAPDS, STR primers target bits of "junk" DNA that accumulate in the genome over evolutionary time, usually in the form of repeated chains of gibberish nucleotides. Because short tandem repeats play no useful role in an organism's continuation of life — at least none that we know of — they are more prone to change rapidly through mutation. High rates of mutation in more functional DNA is usually bad news. Even so, rapidly changing DNA is rather useful in establishing relationships between very closely related groups or individuals. Consequently they have been widely used to sort out the finer details among shorebird populations.

Some researchers are taking molecular marking of migratory birds one step further by identifying the birds' unwanted cargo — in this case, blood parasites. Studies of willow warblers (*Phylloscopus trochilus*) in Finland suggest that parasites could be more useful for geographically linking breeding and wintering grounds than attributes of the birds themselves. Parasites bear the genetic signature of where the host acquired them. Parasite populations may demonstrate greater genetic divergence because they are more geographically isolated from one another — most parasites cannot get around on their own, requiring hosts to transport them. By typing the species or population of a parasite where it is most infective, it is potentially possible to trace the geographic movements of its hosts.

Tracking individual birds through the seasons is another matter altogether. In the field, wildlife biologists often rely on radio telemetry to determine what their individual study animals are doing and when and where they are doing it. They affix tiny battery-powered transmitters housed in collars, tags or miniature backpacks, each tuned to a different frequency, to their various charges and then track them using a radio receiver. Telemetry of this nature works wonders in a local area but is considerably less useful over great distances, because it requires the tracker to find and sometimes follow the animal.

More recently, however, bird migration research discovered satellite tracking. Satellite tracking still requires individuals to be captured and fitted with tiny transmitters, but in this case information regarding the animal's whereabouts can be uploaded in near real time directly to the researcher, via the ARGOS (Advanced Research and Global Observation Satellite) system. Each ARGOS satellite orbits our planet every 102 minutes at an altitude of about 525 miles (850 km). An individual's global position can be fixed with an accuracy of about 500 feet (150 m) by at least one of these satellites at virtually any time. In addition to providing wildlife researchers with tracking options, ARGOS also monitors meteorological, oceanographic and atmospheric

Biologists at Cape Crozier on Antarctica's Ross Island attach satellite transmitters to emperor penguins (*Aptenodytes forsteri*) to track their seasonal movements. Information regarding a bird's whereabouts can be uploaded in near real time directly to the researcher.

conditions, from arctic ice to El Niño events to ionizing magnetic storms. Some high-tech transmitters for avian research contain microprocessors that also collect data on air temperature, light intensity, flight speed, altitude and flight inclination. Long-life batteries can provide months or even years of almost continuously streaming data; the transmitters are designed to fall off at about the time their batteries wear out.

Avian migration studies have embraced satellite technology with gusto because it can track an individual's movements between known and unknown breeding and wintering distributions, locate stopover and staging areas, and plot the course between all points in both space and time. Dozens of migratory bird species have been tracked this way since its inception, including penguins, albatrosses, cranes, birds of prey, waterfowl and shorebirds. Moreover, the value of satellite tracking to conservation workers is immeasurable. For example, massive declines in populations of Swainson's hawks (*Buteo swainsoni*) returning to their breeding grounds in western North America during the late 1990s prompted a search for a wintering site in South America. Researchers were shocked by what they found. The northern declines were reflecting the annual demise of thousands of wintering hawks—at least 6,000 in two years—on the pampas grasslands of Argentina, where a highly toxic pesticide called monocrotophos was being used to control grasshopper outbreaks; Swainson's hawks feed extensively on locusts in winter. Satellite tracking also discovered an unknown breeding population

Wandering albatrosses travel thousands of miles above the southern oceans by soaring almost effortlessly on their long, narrow wings. They have the largest wingspan of any living bird.

of Siberian cranes (*Grus leucogeranus*) when one of this critically endangered species was tracked as it flew north from the south Caspian Sea. Not only did its movements lead to a fragment population breeding in Russia, they also demonstrated the importance of the Volga River delta as critical stopover habitat.

Satellite tracking has allowed us to witness some miracles of avian seasonal movement. Wandering albatrosses (*Diomedea exulans*) are not so named without cause. This chunky seabird—now considered vulnerable to extinction—has the largest wingspan of any living bird, about 10 feet (3 m), and it uses these long, narrow-chorded wings to glide effortlessly above the waves of the southern oceans with barely a wing-beat. When not breeding, wandering albatrosses wander, taking mysteriously long voyages apparently to nowhere. Even when they have a chick in the nest, one albatross parent will frequently take an extended hiatus to fly and feed. Researchers wanted to find out where these birds go when they leave land, so they affixed satellite-tracking transmitters to a number of individuals. The data revealed that in a single foraging voyage, wandering albatrosses could cover a circuitous route of almost 10,000 miles (15,000 km) at speeds of up to 50 miles (80 km) per hour. During the off-season, one bird wandered about 31,000 miles (50,000 km) in 200 days.

The albatross's endurance and speed on the wing have been used to raise both awareness and funding on behalf of these imperiled birds. Albatross numbers are declining dramatically because of longline fishing, which kills more than 300,000 seabirds each year, a third of them albatrosses. Commercial longliners catch tuna, swordfish and other large pelagic (open-sea) species by dragging behind their boats fishing lines that are sometimes 60 miles (100 km) or more long. The lines are studded with thousands of razor-sharp baited hooks that snag hapless birds and drag them underwater. Unable to free themselves, they perish by drowning. Some estimates suggest that an albatross dies this way every five minutes. Longline fishing has come under considerable scrutiny in recent years, but it is still widely practiced in many parts of the world. Regrettably, all 21 albatross species may be facing extinction in the not-so-distant future.

To focus attention on the plight of the albatross, the Big Bird Race was born. The event was the brainchild of an Australian conservationist, Tim Nevard, and was supported by numerous conservation organizations, including Bird Life International, the Royal Society for the Protection of Birds, and the U.K.-based Conservation Foundation. In spring 2004, 18 Tasmanian shy albatrosses (*Thalassarche cauta*) were moved from three Australian islands, tagged with satellite transmitters, and released to begin a 6,000-mile (9,600 km), 11-week transoceanic journey to their wintering grounds on the Cape of Good Hope, at the southern tip of Africa. Avid bettors and birders were encouraged to contribute monetary support by choosing their favorite competitor, assisted by the world's largest bookmaker, Ladbrokes. Celebrity supporters included Sir David Attenborough, Olivia Newton-John and Queen Noor of Jordan. The 2004 winner, a gawky female named Aphrodite, was sponsored by former model Jerry Hall, ex-wife of Rolling Stones rocker Mick Jagger. Prince Philip presented the winner with the Duke of Edinburgh's Challenge Cup, which he had donated for this event.

The following year, however, the Big Bird Race ended in tragedy: all 17 contestants vanished at sea somewhere off the coast of Western Australia. Experts believe that the travel-hungry birds fell prey to their greatest nemesis—longline fishermen. Recent research has indicated that longline fishing in Australian waters catches about 45 species of marine animals, most of which have no commercial value. Known as bycatch, these so-called useless turtles, sharks, stingrays, marlin, sunfish, seabirds and marine mammals may represent a greater portion of the catch than the actual target species. Although the demise of the 2005 racing albatrosses was tragic, we can hope that they did not die needlessly; perhaps their passing contributed, at least in some small way, to the end of this destructive practice.

Observing, marking and tracking birds through the centuries has revealed considerable information about the *where* in our original query. These activities demonstrated that migratory bird species typically follow predictable patterns of movement through characteristic travel corridors. The routes are often influenced by the shapes of land masses and by topographical features such as mountain ranges, bodies of water and deserts that may prohibit a route "as the crow flies." In North America, most migratory land birds' routes are oriented north/south, not only because of the continent's shape but also because most of the barriers to movement, including the Rocky and Appalachian mountains, run more or less north/south, as does the land connection between the Americas. This is also the case for the handful of New World austral migrants—that small minority of birds that migrate north from the Southern Hemisphere in autumn—such as the fuscous flycatcher (*Cnemotriccus fuscatus*) and the white-crested elaenia (*Elaenia albiceps*), which breed in temperate South America and winter in the warmer tropical latitudes. In Europe and Asia, however, many avian migration corridors run east/west, following the orientation of major obstacles such as the Alps and the Himalayas, the Mediterranean Sea and the deserts of the Middle East and northern Africa. (It is no surprise that our own species' early trade routes across Eurasia were also oriented primarily in this east/west direction.)

One would think that, unlike humans, birds would be unfazed by obstacles as trivial as mountain ranges. But even though birds can fly, barriers can have long-lasting influence on the evolution of travel routes. Migration behavior reflects the ecological balance sheet in many ways. Flight is energetically expensive, and birds no doubt want to get as far as possible with the smallest investment of resources. In some cases it may be "cheaper" to fly around an obstacle than to pass over or across it, particularly if overcoming the barrier requires long stretches of nonstop flight. In addition, broad-winged birds such as birds of prey, storks and cranes, which save energy by soaring, are better served by traveling over land as much as possible. These species frequently use thermal currents—rising columns of heated air created by the sun warming the earth's surface—to gain free elevation, and thermals do not form over water. Consequently we often see flocks of migrant birds making detours around significant obstacles. For example, many European species bound for African wintering grounds choose to travel around either end of the Mediterranean Sea rather than cross it. Birdwatchers are well aware that the straits of Gibraltar and Bosporus are ideal locations for viewing thousands of migrating birds. In some situations, a significant barrier simply marks the end of a species' migration journey, provided that the stopping point offers the resources necessary to pass the winter. Perhaps this explains

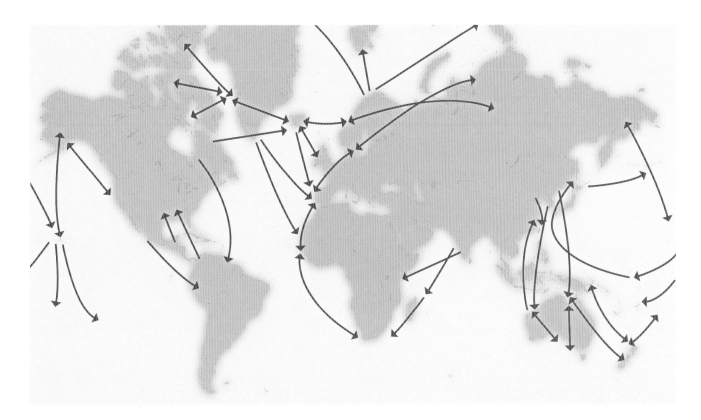

why so many species winter in the rich marshes and mudflats ringing the Gulf of Mexico rather than traveling on to South America.

Many birds do choose to cross the world's most daunting obstacles, but even these species do so in such predictably energy-conserving ways that distinct patterns in their movements can be observed. In a 2000 study, migration ecologists Robert Diehl and Ron Larkin used the NEXRAD weather surveillance system to map the patterns of birds crossing the Great Lakes during spring and autumn migration. The Great Lakes measure about 96,000 square miles (250,000 sq km) in area and extend 900 miles (1,400 km) from east to west. The researchers found that birds seemed to cross the lakes at regular locations that would effectively shorten their journey over open water. In particular, southbound clouds of birds were seen departing from peninsulas and other landforms that extend out into the lakes, such as Lake Erie's Point Pelee and Long Point and Lake Superior's Sibley Peninsula. During spring migration, northbound birds passing over the water frequently oriented toward these same features to reduce their time to landfall.

Large numbers of southbound migratory birds have also been recorded in the skies above Bermuda. Bermuda is in the Atlantic Ocean about 670 miles (1,100 km) east-southeast of Cape Hatteras, North Carolina. Only about 20 square miles (53 sq km) in extent, this tiny atoll would be a mere speck to a bird passing overhead, but this section of ocean is of considerable importance. Some shorebirds and waders, and even a few songbird species, fly to South America by a transoceanic route rather than crossing the Gulf of Mexico. These birds depart in a broad front from staging areas in northeastern North America and travel southeast over the Atlantic Ocean, taking advantage of passing cold fronts. Just south of Bermuda they catch the northeasterly trade winds, which push them southwest toward the South American coast. Although this route may seem less efficient than a more direct passage across the Gulf, its existence demonstrates otherwise. For some species, such as the American golden plover (*Pluvialis dominica*), the transoceanic route represents the best compromise between the length of the detour and the energy saved by taking advantage of persistent tailwinds.

Birds in passage also need feeding and roosting habitat en route to their ultimate destination. Traditional migration corridors are commonly established along lines of these crucial resources, forming the world's great continental flyways. Perhaps the most obvious and widely used flyways occur in North America, where the shape of the continent and its topographic features conspire to funnel birds along four major travel routes: the Pacific, Central, Mississippi and Atlantic flyways. The North American flyway concept was developed in the 1930s by biologist Frederick Lincoln (1892–1960) of the U.S. Bureau of Biological Survey (now the U.S. Fish and Wildlife Service). When Lincoln joined the Bureau in 1920, he was tasked with organizing the U.S. Bird Banding Office, which had taken over primary responsibility for tagging birds and recording banding returns from the American Bird Banding Association that same year. Lincoln was adamant that uniform procedures be imposed on all U.S. banding activities to safeguard the scientific merit of data being collected across the country. Consequently he developed robust numbering schemes and record-keeping methods, and he also formulated the statistical "Lincoln Index," based on marking and recapturing marked individuals, that is still used to estimate population sizes. Lincoln devised the North American flyways concept in 1935, using data collected and collated from banded waterfowl.

The North American flyways system is something of an oversimplification; certainly not all migratory birds adhere to such rigid travel corridors. Nevertheless, many species do choose these routes to access the plentiful resources that they offer. The Central and Mississippi flyways provide historically abundant wetland and riparian habitats, respectively, to many waterfowl species and to songbirds such as the boldly marked Harris's sparrow (*Zonotrichia querula*) and spectacular scarlet tanager (*Piranga olivacea*). The Atlantic and Pacific flyways offer abundant food along the east and west coasts for shorebirds, including purple sandpipers (*Calidris maritima*),

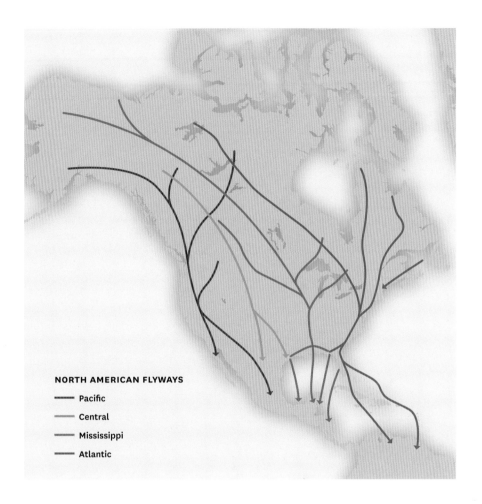

NORTH AMERICAN FLYWAYS

—— Pacific

—— Central

----- Mississippi

—— Atlantic

North American migratory birds frequently travel along traditional corridors (known as flyways) that offer abundant food resources and favorable environmental conditions enroute.

wandering tattlers (*Tringa incana*) and ruddy turnstones (*Arenaria interpres*). These migrants get the added bonus of easy landmark orientation and ocean breezes that provide a little extra lift for weary travelers.

Perhaps the benefits conferred by coastlines produced some of the longest migration corridors in the world: the circular routes that skirt the great oceans. Ornithologists think that circuitous travel routes—the journey is known as loop migration, or *Schleifenzug*—provide migrants with a bounty of resources from summer to winter and back again, in a way that a more linear journey would not. For example, Arctic loons (*Gavia arctica*), known as black-throated divers outside North America, are large, heavy birds with relatively small wings that require open water for landing, feeding and becoming airborne again. Their long, looping migratory route guarantees that open water will be available throughout the year. Even some land birds such as diminutive Connecticut warblers (*Oporornis agilis*) and palm warblers (*Dendroica palmarum*) use a similar strategy to optimize food resources and weather conditions en route.

Ornithologists suggest that, of all animal species, the bar-tailed godwit — a medium-sized brownish shorebird — makes the longest migratory journey without pausing to feed.

The looping coastal routes traveled by shorebirds and seabirds are those that call for the greatest feats of endurance. Sooty shearwaters (*Puffinus griseus*) circumscribe the Pacific Ocean from their breeding sites in Australia and New Zealand, north to the Pacific rim of Asia to Japan, west to Alaska, and then south along North America's Pacific Coast. An international team of biologists led by Scott Shaffer of the University of California tracked the seasonal movements of 19 sooty shearwaters in 2005. They discovered that the birds traced a looping figure-eight route that extended from the Bering Sea to the waters of the Antarctic and measured on average about 40,000 miles (64,000 km). The journey lasted about 200 days, with some individuals covering about 560 miles (900 km) per day.

Bar-tailed godwits (*Limosa lapponica*) follow a similar course north to Alaska from Australia and New Zealand, but then turn sharply south to finish their circuitous journey by directly crossing the Pacific Ocean. Individuals are seldom seen leaving the north, so details of their route south remained a mystery until the advent of satellite tracking. In 2007 U.S. Geological Survey biologist Robert Gill and his research team were flabbergasted when they

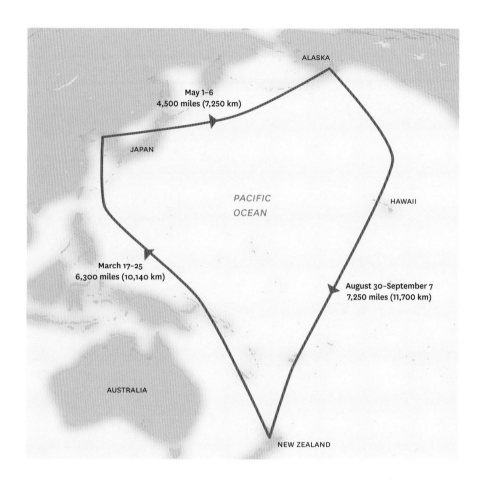

In 2007, satellite tracking revealed the impressive journey of a female bar-tailed godwit called E7 whose southbound nonstop migration from Alaska to New Zealand — a distance of 7,250 miles (11,700 km) — was accomplished in only eight days.

discovered that one female bar-tailed godwit, named simply E7, had left Alaska on August 30 and arrived in New Zealand eight days later after a nonstop oceanic crossing measuring 7,250 miles (11,700 km) — the longest continuous flight in avian history. She averaged 35 miles (56 km) per hour riding tailwinds that pushed her toward the southwest, and fueled the entire flapping flight by burning body fat, even sleeping on the wing by shutting down half her brain in a mystical reverie.

Unfortunately, the future of these dauntless voyagers is uncertain. Recent population censuses indicate that godwit populations may number half of what they were in the 1990s. The primary cause of decline is catastrophic loss of critical stopover and staging habitats on the Asian coast near the Yellow Sea. Wetlands in this region, used by two million shorebirds annually, are being drained at an alarming rate as land is claimed for other purposes; approximately half have already been lost, with an estimated 40 percent of what remains scheduled for conversion in the future. Without access to reliable food sources before departure, godwits and other migratory species will have insufficient fuel to complete their arduous journey.

It is no surprise that patterns of migration are designed to provide birds with basic requirements en route and the means to get where they are going in the most effective manner. Moreover, their choice of destination usually makes ecological and evolutionary sense: forest birds often winter in forests, and wetland birds seek out marshes and mudflats. One hypothesis to explain the movement of northern breeders such as the Arctic tern (*Sterna paradisaea*) to wintering grounds so far south is that only Antarctica provides similar habitat in December as north of 60° latitude does during July.

The apparent dedication of most migratory birds to their chosen route and their wintering destination suggests that they have traveled these corridors for an eternity. However, this is not the case. For one thing, the continents are continuously moving around on our planet through a geological phenomenon known as plate tectonics. The outer skin of the earth, its crust, is fractured into about seven major plates, most of which possess a land mass above sea level that appears to us as a continent. These plates are pushed along as new crust is formed by seafloor spreading at the margins of some — such as the Mid-Atlantic Ridge — while being destroyed by subduction at others. Subduction occurs where one plate grinds into another, as it does in northern India, causing the underneath plate to be consumed by intense heat. The overriding plates are often pushed up relatively rapidly — geologically speaking — to form the world's great mountain ranges, including the Himalayas and the Andes. Although their movement is not discernible to us as we ride the drifting continents, rest assured that North Americans are traveling away from Europeans at about the same speed that our fingernails are growing — a thought to ponder with each passing manicure.

Back in the earlier days of avian migration, the patchwork of continents and seas across the earth's surface would not have appeared as it does today. Many current barriers to movement did not yet exist; for example, the Himalayan Mountains, which include the world's tallest peaks, reached their current height only within the past few million years. They are, in fact, still growing as the Indian Plate continues to be driven under the Eurasian Plate; some geologists estimate that Mount Everest has risen as much as 12 feet (3.6 m) in the past century. Other barriers to migration, however, would have been more formidable in the past, including the ancient Appalachian belt. This mountain range stopped building about 250 million years ago and has since decreased considerably in size after millions of years of erosion. Of course, landforms with different elevations in the past would have had different climate regimes, and accordingly different patterns of vegetation.

The northern breeding distribution of temperate migrants has also been affected by the cyclical alternation of glacial and interglacial periods that has characterized the Pleistocene epoch for the past two million years. Some

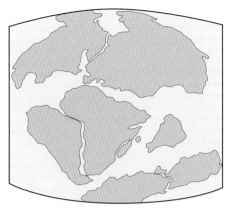

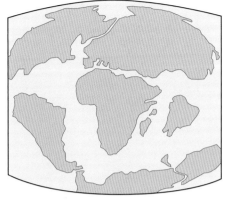

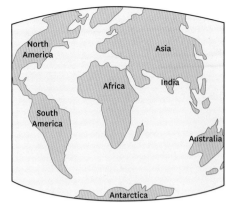

JURASSIC (150 MILLION YEARS AGO)   CRETACEOUS (65 MILLION YEARS AGO)   PRESENT DAY

geologists believe that the Pleistocene ended when the continental glaciers of the last great ice age—the Wisconsin—receded; others propose that the moderate temperatures we enjoy today merely indicate an interglacial period. Regardless, only 18,000 years ago the Laurentide ice sheet over Montreal, Quebec, was about 2 miles (3 km) thick—unquestionably no breeding habitat for bluebirds. In Europe the ice sheet covered Greenland, Scandinavia and most of the United Kingdom, extending as far south as the Alps. To the south of the ice front were arctic-like tundra and steppes; average global temperatures were 8° to 11°F (4°–5°C) cooler than they are today.

Pleistocene glaciations no doubt had an enormous effect on avian migration. Paleoecologists have suggested that the ice coverage and changes to vegetation—no forests, for example—south of the glacial front in Europe probably reduced the number of breeding birds on the continent to less than half. The severe climate may also have made it necessary for more species to migrate south to Africa, as they do today. Fortunately the Sahara Desert was much less arid and considerably more vegetated during the Pleistocene; it was punctuated by many lakes, six of which had surface areas larger than that of Belgium. Rather than being a barrier to migration, the Sahara region would have been a winter haven for many of the migratory birds that nested on the European tundra.

During glacial peaks, the North American ice sheets extended much farther south than those in Europe and Asia, reaching what is now the central Midwestern states at about 40°N latitude. Most of North America's migratory waterfowl, raptors, shorebirds and boreal songbirds currently nest above 35°N, so breeding birds would have been pushed south with the advancing glaciers, seeking refuge in the southern states and Mexico. Indeed, the Pleistocene avifauna of Mexico comprised many species characteristic of today's north; one late Pleistocene cave in Nuevo León contained fossils of several species associated with temperate latitudes, including the American

Throughout time, the continents have occupied different positions on our planet as a result of a geological phenomenon known as plate tectonics.

During the last Pleistocene glaciation, ice sheets as thick as 2 miles (3 km) covered much of North America and northern Eurasia.

woodcock (*Scolopax minor*) and pinyon jay (*Gymnorhinus cyanocephalus*). As in Europe, birds entrenched in glacial refugia probably migrated shorter distances, if they demonstrated any seasonal movements at all.

The advance of the glaciers likely fractured populations of some more widely distributed species, allowing these isolated groups to pursue their own evolutionary trajectories. For example, the yellow-rumped warbler (*Dendroica coronata*), a common North American songbird, occurs as four distinct subspecies: two migratory North American breeders (the myrtle warbler, *D. c. coronata,* and Audubon's warbler, *D. c. auduboni*) and two sedentary populations in Mexico (*D. c. nigrifrons*) and Guatemala (*D. c. goldmani*). Ornithologist Borja Milá and colleagues at the University of California suggest that the migrant group diverged from sedentary populations in Mexico in the early Pleistocene, then were isolated from one another when they were confined to separate fragments of forest habitat that survived in the south during maximum glaciation.

Current patterns of migration in the Northern Hemisphere—particularly those long-distance routes—may thus have evolved after the Pleistocene glaciations. As average temperatures rose and snow and ice cover receded to the north, birds could expand their ranges accordingly. Novel plant species and vegetation types colonized the once barren landscape, offering these voyagers pristine habitat where competition was mild and resources were bountiful. Some landscape features on which many migrating birds depend, such as prairie potholes, were formed as the continental glaciers retreated, when wayward chunks of ice melted to fill new depressions in the topography.

The current breeding distribution of yellow-rumped warblers is typical of many forest-dwelling North American birds, including fox sparrows (*Passerella iliaca*), sapsuckers (*Sphyrapicus* species) and vireos (*Vireo* species), reflecting postglacial expansion up both sides of the continent, with the eastern group continuing west across the boreal zone to Alaska. Many avian species seem to have maintained a connection to their glacial refugia as wintering habitat. Audubon's warbler, the western subspecies of yellow-rumped warbler, still winters in the highlands of western Mexico alongside its nonmigratory kin *D. c. nigrifrons*. But why it "chose" to migrate rather than live sympatrically with its closest relatives is a story that has yet to be told.

The last part of our equation, the *why* of bird migration, is perhaps the most compelling of the five Ws, and may be the single topic in avian migration that has garnered the most research — and the least consensus among researchers. To understand why some bird species evolved to migrate and others did not, we must turn again to the ecological balance sheet. Migration certainly has its benefits, but for the behavior to arise and then persist in a population or species, the benefits must outweigh the potential costs. From an evolutionary point of view, the simplest way to assess this cost is by looking at mortality.

Migration is a dangerous business. It has been estimated that approximately half of the birds that leave their nesting grounds in autumn do not return the following spring. One might guess from this figure that the wintering grounds pose risks that do not exist on the migrants' home turf. However, studies of stable black-throated blue warbler populations throughout the species' annual cycle suggest that about 15 times more individuals die during the migratory passage than in their winter homes, and death during migration appears to account for about 85 percent of total annual mortality. Although these figures cannot be applied universally across all bird species — songbirds may be less robust than larger species — one cannot dispute the fact that migration is hazardous.

Migrants perish for a host of reasons: exhaustion, starvation, dehydration, inclement weather, poisoning, disease, collisions with human-made structures, hunting and predation. Some avian predators, such as the endangered Eleonora's falcon (*Falco eleonorae*), time their breeding season to coincide with the peak supply of weary songbirds passing through their Mediterranean

Eleonora's falcons (*Falco eleonorae*) time their nesting season to coincide with the influx of travel-weary migrants into their Mediterranean island breeding territories — thus providing ample food for their hungry chicks.

island territories on their autumn migration between Eurasia and Africa. It has been estimated that this species alone captures about 1.6 million migratory songbirds in a 60-day hunting period to feed its own chicks. Predation in more general terms is likely responsible for about 10 percent of mortality in some migratory songbird species, including chaffinches (*Fringilla coelebs*) and bramblings (*F. montifringilla*) — yet they continue to migrate.

Ornithologist John Rappole of the Smithsonian Institution once summarized possible contributing factors to the evolution of migration in birds. They include climatic shifts during the Pleistocene (or more recently) that could have changed sea levels or modified other environmental conditions; local changes due to other causes; competition for resources between members of the same species or among different species; unpredictable food sources that vary seasonally or in abundance; or favorable resources available elsewhere. Added to this list is the "migration threshold" hypothesis postulated by migration ecologist Robin Baker in 1978, which suggests that birds have a genetically determined migration threshold: if local conditions deteriorate to some predetermined level, they will become migratory. From the cost-benefit point of view, when the expected gain in ecological fitness from moving — in terms of things like longevity and reproductive success — is higher than it is for staying put, then it is time to hit the road. Despite the apparent disparity between these theories (and the almost unmanageable inventory of variables involved), they have one thing in common: they all suggest that something—food or climate presumably being among the most powerful motivators—prompted birds to migrate. But did birds evolve migration to exploit better resources for breeding, or did they do so to improve winter survival by fleeing bad weather?

Historically, most people have focused on the autumn trip south in their attempts to explain the seasonal passage of birds. But this view may contain just a dash of anthropomorphism—where would *we* go, what would *we* do? Escaping the northern winters seems a likely answer; it is true that some places are perfectly acceptable for habitation during part of year but exceedingly difficult at other times. But since migration occurs at such great expense, for it to evolve under this model, a higher cost would have to be associated with staying on the breeding grounds through the winter than with vacating them and traveling elsewhere.

Several years ago, Dutch biologists Popko Wiersma and Theunis Piersma examined the energy regimes of migratory red knots (*Calidris canutus*) to determine if there truly was a benefit to wintering at more southerly latitudes. Birds, of course, have no access to central heating, so they must maintain a high metabolic rate to sustain a high enough body temperature to survive in cold weather. Birds have an average body temperature of around 104°F (40°C). If their core temperature drops too low, the usual consequences of hypothermia affect most species.

The researchers used heated taxidermic mounts of red knots to extrapolate heat loss from the bodies of real birds under various conditions of ambient air temperature, wind speed and solar radiation, both in the laboratory and in traditional red knot breeding and wintering locations. They also simulated behaviors that red knots and other avian species use to reduce heat loss in inclement weather, such as facing into the wind and gathering in flocks. In this case the mounted red knots were placed among a "flock" of decoys resembling Eurasian golden plovers (*Pluvialis apricaria*) and bar-tailed godwits. The study clearly demonstrated that red knots wintering at high latitudes would have to maintain a metabolic rate four or five times greater than their normal summer resting rate—something like bicycling in the Tour de France through the entire winter. It was suggested that real knots wintering in the Netherlands' Wadden Sea—the most northerly nonbreeding distribution for this species—are functioning near the limit of their endurance. Birds that choose to winter in West Africa use about 40 percent less energy per day than if they stay in the north. Even the trip to Africa requires less energy than staying put, because the birds can take advantage of considerable tailwinds during their passage.

But if the mild living conditions in West Africa are so beneficial, why not just stay there year-round? Why migrate at all? These questions reflect the other side of the migration coin. Traveling to breed confers distinct advantages; was this the evolutionary force that fueled migration in so many species? The concept that northern-breeding birds are ex-tropicals that struck out to find better breeding conditions has been around since Aristotle's time. Just as some habitats are unsuitable for wintering, others—while excellent for winter survival—may be inappropriate for breeding. These ideas were summarized in the "southern ancestral home" hypothesis of American ornithologist George Cox in 1966.

Despite the nice weather, the tropics do have their challenges. For one thing, predation rates on eggs and chicks appear to correlate with latitude. Birds breeding in the tropics lose considerably more young to predators than those that breed at temperate latitudes—up to 80 percent loss along some tropical forest-edge boundaries. The fundamental difference between the two biomes may be the prevalence of tropical mammals that are particularly effective at working edge habitats, where nearby open areas provide easy access. Parasites are also more common at tropical latitudes because their abundance is not reduced seasonally by freezing temperatures, and heavy parasite loads have a critical impact on mortality rates in juvenile birds.

Adult birds, in contrast, have very good survivability in the tropics. Typically they suffer less predation than younger birds because they can escape capture, and of course there is virtually no overwinter mortality; tropical birds that survive to breeding age live a relatively long time. Some manakins—compact, short-tailed subtropical and tropical birds related to flycatchers—have an estimated annual adult survival rate of 85 to 90 percent, compared to about 40 percent for similar-sized European and North American songbirds. One female golden-headed manakin (*Pipra erythrocephala*) was reported to have raised chicks in at least 11 breeding seasons, which researchers studying this species deemed not unusual.

But high adult survivability has inherent problems. Before they can reproduce, most avian species need a breeding territory that provides all the necessities of life: nesting and roosting sites, display grounds, food and other resources for themselves and their young. With no appropriate space, individuals will delay breeding until they can secure one. In the tropics, most breeding birds can lay claim to their patch of turf for many years; and in territorial challenges, the incumbent will typically prevail. Finding a breeding territory in the tropics has been likened to trying to rent an apartment in a building where no one dies and no one ever moves out. For young birds of breeding age, this can mean waiting several years for an opening.

On the other hand, seasonal abundance in the temperate north offers breeding birds a wealth of resources. The short summer encourages animals

Tropical breeding birds lose considerably more young to predation than do birds that nest at temperate latitudes — up to 80 percent loss along some tropical forest edges.

and plants to breed rapidly and productively before the arrival of autumn. From a bird's point of view, this provides an almost explosive bloom of seed- and fruit-bearing plants, as well as insects and other palatable invertebrates (most Canadians are all too familiar with the rapid appearance of hordes of mosquitoes and blackflies in the first warm days of summer). Food resources in the tropics are available year-round, but on average, they are substantially less abundant.

Temperate and arctic latitudes also offer space aplenty, in part because considerably fewer species make the north their summer home. Only about 60 species nest in Greenland, which is at about 70°N latitude. Farther south, in Maine and Pennsylvania — the "northern 40s" — there are about 175 to 185 breeding bird species. Tropical Colombia, which straddles the equator, has as many as 1,865 avian species, arguably more than any other country in the world. Within most tropical ecosystems, breeding birds occur at near carrying-capacity densities (carrying capacity is the number of individuals that can be sustained by available resources). In contrast, birds nesting at higher latitudes occur at much lower densities, which means less competition for resources and the potential for larger, more profitable breeding territories. As well, temperate species usually begin breeding earlier in life than their tropical counterparts, because they are able to secure a territory as soon as they mature enough to use it; earlier breeding usually results in greater lifetime reproductive output. Lower nesting densities have the added benefit of relatively less predation, because predator densities correlate ecologically with the density of available prey — in this case, eggs and chicks.

The long daylight hours of higher latitudes provide birds ample time to provision their young. This has favored the evolution of larger average clutch sizes for temperate breeding species of many songbirds, hawks, owls, terns, coots, grebes and gallinaceous (chicken-like) birds than for their tropical cousins. Some ornithologists believe that clutch size is directly related to parents' increased ability to feed more chicks where food is plentiful. Others, however, cite lower predation rates as a factor in the evolution of larger clutch sizes — larger clutches are noisier and the frequent to-and-fro activities of the parents make a bountiful nest more conspicuous to the watchful eyes of predators. Regardless of the cause, tropical songbirds usually have clutches of only one or two eggs, while temperate species frequently lay four or five. For the proto-migratory tropical bird, the distant north no doubt represented an irresistible opportunity to tap unexploited and underutilized breeding niches. The primary problem, of course, was getting there.

With the *who, what, when, where* and *why* of avian migration dealt with, we are left to determine a paradigm for how this remarkable behavior evolved. Migration seems unspeakably complicated: it requires genetically programmed or learned knowledge of time and physical space, physiological adaptations for fuel storage and metabolism, and the behavioral means to adjust to continually changing conditions. Yet migratory behavior can be repeatedly gained and lost within an avian lineage. For example, some species groups, including the Old World warbler genera *Sylvia* and *Phylloscopus,* have a mixed bag of migratory and nonmigratory species scattered throughout their phylogenetic past, with frequent occasions where nonmigratory lineages became migratory.

Migration has also evolved more than once in some individual species. Northernmost blackcaps (*Sylvia atricapilla*), which breed in Scandinavia and Russia, are "fully expressed" long-distance migrants that winter in Africa. Individuals from Portugal and Spain, however, are sedentary. In between these latitudinal extremes are populations with mixed strategies of short- and middle-distance migration. In the past four decades, some blackcaps that summer in England have decided not to migrate at all, probably because extra provisions from bird feeders have allowed them to improve overwinter survival. Avian ecologist Stuart Bearhop and his colleagues at the University of Exeter have determined that these sedentary birds are more likely to choose mates from among themselves rather than from the migratory individuals that arrive in spring. He predicts that this strategy, called assortative mating, may be the first step in the formation of two separate species from this one warbler species.

Some birds, such as blackcaps, exhibit mixed migration strategies which suggest that the behavior evolved independently more than once within the species.

Blackcaps are not the only avian species that demonstrates these mixed tendencies in seasonal movements; countless others are distributed both around the world and within many avian families. Reflecting upon the wanderings of *Hesperornis* during the Cretaceous period and the hypothesis of a migration threshold, it is not unreasonable to conclude that the behavioral, anatomical and physiological toolkit for migration may be present in all birds—being in some way part of what they need for day-to-day survival—and that "becoming migratory" simply requires flipping some environmentally activated switch.

Certainly some avian species are more likely to evolve migration than others. The "evolutionary precursor" hypothesis, proposed by Douglas Levey and Gary Stiles of the University of Florida in 1992, suggests that birds that historically occupied particular habitats (such as open or edge habitats) and ate certain types of food (including fruits) would evolve long-distance migration more readily, perhaps because this type of bird might be less resilient to changes in its environment. Likewise, conservation biologist Courtney Conway and graduate student Alice Boyle determined that migratory and sedentary species of flycatchers (suborder Tyranni) differ considerably in the types of habitats and foods they prefer. They also noted associations between open versus closed habitats and insectivorous (insect-eating) versus frugivorous (fruit-eating) species. Furthermore, they found that foraging group size correlates with migration: species of birds that feed alone are more likely to evolve longer-distance migration than those that feed in groups. They concluded that resource variability over time is a key to the evolution of migration in flycatchers, and that foraging in groups—with more eyes to search for those elusive food sources — is just a strategy to avoid having to migrate. Conway and Boyle add that climate probably has very little to do with it; they later renamed their premise the "resource variability" hypothesis.

Numerous studies have shown that migration can evolve very quickly within an otherwise sedentary population. In 1940, house finches (*Carpodacus mexicanus*) — pleasant little red-and-brown-striped songbirds from the American southwest — were being sold illegally in New York City as "Hollywood finches" to caged-bird fanciers. When local wildlife authorities threatened legal action under the Migratory Bird Treaty Act (which prohibits, among other things, possession and sale of wild birds), the contraband birds were released into the wilds of Long Island. They thrived, and an eastern population was born. It is believed that the captive birds were taken originally from southern California, where the finches are nonmigratory. However, by the 1960s bird-banding records indicated that almost 40 percent of the introduced eastern population was migrating short distances toward the southwest. As the years passed, their trips grew longer; by the mid-1980s some house finches were traveling to the Gulf Coast and northern Florida to spend their winter. Banding also indicated that not all eastern house finches flew south every autumn: some stayed near their breeding grounds to tough out the winter, while others migrated in some years and not in others. When researchers took a closer look at the parent population in California, they discovered that some of the western birds also moved seasonally, in ways consistent with some underlying migratory knowledge, indicating that the roots of the behavior had always been present. This behavior, known as partial migration, is observed in many other birds, and it is one mechanism by which a fully migratory species is thought to evolve.

Without a doubt, many (if not all) birds have some onboard genetic programming that gives them an innate urge to move seasonally and the ability to switch on the autopilot in order to get somewhere for the first time. Biologists have suggested that migratory animals possess some type of syndrome — an ancient suite of abilities and traits — that provides a platform for the operation of natural selection and other evolutionary mechanisms. Genetic variation between individuals and the recombination of genetic material that occurs during reproduction have provided the stuff of evolution for the past 1.5 billion years on earth. If there truly is a threshold of environmental factors that stimulates migration in birds, then genetic variation within a species — the individual's "genetic tolerance" to respond to these changes — could produce a mixed population in which some individuals are migratory and some are not.

Mixed-strategy populations of European robins in southern Germany are apparently maintained by unpredictable winter weather. Mild winters favor nonmigratory individuals because it is better to stay put if sufficient food is available, but harsh winters improve the survivability of robins that move south to avoid them. Researcher Herbert Biebach of the Max Plank Institute in Leipzig determined that migratory behavior was heritable in this species, and that clutches often contained young that were genetically programmed for both strategies—a hedge against total wipeout if sustained environmental conditions tipped the balance strongly in either direction. However, the ratios between migratory and nonmigratory offspring were not the same in all pairings: two migratory parents produced migratory offspring about 90 percent of the time. Studies with blackcaps similarly revealed that partial migration in populations is due to genetic polymorphism (a mixture of individuals with slightly different DNA) and that matings between migratory individuals produce increasing numbers of migratory offspring. These birds seem to possess a lower threshold for changing environmental factors, including breeding density and food availability. If, for instance, local conditions favor the survival or reproductive success of migratory individuals, so more of these birds live to produce more of their kind—natural selection in action—then a population could become primarily migratory within a few generations. Loss of migration could occur by this same mechanism; there are many cases of ex-migratory birds such as Canada geese (*Branta canadensis*) giving up the urge to travel under human-modified environmental conditions.

Recent genetic research on chipping sparrows (*Spizella passerina*) at the University of California has suggested that long-distance migration evolved in this species' rapidly expanding populations after the last Pleistocene glaciation. Seasonal movements appear to have begun in earnest once the species' northern front reached latitudes where harsh winter conditions favored a retreat to the south. Partially migratory populations may have been an intermediate step. If untenable winter conditions in the north led to the extinction of nonmigratory individuals in that population, what remained would be a migratory species.

Some models of the evolution of long-distance migration theorize that individuals returning to the south in winter "leapfrog" over the ancestral sedentary population that may still reside there, avoiding intraspecies competition for resources on the wintering grounds. Lack of contact between closely related individuals in both winter and summer creates reproductive isolation, which in turn creates species. Many avian species seem to demonstrate this evolutionary legacy. The blue-gray gnatcatcher (*Polioptila caerulea*), for example, is the only member of its lineage that has successfully escaped the crowded tropics, by evolving a means to exploit bountiful temperate resources.

Can these models, syndromes and hypotheses predict future changes in the migratory behavior of birds? If environmental change is the primary mechanism behind the evolution of migration, then perhaps they can. Even small changes in the global climate can affect the timing of migration and the routes and destinations chosen by the birds. Changing climates also affect the distribution and availability of critical resources, such as food and water and suitable nesting and wintering habitats. If a species is able to adjust to environmental changes in winter and summer and along the migratory route, then it will persist. For example, changes in global climate caused by the greenhouse effect have resulted in some western hummingbirds, including the migratory rufous hummingbird (*Selasphorus rufus*), showing up in the eastern United States in winter. Not long ago they would have perished at these latitudes, but now they do not. And hummingbirds are not the only ones. Dozens of avian species are experiencing shifts in their migration routes — unfortunately, not all of them favorable. Some species seem constrained when it comes to change; for example, Swainson's thrushes (*Catharus ustulatus*) are an interesting case. A recently established migratory population that breeds in Alaska takes an unusual detour in its migration journey that seems to follow some ancient pathway rather than the most direct, cost-effective route. Perhaps this population lacks the genetic blueprint required to modify its route, and insufficient genetic variation could bring doom during times of rapid environmental change.

Human-induced global climate change is creating shifts in migration timing and the distribution and abundance of resources available to migrants. Many birds are arriving earlier on the breeding grounds in spring; it is their ingrained nature to take advantage of whatever the relatively short breeding season has to offer. But sometimes conditions there are not yet consistently profitable: around the world, global climate change is affecting growing seasons, distribution patterns and the phenology (timing) of flowering and fruiting in plants. Plants are the base of the food chain on which other life depends, and insects and other invertebrates — indeed, all life on our planet — have been accordingly affected. The pied flycatcher (*Ficedula hypoleuca*) is only one of many avian species already out of sync with its primary food source. Again, some species will win and others will not.

Birds' innate drive to move through the seasons has been part of their legacy for many millions of years. Through time they have weathered ice ages; continental drift and mountain building; changes in sea level, ocean currents and precipitation patterns; and distributional shifts of resources, parasites, predators and competitors. The big difference between these background perturbations and the human-created challenges they face now is the rapidity with which the effects are kicking in. Let us hope they can keep up with us.

Shrikes

Anomalous migratory songbirds

Although they are songbirds, shrikes have evolved a feeding style that emulates some classic birds of prey, including hawks, harriers and kestrels, swooping down in rapid pursuit from an elevated hunting perch to catch insects, birds and small mammals.

For most people, the word songbird conjures up a vision of a brightly clad, diminutive bird flitting from twig to twig, happily twittering out a carefree tune. From a strictly taxonomic point of view, songbirds represent the avian order Passeriformes, a conglomerate of about 5,500 species — more than half of all living birds — that descended from an obscure common ancestor tens of millions of years ago. They are united systematically by a variety of shared traits that include the divergent structure of their feet and their forelimb and thigh muscles. Amid some debate, ornithologists have attributed

their success on our planet to features such as their small size, intelligence and rapid rates of speciation (formation of new species). To most of us, songbirds — be they finches, sparrows, thrushes or warblers — appear to be quite similar to one another in appearance and habits.

Among the vast multitude of songbirds, some stand apart from the other 5,000-plus species, and shrikes are among them. About 30 species of shrikes comprise the family Laniidae. They are typically blackbird-sized — about 8 to 12 inches (20–30 cm) in length — with generally gray, black and white plumage. Some phylogenetic analyses suggest that shrikes are most closely related to crows and jays, but shrikes have a unique way of making a living. They frequent open country habitats such as agricultural fields, grasslands and steppes, which are well suited to their foraging behavior. Although they are songbirds, they have evolved a feeding style that emulates some classic diurnal birds of prey, including hawks, harriers and kestrels.

Shrikes catch insects, birds and small mammals by swooping down in rapid pursuit from an elevated hunting perch; they drive the prey into the ground, where they dispatch it using their hawk-like hooked bill to make a few sudden jabs to the base of the neck. This bill is also well suited for subsequently tearing flesh into bite-sized pieces. Unlike true birds of prey, however, shrikes' feet — being songbird feet — do not have strong curved talons for maintaining a good purchase on the meat. But evolution rarely gives up easily, and shrikes have developed an extraordinary way to circumvent this problem. Once it is killed, shrikes transport their prey to a shrub, tree or fence line, where they impale the body on a twig, thorn or barbed wire. In some locales they are known as "butcher birds" because their rows of dangling prey are reminiscent of meat-shop windows.

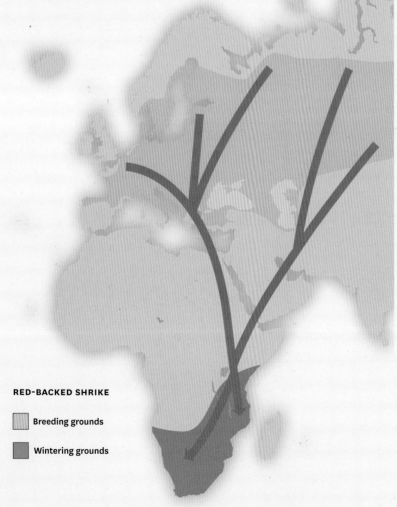

RED-BACKED SHRIKE

Breeding grounds

Wintering grounds

Lacking the strong talons of birds of prey, shrikes impale the bodies of their prey on twigs, thorns and barbed wire.

There are several species of shrikes among the migratory avifauna of the Old World, including the red-backed (*Lanius collurio*), lesser grey (*L. minor*), great grey (*L. excubitor*), masked (*L. nubicus*) and woodchat (*L. senator*) shrikes. Some species travel extensively during their nocturnal migrations to destinations as distant as the southern tip of Africa, making stopovers along the way to rest and feed during daylight hours, when their prey is active. In the breeding season many shrikes rely on other songbirds for provisioning their young; great grey shrikes, for example, regularly prey upon skylarks (*Alauda arvensis*), and their presence may even affect the distribution and density of nesting pairs. In the autumn these predators have the added benefit of being able to prey on migrants that are making the trip at the same time. Although studies are scarce, it is generally thought that other songbird species comprise an important food source for migrating shrikes, particularly when environmental conditions do not favor proliferation of other prey types such as beetles and grasshoppers.

But shrikes are not the only avian predators to take advantage of the glut of avian food available during migration. A few authentic birds of prey, including Eleonora's falcons, time their breeding to coordinate with huge waves of exhausted migrants passing through their nesting territory each autumn; both parents and chicks thrive on this easily accessible food. But Mother Nature often displays a morbid sense of humor. In a quantitative analysis of prey taken by Eleanora's falcons along the Mediterranean Sea, researcher Hartmut Walter of the University of California discovered that among the most commonly killed prey items — comprising some 15 to 20 percent of all prey taken — were red-backed, woodchat and lesser grey shrikes. What goes around comes around, it seems.

Arctic Terns
A life in the sun

The Arctic tern has one of the longest round-trip migratory routes of any bird species: about 25,000 miles (40,000 km). But why migrate so far? What precious resources require such a monumental journey?

Seasonal migration allows birds to thrive throughout the calendar year in the environmental conditions to which they are best suited. We are accustomed to think of birds spending their summers in pleasant temperate climes and their winters in the exotic and sultry tropics. When it comes to migration, however, a few birds seek something different.

The Arctic tern (*Sterna paradisaea*) has one of the longest round-trip migratory routes of any bird species: about 25,000 miles (40,000 km) from their breeding colonies in the high Arctic—as far north as Cape Morris Jessup at 84°N latitude—to their molting and nonbreeding grounds on the ice packs of Antarctica at

around 78°S. Their journey is extraordinary. In late August, when some of the younger birds are only a week past fledging, terns leave their summer homes in small flocks. Their southerly route begins in the eastern North Atlantic and takes them past western Africa; a small percentage of the migrants splits off near the equator and heads west toward the South American coast. Most individuals, however, continue to hug the African shoreline, where their food is abundant, and from there fly south to the coast of Antarctica. They spend the austral summer (December to March) between 30°W and 90°E longitude—more or less due south of Africa and western Asia—where they molt and feed heavily on krill, which is plentiful among the pack ice. Their return to the north begins in March or April. They travel more rapidly toward their breeding grounds than they did the previous autumn, moving in a broad front in which some individuals retrace their southbound route and others fly mid-ocean—sightings near Bermuda are common in April and May. By June the adult birds are nesting among the rocks and low grasses of the treeless Far North. Nonbreeding juvenile birds, like all tern species, wait until their second year of life to take a mate. They choose not to travel so far; most drop out of the wave of northward migrants as they pass central South America. Many will spend their summer feeding in the Humboldt Current off the western coast of Peru.

The spectacular journey of the Arctic tern represents a distance equal to about 54 million body lengths of this pretty, seemingly delicate white bird. What is even more astonishing from our point of view is that the tern travels its path with apparent ease. Arctic terns are long-lived

An Arctic tern chick nestles under one parent's wing for warmth while the other parent offers a small fish, one of the bird's preferred food types.

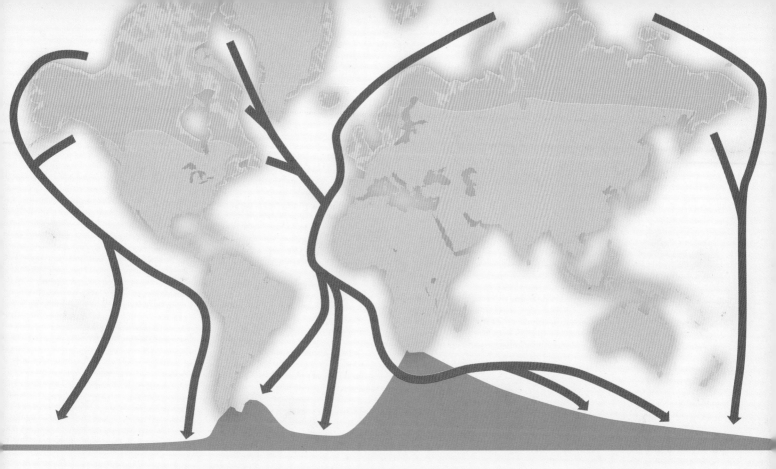

ARCTIC TERN

Breeding grounds

Wintering grounds

birds—many individuals live 25 to 30 years or more—and adult annual survival rates approach 90 percent. By comparison, banding data indicate that many other migratory bird species have annual return rates of about 45 percent or less. Thus, over a lifetime, an Arctic tern may migrate more than 600,000 miles (1 million km). But why migrate so far? What precious resources require such a monumental journey?

Thomas Alerstam and his colleagues at the University of Lund in Sweden suggest that Arctic terns may be exploiting peaks in solar energy that reach the earth's surface, or at least utilizing seasonal blooms of resource abundance associated with them. In grade-school science we learned about the food chain, an oversimplified version of the trophic (feeding) relationships between plants and animals in an ecosystem. At the bottom of the food chain are plants, also known as primary producers. They are so named because, in most systems, they are the means by which solar energy is captured and converted into a form usable by beings higher up in the food chain. Plants use a biochemical process called photosynthesis to produce simple

carbohydrates from carbon dioxide, water and light. Theoretically, more solar energy supports a greater biomass of primary producers, which in turn favors proliferation of herbivores (plant eaters) that ultimately feed the primary and secondary carnivores (meat eaters) located near the top of the chain.

What does all this have to do with the Arctic tern? Arctic terns are carnivores that feed on a variety of schooling fish, small crustaceans and zooplankton (krill), usually by shallow plunge-diving or picking up food items located near the ocean's surface. They are experts at seeking out areas of food abundance and frequently make localized movements to the best feeding grounds. Moreover, their breeding distribution in the north, their nonbreeding range in the south, and even the route they travel in between seem to favor areas of the earth's surface that receive 800 to 1,100 calories of solar energy per square centimeter per day—the most on the planet—when they are present. So although it would seem at first glance that the Arctic tern is a bird of snow, ice and all things polar, it is in fact a bird of the sun.

CHAPTER 3

The *The* **PHENOMENON** *of* **FLIGHT**

One swallow does not make a summer, but one skein of
geese, cleaving the murk of a March thaw, is the spring.

ALDO LEOPOLD

Our world is bountiful with avian species—almost 10,000 by a recent tally—equal to all the mammals and amphibians put together, and three times the count of reptiles. In fact, birds are second only to bony fish (Osteichthyes) in being the most abundant vertebrate group in terms of the number of species. Yet somehow this statistic often escapes us. After all, the bee hummingbird (*Mellisuga helenae*) does not seem *that* much different from the great bustard (*Otis tarda*). Both are bipedal vertebrates with forelimbs molded into wings for flight; both have large eyes, toothless bills and scaly feet; both lack external ears and genitals and their streamlined bodies are cloaked in smooth feathers. But these two species are polar opposites, the mouse and whale of the avian realm: they are the lightest and heaviest birds that fly. And although their size differs by only a few orders of magnitude—not 55 million times, like their mammal counterparts—their ecology and life history are just as dissimilar as the mouse's and the whale's. Hummingbirds and bustards only seem more similar because they display the legacy of the design constraints associated with powered flight.

Bosque del Apache National Wildlife Refuge in central New Mexico is winter home to a multitude of migratory birds, including approximately 30,000 snow geese (*Chen caerulescens*).

Birds are defined by flight. Both inside and outside, their structures have been modified by evolution to reduce weight and increase strength. Their physiology has been retooled to endure relentless miles of travel with little sustenance. Their nervous systems have been honed to receive and process spatial information rapidly and accurately as they hurtle through a three-dimensional environment. By relative measure, birds can travel farther and faster than an SR-1 supersonic jet aircraft; they put up with roll rates and G-forces many times greater than the most experienced military pilots can tolerate, and do so many hundreds of times per day. Birds are also more fuel-efficient and more aerobatic, capable of precise, rapid corrections in flight, and they require little maintenance and rarely crash. Birds are the ultimate flying machines. And why not? No aircraft manufacturer has ever had the benefit of 150 million years of research and development.

Until humans manage to build a time machine, we can only guess precisely how flight evolved in birds. Fossil evidence is only circumstantial: paleontologists share the challenges of forensic scientists as they try to build animals from bits of femur. For fossilization to occur, a precise set of circumstances must exist at the time of the organism's death. For one thing, the remains must be buried quickly in layers of sediment. Gradually organic materials in the animal's body are replaced by silica and other minerals from its surroundings; over millions of years the great weight of sediments accumulating overtop presses the lower layers together to form a tomb of sedimentary rock. Fossilization is thus an extremely rare process; regrettably, most of earth's life has simply vanished without leaving a trace. Fortunately for paleornithologists, however, the required elements came together perfectly one day during the late Jurassic period, some 150 million years ago.

We knew nothing about this red-letter day until 1877. Workers were busy at the Solnhofen limestone mines in Bavaria, midway between Nuremberg and Munich, quarrying fine-grained stone for the lithography industry (lithography is a process that uses pigment on a smooth stone surface to make fine-quality prints). According to one version of the story, a quarryhand named Jakob Niemeyer was splitting layers of stone, like the thick leaves of a book, when he revealed the fossil of a bird — or something very like a bird — that had been preserved almost to perfection. Niemeyer traded the fossil to a farmer named Johann Dörr, who failed to recognize the specimen's scientific merit, suggesting that it was some aberrant flying reptile, perhaps the pterosaur *Pterodactlyus*. Dörr sold it to a tax consultant named Ernst Otto Häberlein for 2,000 German marks. Although his father had amassed an impressive private collection of fossils, Häberlein chose not to keep this find, and in 1881 offered it for sale to the highest bidder. The interested parties included Othniel Charles Marsh, a vertebrate paleontologist at Yale University's

Peabody Museum. However, German institutions, unwilling to lose important specimens to collections outside the country, initiated negotiations to secure the fossil. It was ultimately purchased by the industrial magnate Ernst Werner von Siemens, founder of the corporation that bears his name; he resold the fossil for 20,000 marks to the Prussian Ministry of Culture, which presented it to the Humboldt Museum für Naturkunde in Berlin.

Within years this fossil, dubbed *Archaeopteryx* (meaning "ancient wing"), would become the most significant natural history specimen in existence — the Rosetta Stone of paleontology. It also became a poster child for the emerging evolution movement, which had begun only two decades earlier with the publication of Charles Darwin's *On the Origin of Species.* *Archaeopteryx* was not an ancient flying reptile like *Pterodactlyus,* but neither was it a bird. It was a perfect combination of both, a mosaic of teeth and feathers and bones that gave paleornithologists a 150-million-year-old missing link between modern birds and their reptilian ancestors. Museums around the world scurried to reexamine their existing collections in light of this astounding discovery. Other specimens of *Archaeopteryx* were indeed out there, including a pristine fossil of a single flight feather that had been found in the Solnhofen mines some years earlier.

What makes the Berlin specimen of *Archaeopteryx* so impressive is the clarity of its feather impressions. Stripped of these, it looks very much like the chicken-sized theropod dinosaur *Compsognathus,* with a long, bony reptilian tail; fingers tipped with claws; and a jaw full of sharp teeth. However, *Archaeopteryx*'s outstretched forelimbs bore dozens of flight feathers, so precisely preserved in stone that they can be counted and categorized like the wing feathers of modern birds. Its tail also possessed feathers, not arranged like a fan on vestigial tail bones, as they are on existing species, but attached to each elongated vertebra to form a feathered paddle-like appendage. Its entire body was garbed in a feather coat that smoothed its contours and provided insulation from the elements.

Of course, when we think about feathers, we naturally think about flight. Despite the somewhat reptilian features of *Archaeopteryx*'s skeleton, could it fly? The most significant clue came from an examination of the feather impressions, including the single fossil feather. Birds possess a battery of many different feather types; some of them function in flight and some do not. Flight feathers, the prominent feathers on the wings and tail of volant birds, are specifically configured for their aerodynamic function. They are strong but flexible, curved in cross-section, and supported along their length by a central spine, called a rachis, that is bounded on both sides by web-like vanes. One key to aerodynamic function is the relative width of these vanes. Modern birds that fly have asymmetrical vanes; in other words, the vane on the leading edge of the feather — the one that faces forward when the wing is outstretched — is narrower than the vane on its trailing edge. This has to do with the feathers' function as airfoils, which will be described later in more detail. All modern flying birds show some asymmetry in their flight feathers, while flightless birds such as ostriches and emus have symmetrical feather vanes, that is, both are more or less the same width. Although they evolved from flighted ancestors, flightless birds lost their asymmetrical vanes, along with their ability to fly, when they followed their own evolutionary trajectory.

Archaeopteryx had asymmetrical vanes — therefore it flew. Precisely how well it flew has been the topic of heated debate, but without a time machine we will never know how much its reptilian features compromised its ability to behave like a bird. On the other hand, the not-so-perfect flight configuration of *Archaeopteryx* has provided considerable insight into the evolution of flight itself. Evolutionary innovations such as the ability to fly do not appear *de novo* in their finished form; they must progress through intermediate developmental stages that are themselves adaptive. If a design does not work for some purpose, it is unlikely to last long enough to be modified further by evolutionary influences.

Nevertheless, transitional innovations do not necessarily serve the same function as their ultimate forms. For example, feathers evolved from the scales of birds' reptilian ancestors. But long before the complex structure of flight feathers came about, simpler designs functioned perfectly well to insulate small, active proto-birds from the cold. A feathered body covering likely evolved along with endothermy: maintaining a high body temperature requires a lot of food, so there is considerable benefit to reducing heat loss. A myriad of small feathered theropod dinosaurs, including *Sinocalliopteryx* and *Sinosauropteryx,* have recently been unearthed in fossil beds in China. These reptiles did not use their feathers for flight, because they lacked the rigid structure of vaned feathers, more closely resembling the down feathers that modern birds wear under their outer coat. Hence it follows that proto-birds did not just leap into the air one day to become flying vertebrates. So how did it happen?

The truth may ultimately be explained by one of two proposed hypotheses, or more likely a combination of both. The arboreal hypothesis — first championed by the same Othniel C. Marsh who lobbied to acquire the Berlin *Archeopteryx* — suggests that birds started out as tree-climbing animals, then later evolved wings to assist in controlled glides to the ground or to lower branches. This premise has the advantage that gravity would initiate takeoff, which is perhaps the most difficult part of flying. However, proponents of this hypothesis fail to explain how complex feathered wings could evolve from structures used primarily for gliding. Other gliding vertebrates—for example, flying squirrels and sugar gliders—use sail-like skin folds extended between their outstretched limbs to glide between trees. *Draco* lizards extend fanlike structures that are supported by elongated ribs. Birds, however, fly by flapping their front limbs; gliding membranes along the length of the body are simply not conducive to the evolution of feathered wings.

The cursorial hypothesis—first developed by Samuel Wendell Williston, Marsh's assistant at Yale University—suggests that birds began as small bipedal running dinosaurs that used their forelimbs to catch insects or other small prey, and that flight began as a series of short jumps into the air. Any increase in the surface area of the forelimbs, perhaps by elongation of the contour feathers already covering them, would increase the height of the jump and overall stability by providing a little more lift. Eventually arms would become wings and jumps would lead to flight. Research simulations suggest that this running-and-jumping mode of foraging could indeed yield more food captures. It is generally accepted that birds' ancestors were small, agile theropod dinosaurs—characteristically bipedal species such as *Velociraptor*—so this hypothesis makes sense. However, because of the added resistance when sweeping them through the air, some paleontologists doubt that oversized feathered forelimbs would offer an advantage for catching prey. They also feel that the ground speed required for takeoff would exceed the maximum running speeds of existing lizards and cursorial (running) birds by a factor of three. It is possible, however, that proto-birds used wind speed to increase lift during takeoff, taxiing into a headwind just like aircraft—and albatrosses.

More recently, paleornithologists have proposed a third model—the "pouncing proavis" hypothesis—which combines some elements of the previous two. This model describes proto-birds as small, active ambush predators that hid on elevated perches such as a shrubs or boulders, then jumped or swooped down to capture prey. Additional lift would allow longer and more controlled swoops, particularly if feather and wing development focused on the "hands," the location of primary flight feathers responsible for forward thrust in modern birds. This hypothesis implies a gentler, more gradual approach to the evolution of flight; even the intermediate stages of feather and wing development would provide some adaptive advantage to the animal sporting them.

Perhaps this is how *Archaeopteryx* flew. During the Jurassic period, the Solnhofen area was an island archipelago in the ancient Tethys Sea, with placid lagoons surrounded by shrubs and other low plants, but no trees. *Archaeopteryx* lacked some of the skeletal design elements that modern birds use to take off from a standing start (such as the triosseal canal, explained below), so it may have used a low swoop to get into the air. Nonetheless, the

Birds have evolved myriad anatomical innovations designed specifically to reduce weight, such as this Atlantic puffin's (*Fratercula arctica*) specialized bill, which is considerably lighter than a heavy jaw and teeth.

rest of its anatomy, including its asymmetrical flight feathers, suggests that, once airborne, *Archaeopteryx* was capable of powered flapping flight some 150 million years ago.

Since *Archaeopteryx*'s time, evolution — ever the tireless tinkerer — has continued to perfect avian design. Birds are unique among other creatures that are capable of powered flight: insects use chitinous outgrowths of their exoskeleton, and pterosaurs (flying reptiles of the Mesozoic era) and bats have leathery wings stretched between their fingers. But with evolutionary retooling come gains and losses. Birds' fully feathered forelimbs no longer sport hands with claws, so they have developed a myriad of specialized bill types for food capture and manipulation. Modern birds have no teeth and their jawbones are lightly built (although seed crushers have powerful muscles and bladelike mandibles to crack even the toughest nuts). Virtually every body component has also been modified to reduce weight and increase

power and strength, including their reproductive systems. Most female birds have a reproductive tract on only one side of the body, not on both sides like other vertebrates. Discarding the redundant part of the system not only reduces excess baggage, it also eliminates the hazards of having two fragile eggs in paired oviducts at any one time. Likewise, male birds reduce weight by shrinking their reproductive organs in winter to thousandths of their operational size during the breeding season; hormones and increasing day length trigger their renewed function in spring.

Perhaps the greatest weight-saving and strength-enhancing measures in birds are reflected in their highly modified skeletons. First, the bones of the skull and body are pneumaticized, or hollow, although strengthened by internal reinforcements. For instance, inside the longer bones of vultures are diagonal struts that form repeated W patterns, resembling the trusses used to strengthen airplane wings and the structural steel of bridges. The resulting weight reduction is considerable. The magnificent frigatebird (*Fregata magnificens*), a large black bird of the southern oceans, has a wingspan of about 7 feet (2.1 m), yet its entire skeleton, including the skull, weighs only about 4 ounces (113 g), much less than a small can of tuna.

Fused body elements also increase strength with little added weight. The bird's manus (hand), which supports the flight feathers responsible for the powerful thrust-producing downstroke, contains only a few elements—not dozens like the human hand and wrist—most of which are fused into a single sturdy bone. Furthermore, the tail is supported by vertebrae fused into a distinctively avian attribute called the pygostyle; this blade-like structure provides attachment surfaces for the intricate musculature that moves and orients the tail feathers. The rib cage and pelvis are also extensively fused to brace against the crushing pressures of wing stroke and landing, respectively.

On the largest scale, a volant bird's entire body has been configured for flight and every part serves an aerodynamic purpose. Flying birds have a fuselage like an aircraft's: streamlined, with a rounded leading surface (the head) and a trailing edge that tapers to a fine point (the tail), creating the smallest amount of drag per unit of body volume. To maintain the smooth flow of air, the legs and feet—the undercarriage needed for pushing off or taxiing—quickly align into position after takeoff to further reduce drag. An osprey fishing offers a good example of the importance of streamlining. The osprey (*Pandion haliaetus*) is a large—24 inches (60 cm) long, weighing 3 to 4.4 pounds (1.4–2.0 kg)—flashy brown and white bird of prey that plunges dramatically into the water to catch fish with its feet. It prefers a substantial dinner, sometimes taking fish as large as 2 pounds (900 g). Becoming airborne carrying a heavy, wriggling fish often requires considerable effort.

OPPOSITE After a fish is captured, the osprey orients its heavy, wriggling prey in line with its own body to reduce drag and increase flight efficiency.

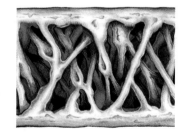

Birds' lightweight hollow bones are reinforced internally by diagonal struts that resemble those used to strengthen bridges and aircraft wings.

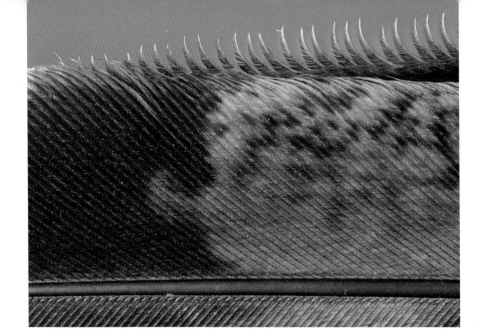

Flight feathers have a rigid central rachis that supports flexible vanes. Owl flight feathers, such as those of the long-eared owl (*Asio otus*) shown here, also possess fringe-like projections on their leading edge that contribute to silent flight.

However, after only a brief moment of frenetic flapping, the osprey adjusts its grasp on its prey to turn its head forward into the slipstream that flows over its body in flight. The fish slung below melds into the aerodynamic shape of the bird carrying it, and the osprey's wing-beats can slow to a steady, confident pace.

On the smallest scale, a bird's instrument of aerodynamics is the feather. Feathers are the hallmark of the class Aves, and until very recently was the one tried-and-true trait used to define a bird: "If it has feathers, it is a bird. If it does not, it is not a bird." A recent fly in the ointment has been those feathered dinosaurs from China—they certainly have feathers, but they are definitely not birds. We know that evolution tends to produce a multitude of experimental designs, often used for more than one purpose, before one really catches on. Many lineages may have possessed feathers and featherlike structures for warmth but not for flight. The flight feather was a mind-boggling evolutionary innovation, and the complexity of its design suggests that it evolved only once. Modern birds certainly descended from a single ancestral lineage.

Feathers are made of keratin, the tough structural protein that also contributes to hair, fingernails, horns and hooves. Bird keratin, however, is of a type unique to reptiles (remember, birds are reptiles); it comprises the scales of reptilian skin and on birds' legs, as well as claws and beaks. Moreover, feather keratin has a somewhat different molecular constitution from typical reptilian keratin that makes it more resistant to wear. Many birds also have granules of the black pigment melanin incorporated into their feather keratin, to make the feathers more durable. This is why we see black flight feathers on the wing tips of many birds such as gulls, terns and cranes; plumage there degrades more quickly from passing rapidly through the air with each wing stroke.

Feathers must be strong, but they must also be flexible and lightweight. The sheer number of feathers in a bird's coat—from about 1,000 in ruby-throated hummingbirds to 25,000 in tundra swans (*Cygnus columbianus*)—dictates parsimony in design. Most of these are contour feathers, which cover the body. To save weight they are arranged in distinctive tracts on the skin, with featherless strips in between hidden by overlapping feathers on top. Even so, its feather coat usually comprises 15 to 20 percent of a bird's total weight.

Though fewer in number, the flight feathers of the wings and tail share a common feature with contour feathers: they are both vaned, with a rigid central rachis. The vanes themselves are a miracle of design. Hold a flight feather up to the light and you will see that it is almost translucent because of spaces between its primary structural components. Run your fingers from tip to base to disrupt the vanes' continuity, then sweep them back to the tip to "mend" the tears that you created. Bend the feather and it will spring back to its original shape. What underlie these phenomenal characteristics are rows and rows of parallel interlocking barbs. Barbs in adjacent rows are locked together by their side branches, which are called barbules. Barbules on the anterior (front) barbs are armed with tiny hooks that latch into ridged plated barbules on the posterior (back) barbs—think Velcro. This microstructure is what confers flexibility and light weight. Superficial feather damage is easily repaired as preening birds repeatedly run their bills along their feathers from the base to the tip, "zipping" all the barbs and barbules back into their proper interlocking positions to restore the feathers' integrity.

The most notable feature of flight feathers is the asymmetrical arrangement of their vanes, which have been crafted by evolution so that each feather functions as a tiny airfoil. Wings are also airfoils, and so is, to some degree, the entire form of the bird in flight; all these features remind us that the design of a bird is dedicated to flight at every level. An airfoil is a structure whose shape generates lift as it passes through the air. In order to fly, a bird (and an aircraft) must be able to generate sufficient lift to overcome the downward effects of gravity operating on its mass. In cross-section, airfoils have a convex top surface and a concave bottom surface. They typically have a thicker rounded leading edge that tapers gently to a thin trailing edge. When air flows over an airfoil, it must travel faster over the longer convex surface than it does over the shorter bottom surface, which produces an area of lower pressure above the airfoil that causes it to rise. Generally, the faster the flow of air over the airfoil, the greater the lift generated, which is why birds that have small wings relative to their body weight—such as mallard

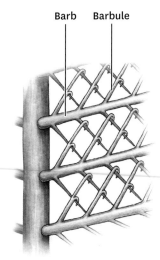

Barb   Barbule

Vaned feathers possess rows of parallel barbs that are locked together by hooked side branches called barbules, a microstructure that confers strength, flexibility and light weight.

Some birds, such as kestrels, can remain stationary in flight because strong winds passing over their wings produce sufficient lift to keep them aloft. This behavior is known as windhovering.

ducks (*Anas platyrhynchos*) — must fly quickly to stay aloft. This phenomenon, called the Bernoulli effect after the Swiss mathematician Daniel Bernoulli (1700–82), also explains how sailboats can move even when the wind is not blowing from directly behind them.

The speed of the air passing over an airfoil can be augmented by wind speed. Both aircraft and birds get an extra boost of lift by taking off into a headwind. Albatrosses are big seabirds with long, narrow wings that can take off only in this manner; consequently they are restricted to the "roaring 40s" — the southern oceans around 40°S latitude, where brisk winds are the status quo. Landing into a headwind is also useful because the extra lift delays stalling at increasingly slower speeds. If the breeze is stiff enough, smaller birds like the kestrel (*Falco tinnunculus*) can remain aloft without flapping their wings. Called windhovering, this hunting technique allows the bird to get a good look at activities of mice, lizards and other small prey on the ground. This remarkable behavior is so characteristic of the kestrel that a common old English name for the species was windhover.

The amount of lift generated by an airfoil can be increased, up to a point, by increasing the angle of attack, which is the orientation of the airfoil relative to the airflow. Typically, tipping a wing back about 5 to 10 degrees from the horizontal will create a sizable benefit, both from the increase in lift generated along the wing's surfaces and from the downward deflection of the airflow by its trailing edge. Newton's Third Law — which states that for every action there is an equal but opposite reaction — reminds us that downward deflection of the air would tend to push the airfoil up. However, increasing the angle of attack by too much, say 15 degrees or more, decreases lift because it creates turbulence on the back half of the airfoil. From a bird's point of view, this decrease in lift can have advantages, particularly when landing. Landing birds must slow their airspeed rapidly while descending. One way to do this is to tip the wings so far back that they lose aerodynamic function, causing the bird to plummet toward the ground in a controlled stall; it maintains enough lift not to crash by opening its wings fully, fanning its tail and spreading its toes. Just before making contact, a little bit of back-flapping (think reverse thrusters) scrubs the last bit of airspeed, and the bird lands safely.

Feathers and body shape aside, certainly the primary airfoils on a bird are its wings. Yet these remarkable structures serve another critical purpose: they are also a bird's engine. And it is the avian form of powered, flapping flight that places birds apart from — and beyond — the flight capabilities of other volant creatures, and humans, as aeronautical innovators. If a duck were an airplane, it would merely hold its wings immobile and kick with its feet, which, of course, it does not.

Birds' wings are akin to other vertebrate forelimbs, regardless of whether they swim, fly, run or use tools. Despite obvious modifications in shape and size, inside the wing are the same bones as in the human arm: metacarpals and phalanges in the hand, radius and ulna in the forearm, and a humerus in the upper arm that connects to the shoulder, or pectoral girdle. Wing bones, however, have been redesigned to provide extreme mobility — wings must fold and stretch, move up and down, and rotate fore and aft. Even the joints between the bones have evolved large, flattened surfaces that allow wings to be tucked neatly against the body when at rest. All these intricate movements require the assistance of about 50-odd different muscles, which are designed to move with maximal strength and minimal energy requirements. Consequently the amount of heavy tissue decreases toward the wing tip, with the greatest muscle mass positioned right next to the body. This is characteristic of virtually all vertebrate biomechanical designs: the largest muscles operating the human leg are located at the hips, not the feet, because less energy is expended to move a limb if the bulk of its weight is positioned near the center of its mass. This paradigm explains many aspects of vertebrate design, such as why you get a better cardiovascular workout if you wear ankle weights when you jog — and why there is never enough meat on a barbecued chicken wing.

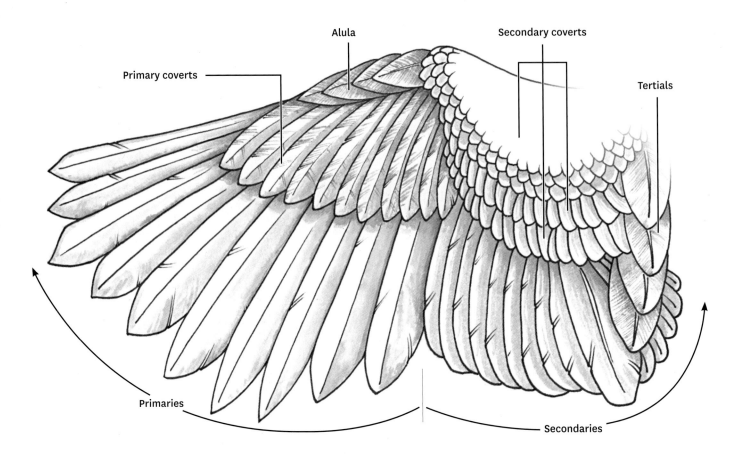

Primary flight feathers generate forward thrust during the downstroke, and secondaries provide a surface area upon which lift is generated. The alula can also be extended to create lift. Rows of coverts cover the bases of these feathers to produce a smooth wing surface without gaps.

On the outside of a bird's wing are different feather groups specifically designed for the various needs of flight. The most prominent are the strong, flexible asymmetrical flight feathers—also called remiges—that line the trailing edge of the wing. On the outer reaches of the wing, connected to the avian hand, are the primary flight feathers. Primaries are typically more robust than other wing feathers because they must be rowed quickly through the air to provide forward thrust. Lift is not the only requirement for flight; without forward thrust to overcome the forces of drag from air resistance, birds would be going nowhere fast. Most birds have 9 to 11 primaries, although the number varies somewhat; grebes, for example, have 12.

Secondary flight feathers are attached the ulna, usually the largest bone in the avian forelimb, which is between wrist and elbow. Secondaries make up most of the wing's area; they function primarily to provide a large surface upon which lift can be generated. The number of secondaries varies considerably depending on the shape of the wing and the life history of the bird that owns it. Nine to 11 secondaries are typical for songbirds, and 11 to 15 for pigeons and doves. Hummingbirds, whose wings have been retooled for hovering, have only 6 secondaries. On the other hand, the long gliding wings of vultures and albatrosses call for 25 and 40 secondaries respectively.

The tertial flight feathers are connected to the humerus, the bone in the upper arm that attaches to the pectoral girdle (shoulder). Tertials are there to fill the space between the secondaries and the bird's body. The alular feathers are attached as a group to the avian thumb, tucked up on the leading edge of the wing near the wrist. In many birds the alula forms a distinct mini-wing that can be manipulated to create a slot between itself and the rest of the wing, providing additional lift under some circumstances. Concealing the bases of the flight feathers where they attach to the wing bones are rows and rows of covert feathers. Overlapping coverts fill the gaps between the flight feathers like tiles on a roof, producing a slick, aerodynamic surface that reduces turbulence in flight. Finally, short contour feathers cloak the front of the wing to provide a smooth, rounded leading edge.

The wings are operated by a miracle of avian engineering. Typically, limbs are manipulated by alternating contractions of opposing muscle groups. In humans the deltoids (in the shoulder) and latissimus dorsi (in the lower back) work against each other to rotate the arm at the shoulder. The standard configuration has muscle mass on each side of the structure that is being maneuvered. This works fine for most vertebrates, but not for birds. Birds need immense muscles to operate their wings, particularly during the downstroke, because that part of the wing-beat cycle produces forward thrust by displacing air. The upstroke, or recovery stroke, that follows serves primarily to return the wings to their original position. Birds reduce their effort on the recovery stroke — why fight air resistance? — by folding their wings slightly and opening the primaries to allow air to pass through. Think of a rowboat: the boat is propelled forward when your pull on the handles digs the oars in deep to displace water (the downstroke). You return the oars to the start of the power-stroke by lifting them out of the water and moving them through the air, which has less resistance (the recovery stroke). Incidentally, hummingbirds can hover because they "row" in both directions, providing power on both downstroke and recovery stroke. Try this in a rowboat and it quickly becomes apparent that you stay in more or less the same place, and get an excellent workout for both your deltoids and latissimus dorsi. Interestingly, when birds row through the air, they produce donut-shaped vortices of turbulence off their wing tips, much like the swirling eddies of water that form at the ends of oars.

If birds had pectoral girdles like those of nonvolant vertebrates, they would be built like linebackers, with heavy wing musculature on both the dorsal (top/back) and ventral (underside/belly) sides of their body, which would compromise their center of gravity and aerodynamic shape. Fortunately,

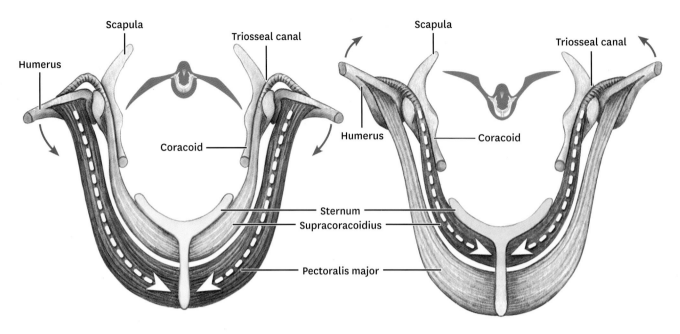

DOWNSTROKE

UPSTROKE

Scapula

Humerus

Triosseal canal

Coracoid

Scapula

Triosseal canal

Humerus

Coracoid

Sternum

Supracoracoidius

Pectoralis major

Both the upstroke and the downstroke of the wing are effected by the contraction of flight muscles attached to the sternum's keel, shown here in cross section.

the avian pectoral girdle and sternum (breastbone) have been entirely redesigned to better suit their purposes. Birds have two primary flight muscles, the pectoralis major and the supracoracoideus, both of which originate on the sternum and operate the wing from the underside of the body. In volant birds, the sternum has a deep keel, not unlike the underside of a sailboat, that provides a large surface for muscle attachment. Usually, the deeper the keel, the stronger the flier. Domestic chickens are poor fliers, a fact that may be verified while preparing Sunday dinner. The white meat of chicken is made up of the pectoralis major and supracoracoideus muscles. When carving the bird, you can clearly see that this breast meat is attached to a long, keel-shaped bone that runs down the midline below the neck. This is the sternum, which in chickens is rather shallow and underdeveloped—ergo, poor flight capability. This bone is often not really bone at all, but cartilage, like the tip of your nose; this speaks volumes about the commercial poultry industry, which has perfected mass production of full-sized chickens that are apparently not yet old enough for their bones to be entirely ossified.

The pectoralis major, which powers the downstroke, is the larger of the two flight muscles and is visible directly under the skin. In some strong fliers like pigeons, this muscle alone may encompass 15 to 20 percent of the bird's entire body weight. Beneath the pectoralis lies the smaller supracoracoideus, which terminates in an obvious tendon—a sometimes problematic feature when preparing poultry for the skillet—that contributes to the elegant pulley system that allows birds to carry virtually all their flight muscles on the underside. The tendon passes up through a bony structure known as the triosseal canal, which is formed by the junction of three bones that contribute to the avian pectoral girdle — the coracoid, scapula and furcula — and then attaches to the top side of the humerus. The pectoralis major, on the other hand, inserts on the underside of the humerus.

When the pectoralis major contracts, it pulls the wing down, but the real elegance of the design can be seen on the recovery stroke. Because the supracoracoideus muscle inserts on the top of the humerus, its contraction causes the wing to snap up, even though the muscle is technically pulling from beneath. This maneuver is called the wing flip. Decades ago, studies of surgically altered pigeons demonstrated that the wing flip is critically important for taking off from a standing start: it rapidly snaps the wings into a position where they can create the major downstrokes required to get airborne. Once in the air, the wing stroke can be recovered more easily, simply by allowing air resistance to push the wings back. All modern volant birds have this tendon-pulley apparatus, but *Archaeopteryx* did not — a primary reason why paleornithologists are stymied when trying to reconstruct its flight capabilities.

Another key feature of the avian pectoral girdle — which *Archaeopteryx* and some theropod dinosaurs did have — is the furcula. In the chicken dinner realm this is better known as the wishbone, the equivalent of the mammalian clavicles, or collarbones. In addition to forming a section of the triosseal canal at its upper end, the furcula is also part of a strut-like triangular framework that encloses the chest cavity and resists the wings' crushing pressure as they are repeatedly pulled down. Anyone familiar with the wishbone knows that it must be dried for a day or two before it will snap apart suitably, being otherwise too bendy to work properly. Experiments using European starlings (*Sturnus vulgaris*) demonstrated that the furcula's flexibility allows it to act like a spring, storing energy on the downstroke to be subsequently released on the recovery stroke. The purpose of this may be twofold: first, in providing low-cost energy to assist in wing recovery, and second, in helping to ventilate the lungs and forward air sacs (see chapter 4) with its bellows-like movement.

Their anatomical attributes are common to all birds that fly, and to many of their ancestors. However, the specific nature of flight varies considerably among birds according to the ecological nature and life history of the species, and much of this variation can be diagnosed from wing shape and size. Flight speed, aerial ability and energy consumption all depend on the physical attributes of the wing — in particular, wing loading and aspect ratio.

Wingspans range from about 3 inches (8 cm) in hummingbirds, which weigh about 0.1 ounce (2 g), to around 10 feet (3 m) for a 22-pound (10 kg) albatross. Typically, the larger the bird, the greater the wingspan. However, the true energetic cost of flight is best determined by calculating the bird's wing loading: basically its body weight divided by its wing area. Birds with small wings relative to their body mass—such as auks, loons and grebes, which spend more time diving and swimming than they do flying—have high wing loading: about 2.6 grams per square centimeter for thick-billed murres (*Uria lomvia*). These species must run over the water's surface flapping their wings madly to gain sufficient lift for takeoff. In contrast, herring gulls (*Larus argentatus*), which weigh about the same, have much larger wings, and consequently lower wing loading (approximately 0.42 grams per square centimeter), which confers seemingly effortless flight.

Another key feature is aspect ratio, a measure that summarizes wing shape as a function of its span relative to its chord, or width. In general, birds with long, narrow wings, such as albatrosses and frigatebirds, are described as having high-aspect wings. Birds with stubby, rounded wings, including wrens, doves and pheasants, have low-aspect wings. Biologists, in their endless quest to explain and categorize nature, have identified four major classes of wings. It is important to note, however, that wild things rarely fit gracefully into categories; many species exhibit aspects of two categories or fall somewhere in between. Nonetheless, you can tell a great deal about what a bird does for a living by looking at its wings.

Wings with the lowest aspect ratio are often called elliptical wings, because their substantial width relative to their span confers a somewhat rounded profile. Elliptical wings are suited to steep, explosive takeoffs and rapid flight amid tangles of leaves and branches. Their fast wing-beats are capable of moving a considerable amount of air, producing rapid acceleration, which is particularly useful for species that are viewed as dinner by discerning predators. Elliptical wings are also frequently slotted. When open, the slots—the spaces between the primary feathers—create the appearance of fingers. Wing slotting provides added lift without sacrificing maneuverability, because each primary acts like a separate miniature airfoil. Think of a wide river being forced through a downstream narrows; as the water passes through the confined channel, it is forced to speed up. Slots work in a similar fashion. As the air passes through the spaces between the feathers, it speeds up; greater air speed over an airfoil equals more lift.

Most songbirds have elliptical wings, and very active species are more likely to have prominent wing slotting. For example, gray catbird (*Dumetella carolinensis*) wings have slots along almost half their length. Additional lift is sometimes conferred by well-developed feathers on the alulae, the avian equivalent of thumbs. The alula can function as an additional mini-wing because it can be moved up and forward to open a slot between itself and the leading edge of the main wing. Humans first imitated these

structures—called slats on aircraft wings—in 1919, when they were adapted by the English aircraft manufacturing company Handley Page Ltd. Slats (and alulae) work because they redirect the moving stream of air along the wing's upper surface to smooth out turbulence, allowing the aircraft (or bird) to fly more slowly without stalling. Sitting over the wing of a commercial aircraft on final approach provides an excellent view of slat operation. Or watch a songbird land on a branch and you will see precisely where we got the idea.

European robins (*Erithacus rubecula*), like many songbirds, have elliptical wings, which are well suited for quick takeoffs and rapid flight through vegetation. Slots between primary feathers provide added lift without sacrificing maneuverability.

On the spectrum's opposite end are wings with a high aspect ratio, which are very long and narrow. Perhaps the most extreme configuration is the wings of albatrosses and giant petrels; the wandering albatross has a wingspan of 10 feet (3 m) but the wing chord is typically only about 1 foot (30 cm) at its widest. Unlike elliptical wings, this configuration lacks maneuverability at low speed, because of the size of the span. Furthermore, turbulence created off the trailing edge of their overly narrow wings, as well as the high wing loading characteristic of such large birds, increases stalling speed considerably. These factors make such wings particularly unwieldy during takeoffs and landings, which could be more aptly described as controlled disasters. Many an albatross has tumbled beak-over-heels into a squawking tangle of wings after an aborted takeoff, or performed a spectacular face plant at the end of the runway—hence the epithet "gooney bird." What albatrosses and similar birds are perfectly suited for, however, is dynamic soaring.

High-aspect wings of albatrosses, such as the Campbell albatross (*Thalassarche impavida*), are perfectly adapted for dynamic soaring but are decidedly unsuitable for elegant takeoffs and landings.

The large oceanic birds spend the majority of their life on the wing, many coming to land only to nest. They even feed on the wing, by picking flying fish and jellyfish from the ocean's surface as they glide above it. They could never sustain this lifestyle with flapping flight; indeed, considerable energy is consumed by takeoff alone. However, they are able to stay aloft for weeks on end because they soar effortlessly over the waves on set wings. Even the energy required to hold the wings outstretched is minimized by a wing-bone locking mechanism that allows the radius to slide backward and slip over a bump on the ulna. Wandering albatrosses regularly make extended oceanic feeding forays that last several weeks; during this time they alight on the water only occasionally for a brief snooze of no more than an hour and a half. Albatrosses have also been known to circumnavigate the globe in less than 80 days, rivaling the efforts of Jules Verne's heroic Phileas Fogg.

To perform these miraculous feats, dynamic soaring birds cruise along the windward side of large wave crests, using air deflected up by the swelling waves to provide lift. First they make a shallow dive downwind from an altitude of about 65 feet (20 m), increasing velocity as they descend. Just as the bird reaches the water's surface, it turns gracefully into the wind and ascends skyward as it rides the updraft. When it has again achieved altitude, it turns

Dynamic soaring birds cruise effortlessly along the windward side of cresting waves using resulting updrafts to provide lift. They then steer downwind and descend toward the ocean's surface, where they turn into the wind to gain altitude again.

into the wind once more and repeats the circling dive. Provided that the wind and waves persist — and they always do where soaring birds are found — the process can be repeated almost endlessly with little effort.

Nonetheless, many of the world's greatest long-distance migrants have high-speed wings, which are long and relatively slim, with swept back, un-slotted "hands" — these are the wings of terns, sandpipers and swifts. High-speed wings are best suited to rapid, open-country flying; slots may perform well in vertical and slow-speed flight, but they hamper fuel efficiency in level flapping flight. Unlike a slotted wing, the tapered tip of the high-speed wing generates little drag-producing turbulence in the form of vortices as it passes through the air. On the downside, tapered primaries produce less lift than blunter ones, and they confer somewhat less maneuverability. Consequently, high-speed wings must be flapped almost continuously, and heavier birds with higher wing loading, such as dabbling ducks, must beat their wings very quickly to generate sufficient lift.

What high-speed wings sacrifice in slow-speed performance they regain many times over in blistering speed. The aerial pursuits of the peregrine falcon (*Falco peregrinus*) are well known in North America; swept-back high-speed wings serve this species well as it dives headlong toward prey at up to 200 miles (322 km) an hour. A less well-known swift in India, the white-throated needletail (*Hirundapus caudacutus*) has been clocked at 219 miles (352 km) per hour in level flight — a spectacular accomplishment from an avian family that well deserves its moniker. Even the more pedestrian swifts can perform wonders: common swifts have been known to journey more than 560 miles (900 km) per day during migration, and it has been estimated that chimney swifts (*Chaetura pelagica*) travel over a million miles (1.6 million km) during their lifetime.

While achievable, such speeds are not characteristic of birds during migration, even swifts. On the long haul, birds must choose an optimal speed that allows them to cover the greatest distance over ground while using fuel

Peregrine falcons (*Falco peregrinus*) have long, pointed wings that are well suited for high-speed flight because they produce considerably less drag than other wing types.

(stored fat reserves) with utmost efficiency. Those of us committed to conserving our precious fossil fuel supply know that driving a car at high speed wastes gasoline. Driving slowly is more fuel-efficient, but given the much shorter distances covered at lower speeds and the longer time required to get where you are going (all the while burning fuel), this is not a practical solution either. Studies show that most cars peak in fuel economy at around 50 miles (80 km) per hour. It is much the same for birds. Despite considerable differences among species, optimal cruising speeds for most migrants range from about 25 to 45 miles (40–70 km) per hour.

There are times, however, when avian design favors an alternative strategy—in this case, slotted high-lift wings. Most frequently we see this wing overhead as a distinctive silhouette against an afternoon sky; it is the wing of eagles, hawks and most other birds of prey (except falcons), as well as vultures. Slotted high-lift wings are just what their name implies; they have a relatively low aspect ratio to provide ample surface area for lift generation; they are strongly cambered (curved in cross-section); and they have prominent slotted "fingers." The benefits of these traits to the birds that possess them are twofold: they provide enough power to carry heavy prey aloft and enough lift to soar effortlessly on thermal updrafts.

When the earth is heated by solar radiation, rotating rising columns of warm air called thermals may result; they typically form in predictable areas according to topography. A bird with slotted high-lift wings can exploit these

High-lift slotted wings allow large birds such as turkey vultures to soar slowly and effortlessly. This is a particularly useful strategy for species that spend considerable time aloft searching for food on the ground.

thermals to gain both altitude and horizontal travel virtually free of charge. It enters the thermal near its base, holding its wings outstretched, and circles upward, riding the ascending warm air. It then leaves that thermal current and glides effortlessly down to the base of an adjacent thermal to begin rising again. A soaring bird's weight will cause it to lose altitude at a rate of 3 to 6 feet (1–2 m) per second in still air. However, if the thermal is well established—rising at perhaps 13 feet (4 m) per second—the net direction of movement will be upward. The ability to ride thermals varies from species to species. For example, turkey vultures (*Cathartes aura*), with their longer wings, soar somewhat more easily than the shorter- and rounder-winged black vultures (*Coragyps atratus*), which must wait until later in the day for thermals to be sufficiently robust.

Our knowledge of thermal soaring in birds was pioneered by ornithologist Colin Pennycuick at the University of Bristol. He followed vultures on the Serengeti Plain in East Africa as they traveled via thermals from their night roosts to their daytime feeding grounds. Pennycuick used a motorized glider that could switch, just like the birds, from soaring to powered flight as necessary. He found the vultures could travel about 47 miles (75 km) riding only six thermals that rose to approximately 5,000 feet (1,500 m). Not only did the birds know how to use thermals, they always knew where to find them. This predictability of formation and birds' learned or innate knowledge of thermals have enabled birders to witness vast numbers of birds of

Large, broad-winged birds such as hawks and vultures use rising and rotating columns of warm air to gain altitude with little energetic cost — a process known as thermal soaring.

prey during migration. Each autumn, more than 20,000 southbound hawks and eagles ride the thermals above Hawk Mountain Ridge in the Appalachian Mountains of central eastern Pennsylvania, near Reading and Allentown. Here, "kettles" of birds such as broad-winged hawks (*Buteo platypterus*) present a spectacular display while providing ornithologists with critical information about the well-being of North American raptor populations.

Some migrating birds pursue yet another way to gain a free ride: they fly in formation. We are all familiar with honking V-shaped flocks of geese. Even before the advent of modern science, the great poets of ancient Rome and early-17th-century naturalists recognized the benefits of formation flight. English cleric Edward Topsell (1572–1625) wrote in *The Fowles of Heaven* that he believed V-formations allowed cranes to cut through the air more readily, and that captains of the flock, selected from among the older birds, took turns leading the others. Despite the anthropomorphism, he understood the fundamental reason for formation flying: it saves energy. As the wings move in flight, they produce swirling vortices of air turbulence trailing off their tips — the downwash being more inward and the upwash slightly to the outside. The upwash gives birds flying just off and behind the wingtips of others a bit of added lift. And extra lift saves energy — aircraft flying in a similar formation can save up to 15 percent on fuel by using this strategy. The advantage may be as high as 50 percent in migratory birds, especially large, heavy birds such as geese and storks. Moreover, American white pelicans (*Pelecanus erythrorhynchos*) flying in formation were found to have heart rates 11.4 to 14.5 percent lower than those flying alone under similar circumstances.

Research has also shown that birds know precisely where to position themselves to receive the greatest benefit in formation flying. In one study, 44 skeins of pink-footed geese (*Anser brachyrhynchus*) were assessed to determine the relative placement of flock members in flight. Ornithologists discovered that the spacing between the birds' wingtips averaged 6.7 inches (17 cm), give or

Geese are frequently observed flying in formation while migrating, a behavior that may boast an energy savings as high as 50 percent.

take less than an inch (2.5 cm). The birds were choosing their optimal aerodynamic position very carefully, not by accident, and with great precision. And what about all that honking? Some people suggest that birds flying in formation are communicating important information about their operational status or position to other flock members. No one can lead all the time, and in reality no single bird does. This is because the bird at the head receives no benefit in energy conservation and may tire more quickly than those following behind, just like the athlete leading the cohort in the Boston Marathon or the Tour de France. Watch geese flying overhead and you will occasionally see a weary leader drop back to be replaced by a fresher companion.

From their outward appearance, birds are all about flight, but for every advantage gained, evolution has imposed a cost or constraint. Migration taxes these designs to the utmost, since success also requires both innate knowledge and experience and the physiology for and adaptations to fuel the journey. Migration necessitates flight, of course, but no less than it requires knowing where to go and having the will to get there; even the lowliest sparrow possesses these skills in spades. Perhaps it is birds' command of these attributes that draws us land-bound creatures into flights of fancy as we watch them in the sky above us.

Wheatears
The finer points of wing shape

Evolution has resulted in a vast array of wing shapes, each suited to a species' particular needs. Subtle differences in design can be found even among closely related species.

The unwritten laws of evolution dictate that the characteristics of living things that are necessary for survival are subject to considerable selection pressure. In other words, if something is important, it will be tinkered with on an ongoing basis as it moves toward perfection of design. Over the eons, this fiddling with birds' body plans has resulted in a vast array of wing shapes, each suited to the species' particular needs. Even among closely related species we can observe subtle differences in design that reflect recent evolutionary modifications of a basic theme. Such is the case with wheatears.

Wheatears (genus *Oenanthe*) are songbirds, typically with bold black and white plumage and flamboyant behaviors, that breed predominantly in the Old World, from western Europe and Great Britain eastward across Eurasia to northern Siberia, and south through most of Asia, the Middle East and Africa. They were traditionally considered to be thrushes (family Turdidae), but more recently have been classified among the Old World flycatchers (family Muscicapidae). By one account, their common name—which has nothing to do with either wheat or ears—results from English physician Thomas Bowdler's (1754–1825) rewriting of the works of William Shakespeare to make the more bawdy passages suitable for children. The story maintains that wheatears' previous common name referred inappropriately—according to Bowdler—to the birds' white rumps.

The 20-odd species of wheatears are diverse in their seasonal movements, some being migratory and some not. The northern wheatear (*Oenanthe oenanthe*) has the widest nesting distribution of the genus. It is best known for its relatively recent colonization of Greenland, northeastern Canada and Alaska; it expanded its breeding range east and west following the retreat of the continental glaciers that ended the last ice age, about 10,000 years ago. The fascinating legacy of this range expansion is that northern wheatears continue to migrate back to their traditional wintering grounds in central Africa, regardless of their breeding location. Consequently, some individuals have migratory routes more than 9,300 miles (15,000 km) long. At the other end of the spectrum are species such as the Somali (*O. phillipsi*) and red-breasted (*O. bottae*) wheatears, residents of tropical shrublands and grasslands in Africa and Saudi Arabia, which do not migrate at all.

Although wheatears differ little in their genetic makeup, they vary considerably with regard to their wing shape, in particular the length and relative degree of "pointedness" of their

Northern wheatears — female (left) and male (right) — are long-distance migrants that possess somewhat more pointed wings than closely related sedentary wheatear species.

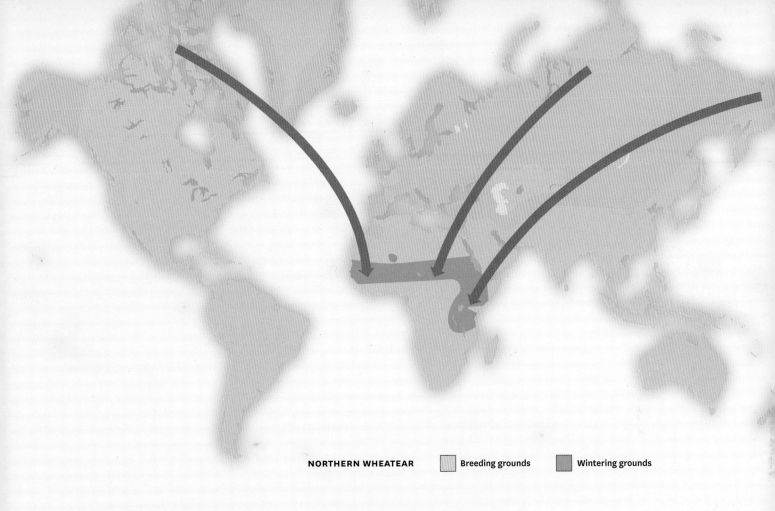

NORTHERN WHEATEAR ☐ Breeding grounds ▓ Wintering grounds

wings. Since long, pointed wings confer better fuel efficiency in flight than short, rounder wings, it is natural to assume that migratory wheatear species will have longer, pointier wings than sedentary species. A recent study demonstrates this elegantly. Researchers at the University of Amsterdam, the Ispahan University of Technology and Université Montpellier compared the migration index—the overlap between breeding and wintering ranges—of all wheatear species with ratios of their wing parameters, including wing length and roundness and the degree of slottedness. Not surprisingly, they found that the long-distance migratory species, such as northern and Isabelline (*O. isabellina*) wheatears, had the wheatear equivalent of the classic high-speed wing. The wings of sedentary species, on the other hand, were more elliptical in shape. The results also suggested that migratory wheatears might be somewhat lighter in weight, relative to their body size, than nonmigratory species, which would confer lower wing-loads on birds that needed to fly farther.

An interesting aside to the extremes of the researchers' data involves desert-dwelling species such as hooded (*O. monacha*) and white-crowned (*O. leucopyga*) wheatears. Although these species are sedentary, their wing shapes lie somewhere between those of the other nonmigratory and migratory species. The researchers suggested that this was because of their need to make frequent and occasionally long foraging flights in order to find sufficient food and water in their harsh, patchy desert habitat. Somewhat improved fuel efficiency and lower wing-loading would benefit these species as well.

It is human nature to imagine evolution as a plodding process that requires millions of years to bring about measurable change, but this is not always the case. Just like the rapid cultural evolution of humans, which can change a bird's common name in the blink of an eye, morphological evolution can fashion a bird's wing according to its needs at a correspondingly blinding speed—relatively speaking.

Dippers
Migrants in another dimension

Altitudinal migrants move up and down rather than across with seasonal change. Rather than heading south when the weather turns cold, these birds move downslope to find more suitable conditions.

We are most accustomed to thinking about bird migration in two dimensions, with movements generally parallel to the earth's surface and more or less north/south. Some species, however, carry out their seasonal journeys in a third dimension that is perpendicular to the others. These birds travel up and down, not across, and are called altitudinal migrants. Altitudinal migrants move for the same reasons as latitudinal migrants, namely a change in the seasons that heralds a suite of difficult circumstances. Rather than heading south when the weather turns cold, these birds move downslope to find more suitable conditions. This works because relative air temperature decreases as altitude—or elevation, in the case of a mountain—increases; temperatures likewise increase closer to sea level.

The premise behind altitudinal migration is a mathematical constant known as the environmental lapse rate, which calculates the effect of increasing altitude on air temperature, thus explaining why the worst weather in the world can be found at the top of a mountain in wintertime. Although the calculation varies with factors such as convection and condensation, the lapse rate predicts a drop in air temperature of about 3.5°F per 1,000 feet (6.5°C per 1,000 m) of increasing altitude, from sea level to almost 7 miles (11 km) up in the troposphere. Hence, when it is 80°F (27°C) at sea level, surface water (lakes, rivers and streams) will be freezing at about 14,000 feet (4,200 m). In the world's temperate zones, where autumn brings cooler temperatures at sea level—50°F (10°C), for example—freezing will occur at about 5,000 feet of elevation. For birds that require open water, this is a critical factor.

A small group of birds that perfectly fits this description are the dippers (family Cinclidae): chunky, short-tailed, thrush-like birds so named for their curious bobbing and dipping movements. Dippers have a unique lifestyle. They live on the banks of swift-moving freshwater mountain streams, where they forage for aquatic insects, other invertebrate prey and small fish by plunging headfirst into the cold rushing water. Of course, many mountain waterfowl do this; what sets dippers apart is that they are songbirds. As such, they lack many of the adaptations that would seem necessary for an aquatic existence—webbed feet, for example. Dippers, however, have their own variation on diving-bird anatomy and physiology. Their short wings are heavily muscled for "flying" underwater in currents strong enough to knock

Dippers are aquatic songbirds that forage for invertebrates and small fish by plunging headfirst into the cold rushing waters of mountain streams.

over a human wader. The sphincter muscles of the iris in their eyes are also enhanced to enable focusing above and below the water's surface. Their plumage is soft and dense to retain body heat, and they have a large preen gland that secretes oil to waterproof their feathers. Dippers also have strong legs and toes that are suited for both clinging to slippery rocks and clambering along the streambed. These birds forage underwater by searching deliberately beneath stones and woody debris, which can take some time. Fortunately, dipper blood has a high concentration of oxygen-storing hemoglobin, and dippers can depress their heart rate up to 69 percent to reduce metabolic needs. As a result, they are able to remain submerged for 30 seconds or more.

The European dipper (*Cinclus cinclus*, also called the white-throated dipper or, rarely, the water ouzel) breeds along highland and mountain streams in the United Kingdom, across Europe and Asia and south to North Africa, although its distribution is highly fragmented because of the specific nature of its preferred habitat. During the summer, dippers can be found nesting and foraging up to 6,500 feet (2,000 m) high in the Alps and the Caucasus Mountains, which divide Europe and Asia, and up to 16,400 feet (5,000 m) in the Himalayas. Technically it is not cold weather that stimulates dippers to move downslope—in Siberia they have been observed foraging in rushing torrents in air temperatures of −40°F (−40°C); it is the lack of open water. When the streams freeze, dippers migrate. And sometimes their seasonal needs simply require traveling downslope, often to near sea level.

Banding studies of European dippers breeding in Sweden and Norway have uncovered another interesting migration pattern. As well as making an altitudinal migration, these dippers fly southeast 430 miles (700 km) or more to winter along streams in southern Sweden, Denmark and Germany. They are the only European short-distance migrants to fly in that direction in autumn; other migratory birds that breed in northern Europe typically fly southwest, toward Great Britain. Why not dippers? The highlands of western England, Wales, Scotland and Ireland offer relatively mild winter weather and plenty of open water. Researchers suggest that it is precisely those conditions that discourage dippers nesting in Europe from wintering in the British Isles. According to the British Trust for Ornithology, 19,000 pairs of European dippers already occupy permanent, year-round streamside territories there. Moreover, they advertise and defend their feeding territories all winter long. Resident birds enjoy the "home-field advantage" under these conditions; a newly arrived migrant would have little hope of acquiring much-needed streamside real estate.

CHAPTER 4

FUELING *the* JOURNEY

*Weight for weight, birds eat more food, consume more
oxygen, move more rapidly, and generate more heat than any
other vertebrates.*

JOEL CARL WELTY

Only two centuries ago, humans began their addiction to fossil fuels. And since that time we have had some difficulty understanding how the rest of the animal kingdom does without them. Yet the animals survive, even thrive, on the basic stuff that Mother Nature endows. Birds are among evolution's greatest engineering miracles in this regard, and we can only marvel at their ability to convert food, air and water into long-distance travel. Just like their anatomy, avian physiology—the inner workings of their bodies—has been honed over the millennia to provide the essence of what is required to endure such voyages.

In principle, fueling flight differs little from walking around the block. Just like our legs, birds' wings must be powered by shortening and stretching specific muscle groups to create forward motion. Our bodies provide the energy required for these activities in the form of rich phosphates (adenosine diphosphate, or ADP) that are released when fats, carbohydrates and proteins are oxidized. Every dieter knows that increased exercise burns up last night's turkey dinner more quickly, and that maintaining a higher activity level requires elevated heart

Mallard ducks (*Anas platyrhynchos*) may spend as much as 40 percent of both day and night hours searching head-down for aquatic vegetation and invertebrates.

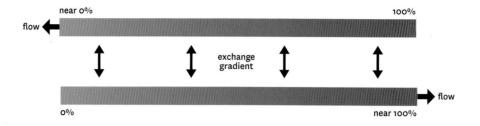

and respiration rates to ensure that the appropriate muscles are adequately supplied with oxygen. The same holds true for birds, although the scale of things differs considerably. Most people get winded by climbing four flights of stairs—imagine flying to Antarctica.

Birds make it all appear so simple because their bodies are designed to do exactly what their ecology and life history demand of them. For example, birds' lungs are structurally superior to those of mammals, conferring a significantly more efficient rate of gas exchange. Mammalian lungs are like blind sacs, and when we breathe normally we exhale only about 10 percent of the air in them. Consequently, when we inhale to refill the lungs, we mix the fresh, oxygenated incoming air with oxygen-depleted residual air, providing a relatively poor venue for oxygen uptake. The avian respiratory system, on the other hand, is a unidirectional flow-through system. Gas exchange does not occur in grapelike alveolar clusters, as in mammals, but in small parallel tubes called parabronchi that pass right through the lung tissue.

Oxygen uptake occurs along the parabronchi by means of a countercurrent exchange mechanism that extracts every molecule of oxygen from the air passing through it. Countercurrent exchange mechanisms are common paradigms in biology; they explain such phenomena as why canids (doglike mammals) have long noses and how geese can stand all day on ice without freezing their feet. Countercurrent exchanges are somewhat analogous to paired railroad tracks, with one serving westbound and the other eastbound traffic. They work because air and blood flow in opposite directions in the system, just like the train tracks. Oxygen molecules in the rich "eastbound" air jump to the "westbound" bloodstream as they move along; the air traveling east thus has lower oxygen content the farther you go down the line. At the same time, the bloodstream increases in oxygen content as it travels west, because it is picking up oxygen as it flows. The molecules continue to jump the tracks even when present in extremely low concentrations, as long as the oxygen content of the bloodstream at that point is even lower—given the choice, they will always move from a more crowded train to a less crowded one. Needless to say, at the "eastern terminus" of the system, where little oxygen remains in the air, there is even less in the blood; having just left the station, it has not acquired any yet.

In this way, birds are able to extract precious oxygen from air that is almost unbreathable by mammals. This point was demonstrated elegantly in a series of experiments: two similarly sized species, white mice (*Mus musculus*) and house sparrows (*Passer domesticus*), were placed inside a pressure chamber. House sparrows are nonmigratory birds that typically stay close to the ground. Nonetheless, when the pressure in the chamber was dropped to simulate an altitude of 20,000 feet (6,100 m), the sparrows fared well—hopping, flying, squabbling among themselves—despite the exceedingly thin air. The mice, on the other hand, lay flat on their bellies, inert and immobile, clinging to their very existence until the experiment was over. This ability to remain fully active under hypoxic (low oxygen) conditions explains how migratory birds can cross otherwise impassable barriers such as mountain ranges and use weather systems to their greatest advantage.

One startling incident occurred on December 9, 1967, when a radar operator in Northern Ireland detected a mysterious echo traveling at high speed over the ocean near the Hebrides Islands. He estimated its altitude at about 26,900 feet (8,200 m) above sea level. When the echo chose not to answer radio queries, a nearby pilot was dispatched to identify the craft. As the pilot closed in on the mystery flier, he found not an airplane but 30 whooper swans (*Cygnus cygnus*) en route to Iceland. A passing weather front generating snow squalls over the sea was providing 112 mile (180 km) per hour tailwinds above 26,000 feet (8,000 m). The resulting speed of the birds was more than 125 miles (200 km) per hour over ground, shortening the duration of their 800-mile (1,300 km) journey to less than seven hours. The air temperature at this altitude was 40° below zero.

Cold temperatures pose little problem for migrating birds. On the contrary, flight muscle activity generates enormous heat loads, and birds suffer more under warmer conditions—from heat stress and excessive water loss—than they do when migrating in cold weather. Flying at high altitudes, however, does require some compromises. Thinner air provides poorer conditions for generating lift, so more power is required to remain aloft: an estimated 50 percent more at 26,000 feet (8,000 m). Nonetheless, if flight conditions at that altitude are clearly favorable, such as for the whooper swans with their galloping tailwind, birds will choose to exploit them.

The ability to fly high can also be an advantage when the route over a mountain range is decidedly shorter than flying around it. Many migratory species, such as demoiselle cranes (*Anthropoides virgo*) and greylag geese (*Anser anser*), routinely fly over the Himalayan Mountains, the west Asian range with the earth's tallest peaks, including Mount Everest, with an elevation of 29,029 feet (8,848 m). One mountaineer recalls seeing a flock of birds pass between him and the full moon as he gazed skyward through his

Demoiselle cranes regularly fly over the Himalayan Mountains, the world's tallest mountain range, when migrating to their wintering grounds on the Indian subcontinent.

telescope. Another heard bar-headed geese (*Anser indicus*) cackling to one another as they easily cleared the peak of Everest. These feats seem even more astonishing when you consider that the geese begin their ascent in spring from the Indian lowlands, which are less than 650 feet (200 m) above sea level and only 93 miles (150 km) away. Thus their acclimatization to the extreme hypoxic conditions at high altitudes, which most humans need weeks to accomplish, takes the geese no more than a couple of hours, if any time at all.

The unidirectional flow-through respiratory system of birds is considerably more complex than a set of lungs interlaced by parabronchial tubules. It also includes several paired sets—three in weaverbirds, six in shorebirds—of thin-walled air sacs that extend into the body cavity and the long, hollow bones of the wings and legs. The sacs, which connect to the respiratory system via the primary and secondary bronchi, serve a multitude of purposes, including providing a means for air to pass one way through the lungs during both inhalation and exhalation. A bird's respiratory system functions like a two-cycle pump: two inhalations and two exhalations are required for a single unit of air to travel through the system. During the first inhalation,

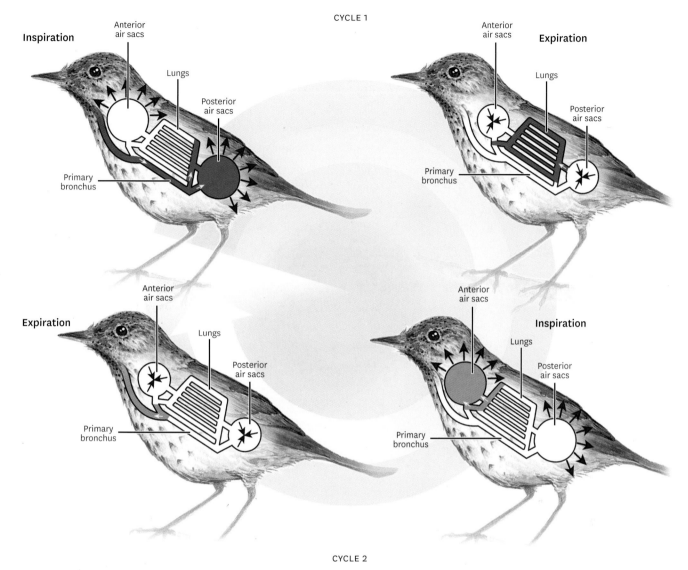

Inspiration

Anterior air sacs

Lungs

Posterior air sacs

Primary bronchus

Expiration

Anterior air sacs

Lungs

Posterior air sacs

Primary bronchus

Expiration

Anterior air sacs

Lungs

Posterior air sacs

Primary bronchus

Inspiration

Anterior air sacs

Lungs

Posterior air sacs

Primary bronchus

CYCLE 2

Avian respiration functions like a two-cycle pump in which a single breath of air requires two inhalations and two exhalations to pass through the system.

the air passes directly to the posterior (rear) air sacs. The first exhalation then moves this air through the parabronchi in the lungs, where it relinquishes its oxygen. During the second inhalation, as another breath is drawn into the posterior air sacs, the first air unit passes forward to the anterior (front) air sacs. Finally, the second exhalation exhausts spent air to the outside as it moves the second batch of inhaled air to the parabronchi. Air sacs have added benefits: increasing buoyancy, functioning as onboard air-conditioning, and providing delicate internal organs with built-in bubble wrap. As a comparison, the entire respiratory system represents about 20 percent of the body volume of ducks, but only about 5 percent in humans.

Birds do not have a diaphragm, the sheet-shaped muscle beneath our rib cage that ventilates our lungs by changing the size of the chest cavity — a muscle we are generally unaware of until its spasms cause bouts of hiccups.

Birds breathe in concert with their wing-beats: pressure changes in the thoracic (chest) cavity and the air sacs are aided by the flexing of the furcula and the up-and-down tilting of the sternum caused by each wing-beat. This makes sense in the most biologically elegant way — the faster you fly, the more quickly you must breathe. Avian respiration rates in flight are commonly 12 to 25 times greater than resting rates, and even the resting rates of birds are relatively high: a house sparrow taking a break breathes about 60 times per minute.

The essential partner to a highly efficient respiratory system is a similarly souped-up cardiovascular system that can quickly deliver well-oxygenated blood to critical muscles and organs. Birds are capable of circulating large volumes of blood rapidly. To begin with, they have four-chambered hearts similar to those of mammals and crocodilians (and likely dinosaurs), but unlike those of other extant reptiles such as lizards and snakes. Four-chambered hearts prevail over the three-chambered variety because there is no mixing in the heart's lower chambers, or ventricles, of well-oxygenated blood coming from the lungs and poorly oxygenated blood returning from the body. This lack of mixing is typically associated with a higher metabolic rate and endothermy. Modern crocodilians seem not to fit this profile until we consider their phylogenetic background: some 245 million years ago crocodilians shared a common ancestor with birds, and through much of the Mesozoic era (250 to 65 million years ago) they were fully terrestrial, bipedal and swift.

Despite the outward similarities, there are differences between avian and mammalian hearts. Bird hearts are considerably larger — 41 percent larger on average — than those of like-sized mammals. The heart of a hummingbird accounts for as much as 4 percent of its entire body mass, while very few small mammals have a heart mass of more than 1 percent. In addition, avian hearts have a much larger stroke volume (the amount of blood pumped in one contraction of the heart muscle) than in mammals. This feature, together with a relatively fast heart rate, produces usefully high arterial blood pressure in birds. Turkeys (*Meleagris gallopavo*) are known to have blood pressure as high as 400 millimeters of mercury (mmHg) — the highest for any vertebrate species; in humans anything over 140 mmHg warrants a quick trip to the doctor. High performance, however, does not come without cost. Aortic rupture and other forms of aneurysm are not an uncommon cause of demise in birds; they likely account for most of the mysterious deaths of wild birds under stressful conditions, particularly after striking windows or being handled by humans.

All these features of avian physiology come into play when we consider metabolic rate, which describes the amount of energy expended during various activities. The basal metabolic rate (BMR) is measured at rest in a neutral environment; it accounts for the energy required only to keep the heart, lungs, brain and other organ systems (except the digestive system) functioning. Anything more requires more energy expenditure and more oxygen use. Birds spend very little time at their basal metabolic level. They must be very active to maintain their busy lives, and migratory birds must be able to sustain this level of activity for long periods of time.

An important study of high-activity metabolic rates and their sustainability used running birds rather than flying birds. In the late 1990s, Matthew Bundel and his colleagues at Harvard University and the University of Bern trained two female greater rheas (*Rhea americana*)—South American relatives of the ostrich (*Struthio camelus*) that are 5 feet (1.5 m) tall—to run flat out on an inclined treadmill while wearing clear plastic hoods over their heads (it took the researchers two years to convince the birds to cooperate). They were able to measure oxygen uptake (using the hood) and rates of lactate accumulation in the muscles, among other things, to determine the birds' maximum metabolic rate and aerobic endurance relative to running mammals such as wolves and horses. They found that that the rheas' metabolic rate peaked at about 36 times their resting rate, so they concluded that birds in general have roughly twice the "aerobic scope" of running mammals. This ability to sustain a high metabolic rate is particularly critical when it comes to flying. Because of limitations of their wing design and the need to cover as much distance as possible in a timely fashion, few birds can fly significantly slower when they are tired, and even cruising flight requires a 15-fold metabolic increase over resting rates. Fortunately, even small migratory songbirds can function at 10 to 25 times their basal metabolic rate for many hours without ill effects. Equivalent-sized mammals, on the other hand, can sustain an activity metabolism of only about five times their BMR.

Activity requires energy, and energy must be supplied in the form of food—this is the price of survival. For birds, three things require energy input above and beyond the requirements for basic existence: reproduction, molt and migration. It is no coincidence that these three activities evolved to occur at times of seasonal resource abundance. For migrants, the greatest energetic cost is perhaps their biannual flight. Flight costs vary considerably between species and depend primarily on two important factors: air speed and body weight. Typically, heavier birds and those that fly at slower speeds have higher flight costs. For example, hovering hummingbirds have among the highest costs, as do hefty pigeons—roughly 13 times those of the world's

Birds of passage feed ravenously before and during migration to stoke up much-needed fat reserves, the fuel that will power them to their destination.

cheapest flyers, albatrosses, which can lock their wings into position and soar almost effortlessly, with very little energy expenditure. Birds that can stay aloft without flapping, even for brief moments between wing-beats, save a significant amount of energy.

Studies have shown that migratory birds may use available energy more efficiently than nonmigratory species. Thrush nightingales (*Luscinia luscinia*) subjected to 12-hour simulated migratory flights in a wind tunnel used only about a third of the energy consumed by nonmigratory finches of approximately the same weight, even though there was no evidence that the nightingales were resorting to energy-saving tricks such as bounding or gliding. A clear explanation for this phenomenon eluded even the primary researchers on this project, although it was suggested that the power requirements for sustained migratory flight may be somewhat less than previously thought, at least when compared to the short bursts of rapid, erratic flight typical of nonmigratory birds engaging in everyday activities such as foraging.

Scientific interest in avian fuel consumption began in earnest in the 1950s, with a myriad of studies designed to determine precisely how much energy is burned per unit of distance flown. However, the question certainly arose much earlier. Lighthouse keepers in the 1800s routinely noted the emaciated condition of many migratory songbirds that died after striking the illuminated towers during their nocturnal passage. Their journals provide valuable information, and indicate that the victims had no access to food after they had left the far shore. This was the assumption made in a study during the 1970s by Russian Academy of Sciences researchers Viktor Dolnik and Valery Gavrilov. Their goal was to measure the amount of body mass lost by migratory songbirds as they flew along the Neringa (Curonian) Spit, a crescent-shaped strip of blowing dunes in western Lithuania that projects into the Baltic Sea.

More than a million migratory songbirds that fly in daylight, including chaffinches, bramblings, pine siskins (*Carduelis pinus*) and Eurasian bullfinches (*Pyrrhula pyrrhula*), use the sand dunes of the Neringa Spit as a safe north-to-south shortcut across the Baltic Sea. During clement weather, the passage takes a little more than an hour. Dolnik and Gavrilov and their team trapped, measured and released migrants at two sites on the spit about 31 miles (50 km) apart. By calculating average flight speed and body mass lost during the journey, the researchers were able to determine flight costs in terms of energy expended in watts. They ranged from 3 to 5.6 watts for the four species, about as much as an incandescent outdoor Christmas light. They also found that more than 63 percent of the mass lost by the birds was from metabolization of fat.

Fat is an extremely good source of energy. In fact, energy is its primary purpose, and many migratory species—insects, fishes, birds and mammals—take on fat reserves prior to departure. In contrast, nonmigratory birds carry little in the way of stored fat throughout much of the year, although they occasionally bulk up when possible in winter or during breeding. For one thing, fat yields more than twice the energy per gram when burned than either protein or carbohydrate. An added advantage is that fat is stored "dry" in birds—without using supplementary water—so it weighs only an eighth as much as would the stored carbohydrates required to produce the same amount of energy. Furthermore, when fat is metabolized, it simply turns into energy, carbon dioxide and water, without producing any nasty by-products such as nitrogenous wastes that must be excreted from the body. The release of water is critical. Termed "metabolic water," the single gram produced by each gram of fat burned is often enough to counteract dehydration in migratory birds traveling in cooler weather. For birds traveling across the Sahara Desert, it means the difference between life and death.

Fat is clearly the way to fly: it is lightweight, readily stored and packed with energy. Birds store most of it subcutaneously (beneath the skin) at several sites on their chest, belly, back and rump, and also in their muscles. The nature of their migratory passage can be predicted from their onboard reserves prior to departure. Short- to medium-distance migrants, and those that are able to conserve energy by soaring or gliding, have fat loads of 10 to 25 percent. Long-distance migrants carry 30 to 35 percent body fat, whereas 3 to 5 percent is typical of nonmigratory birds. Accumulated fat loads may be smaller in autumn than in spring if there are more stops along the way, or where late summer's bounty of fruits and other foods remains plentiful. Arctic-breeding birds such as geese and shorebirds carry extra fat on their northbound journey as a hedge against poor feeding conditions when they arrive at the breeding grounds. Males must have sufficient reserves to fuel courtship and defense of territory, while females' nutritional requirements are perhaps more demanding—they must produce a clutch of eggs not long after making landfall. Birds arriving on their northern breeding grounds in a fat-depleted condition have substantially poorer reproductive success that year.

Prior to departure, and sometimes at major stopovers en route, birds begin the process of fat deposition. Their bodies switch from carbohydrate and protein metabolism to burning primarily fat. They feed ravenously, not by taking in larger meals but by eating almost continuously throughout the day, to ensure that food intake exceeds expenditures on their foraging activities. They frequently move to areas where food is more abundant and faster to procure, and typically switch to choices that are easier to metabolize. When not foraging, premigratory birds reduce their energy consumption by resting quietly or, in the case of hummingbirds, slipping peacefully into torpor, an energy-saving state of hibernation.

Many birds also change from eating protein-rich foods such as insects and other invertebrates to substantially more fruits and grain. Even seemingly unlikely species—cranes, ducks, gulls and shorebirds—can be found foraging in upland areas and among the shrubbery at this time of year. The reasons for this dietary change can be found on the ecological balance sheet. Fruits and grain are often high in unsaturated fatty acids and contain chemical substances that favor lipogenesis, the formation of fats. Furthermore, the time for fat deposition frequently occurs when insect populations are declining, making them more costly to capture. Fruits, on the other hand, are evolutionarily engineered to be eaten—they are brightly colored for easy detection, plentiful and delicious, and they ripen at just the right time. Plants use fruit-eating birds as a primary vehicle for genetic dispersal: 20 minutes after the juicy part is consumed, the indigestible seed is defecated some distance from the parent plant. Fruits and grain also have the advantage of being stationary. Many birds migrate at night to avoid predators and high daytime temperatures, so they must rest for part of the day, and these foods do not run away when they go after them.

The type of food in premigratory birds' diet has much to do with its nutritional value and its availability. For example, birds staging near the Mediterranean Sea generally have access to better-quality fruits than those at higher latitudes, while birds staging on the North American Great Plains may choose ripened grains. Unfortunately, this tendency of birds to feed

Prior to departure, even birds that are primarily carnivorous, such as sandhill cranes (*Grus canadensis*), often switch to a more grain- or fruit-based diet to expedite fat deposition.

ravenously on readily available foods has perpetuated an age-old conflict between farmers and the avian world. Countless migratory birds are destroyed annually as landowners attempt to defend their crops; in 1912, for example, a reported 720,000 bobolinks (*Dolichonyx oryzivorus*) were killed by farmers in the South Carolina rice fields. From a bird's perspective, this is akin to looking down a gun barrel every time you pull off the highway for gasoline. Migratory birds are not an enemy — they are just trying to get home safely. Bearing this in mind, urban and suburban dwellers should consider planting seed- and fruit-bearing shrubs and trees in their gardens to provide passing birds with sustenance in habitats otherwise bereft of resources.

Despite voracious feeding, it still takes some time for birds to accumulate sufficient fat before they depart. This is why they linger for a while — usually several days to several weeks—at critically important stopover and staging locations. Typically they increase their weight by about 3 to 6 percent per day, so a week of hyperphagia (eating to excess) is required to gain 25 percent, and three weeks to a month to double body weight. Some larger birds, including geese, are capable of increasing their body weight by about 10 percent per day.

If fat is the primary source of fuel, larger fat reserves should result in longer flight distances between refueling stops. Numerous scientific studies support this hypothesis, and the red-billed quelea (*Quelea quelea*) offers an elegant example. This African species feeds primarily on the green seeds of unripe savanna grasses, which are available about six weeks after the start of the growing (rainy) season. After their chicks gain independence, queleas leave the breeding grounds with the first rains and migrate to where the rainy season is already six weeks old—and their favorite green seeds are waiting to be plucked from the stems. The distance that quelea populations migrate depends almost entirely on the direction the rain front is moving and its speed. Northern populations need to fly only about 185 miles (300 km)—from Lake Chad to the Benue River in Cameroon—to overtake the slow-moving rains. Birds in northern Botswana travel southeast just over 300 miles (500 km) to the Limpopo Valley. In equatorial Africa, where the rain front moves more quickly, queleas in northern Tanzania need to travel as far as the Shibeli Valley in Somalia, some 750 miles (1,200 km) away, to find sufficient food. Biologists Peter Ward and Peter Jones intensely studied aspects of this peculiar migration during the 1970s, in particular, average body-fat percentages in relation to the distances the birds customarily traveled.

On average, birds burn fat at a rate of about 1 percent per hour, although there is some variation. Species with high-speed wings fly more efficiently than stockier birds with blunt wings. Also, short-distance migrants may use more fuel per hour than long-distance migrants, particularly under adverse flying conditions; Dolnik and Gavrilov determined that southbound chaffinches traveling the Neringa Spit burned more than 2 percent of their body weight per hour. With these variations in mind, we can assume that 10 percent body fat will fuel approximately 10 to 15 hours of sustained flight, enough to cover about 300 to 450 miles (500–750 km) in good weather. Ward and Jones determined that the three quelea populations did indeed carry different amounts of body fat into their migratory journey: 5 percent in Chad birds, 8 percent in Botswana birds and at least 15 percent in birds from northern Tanzania. Not surprisingly, this equates almost perfectly with the estimates of flight distance, with the longer-distance Tanzanian population being somewhat more fuel-efficient than the other two.

A point of biomechanical significance in the quelea story is that the short-distance populations stored only as much extra fat as they would likely need

for their journey, even though it would make sense to carry some in reserve. However, extra fat equals increased body weight, which places added pressure on the flight machinery. Larger birds — cranes, storks and swans, in particular — have less tolerance; body fat of 40 to 50 percent does not occur in these species because the added weight would require about three times more flight power to keep the bird aloft. It is estimated that sustained flapping flight over several hours is feasible only in birds of up to about 25 pounds (12 kg). Beyond that weight, birds typically resort to cost-saving measures such as soaring, gliding and formation flying.

Not all weight gain in premigratory birds can be attributed to fat storage: migrants often "train" before they leave to bulk up their flight muscles. In one study, yellow wagtails (*Motacilla flava*) staging at Lake Chad before their arduous Sahara Desert crossing increased their body weight on average from 14 to 25 grams; further investigation found that about 3 grams of this added weight was increased muscle mass, not fat. The advantages are twofold. First, extra muscle is useful for propelling the bird early in its journey, when it is heaviest. Second, muscle acts like a reserve fuel tank that can be converted to usable energy in case of emergencies. Clearly that reserve tank would be implemented only when fat stores were depleted and the now emaciated bird would no longer need the added power.

A true test of resourcefulness and efficiency can be seen among far-flying migrants that traverse almost unimaginable barriers to perpetuate their species — and there are many. The Arctic tern and bar-tailed godwit are among the best known; their lengthy circuitous journeys trace great elliptical paths across open water, almost from pole to pole. But these are the speed demons of the avian world, with swept-back wings and streamlined bodies built for exactly this purpose. However, countless other species that seem less suited to the task also meet this challenge with no mean effort.

Every autumn a great river of birds passes south across the Gulf of Mexico and the adjacent western Atlantic Ocean on their way to wintering grounds in South America. Once thought to comprise a few species, the vast waves of migrants are now known to include not only waders and shorebirds but also herons, swallows, waterfowl, birds of prey and wood warblers. Even the tiny ruby-throated hummingbird makes this trek each year. Perhaps the best studied of these birds is the blackpoll warbler (*Dendroica striata*), a diminutive black and white wood warbler that breeds in the boreal spruce and fir forests of Alaska and northern Canada. This species has the longest migratory route of any warbler — more than 5,000 miles (8,000 km) — with winter destinations as far away as southern Brazil and northern Bolivia. Its southbound route swings out over the Atlantic, necessitating a nonstop flight of at least 1,800 miles (3,000 km) that takes about 90 hours to achieve. Needless to say, the journey is preceded by a great deal of preparation.

At summer's end, with the northwesterlies at their backs, thousands of blackpolls pour out of their boreal homes en route to the Maritime provinces and New England states. They travel almost exclusively at night, striking out shortly after sunset and flying several hours before settling to rest. By mid-September they have arrived at their coastal staging areas, where they disperse into fall woodlands in search of honeysuckle, yew and pokeberries to supplement their otherwise insectivorous diets. At first they weigh only about 11 grams, but after two or three weeks of ravenous feeding they have almost doubled their body mass. Then the warblers wait. When the autumn rains finally come, they bring a drop in barometric pressure that stimulates the birds to feed one last time. After the depression has passed through, a cool, clear evening follows and the warblers lift off, carrying an energy payload bigger than the rest of their substance combined.

The birds travel southeast over the Atlantic Ocean toward Bermuda. Radar stations have tracked them at about 6,500 feet (2,000 m) altitude, rising to 16,000 feet (5,000 m) or more as they turn south toward the skies above the

West Indies. At that height, headwinds are less frequent and their way seems somewhat easier. When they leave the northern coasts, they have sufficient fuel reserves to fly nonstop for about 110 hours, at average flight speeds of 24 to 28 miles (38–43 km) per hour under predictable weather conditions. If necessary, they can prolong their flight time, avoiding poor weather by slowing from maximum-range speed to minimum-power speed. However, the detrimental effect of this strategy on overall distance flown may prove disastrous if they are unable to make landfall before their fuel is exhausted. As the tiring birds reach the Tropic of Cancer, they feel the lift of the northeastern trade winds and turn southwest to begin their long descent to the South American mainland. Their energy still not depleted, many individuals continue some distance inland to find food, water and rest. The coming weeks will find them still farther south, in the cloud forests or among the mangroves of their winter homes.

Ornithologists Timothy and Janet Williams once suggested that the blackpoll warbler's nonstop flight over the western Atlantic Ocean is equivalent to a human marathon runner completing 50 consecutive 26-mile (42 km) races without consuming any food or water en route and without losing speed from the first to the last leg. During the journey the blackpoll warbler is estimated to burn body fat as slowly as 0.008 gram per hour, possibly the lowest rate among North American songbirds. Mother Nature's technology can in no way be outdone by human invention—if this tiny bird were burning gasoline instead of body fat, it could boast a fuel consumption rating of about 720,000 miles per gallon.

It was once thought that birds migrated because they were hungry. But even in 1720, Baron Ferdinand von Pernau, an avid bird enthusiast and student of avian behavior, was considering this explanation when he wrote, "It is a very strange opinion if some believe the birds would emigrate, driven by hunger alone. Instead they are unusually very fat when they are about to leave us." Of course, we now understand that migration evolved as a means to exploit bountiful seasonal food resources, and day-to-day hunger has nothing to with it. Migratory birds are genetically programmed to move when the time is right, and the ultimate success of migration has much to do with timing. Seasonal movements are merely part of a bird's annual cycle, which is tied fast to the greater importance of reproduction. Spring migration must be timed to deliver the bird to its breeding grounds when conditions are optimal for establishing territories, courting, nesting and nurturing young. Departure from the breeding grounds in late summer or autumn is intimately linked to the readiness of the young to make the journey. Birds

Blackpoll warblers (*Dendroica striata*) fly nonstop over the western Atlantic ocean to travel the 1,800-mile (3,000 km) stretch in about 90 hours. This is equivalent to a human marathon runner completing 50 consecutive races without consuming food or water and without losing speed from the first to the last leg.

have a number of physiological clocks that manage their annual timetable, synchronizing their biological requirements with the state of their external environment.

On the largest scale, all life on earth is sensitive to circannual cycles (from *circa*, "approximate," and *annus*, "year") that match our planet's revolution around the sun and the resulting predictable seasonal changes. Biological entities are also governed by the light/dark cycles of circadian rhythms (from *circa* and *dies*, "day") generated by each rotation of the earth on its axis. At the root of these cycles is the all-important photoperiod: the length of daylight in a single 24-hour day. Information about light in the external environment is recorded not only by the retinas in the eyes but also directly through the skull. Acting on specific regions of the brain—the pineal gland and the hypothalamus—this information initiates cascades of hormones that mark the milestones of a bird's annual cycle.

For example, thyroxin, glucagon, corticosterone and growth hormone all play integral roles in depositing fat and using it as fuel during migration. Sex hormones such as estrogen, progesterone and testosterone are critical in preparing for and inducing breeding. Recent research has determined that melatonin—currently being touted as a cure-all supplement for the ills of humanity—is likely responsible for modulating day/night rhythms and even for directional finding in some species of migratory birds. Melatonin has been called the "hormone of darkness" because its production is inhibited by the presence of light; it can be secreted only at night. Underproduction of melatonin in humans, caused by modern lighting regimes and lack of complete darkness in urban environments, has been linked to a variety of disorders, including autoimmune diseases and cancer.

Bird fanciers through the centuries knew that experimental manipulation of the photoperiod can be used to achieve certain results. The ancient Japanese tradition of *yogai* used candles to lengthen the apparent day of pet

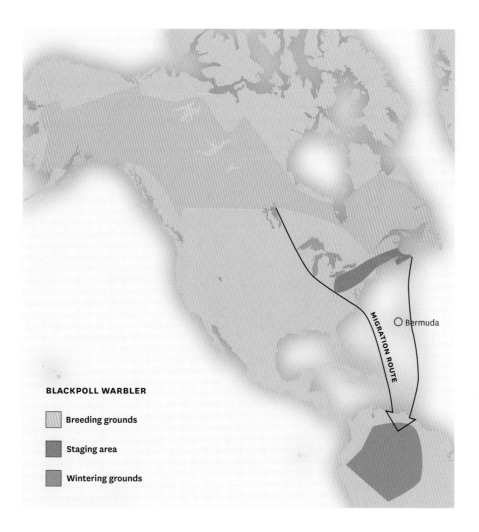

BLACKPOLL WARBLER

Breeding grounds

Staging area

Wintering grounds

MIGRATION ROUTE

○ Bermuda

Blackpoll warblers migrate south from their boreal nesting grounds to stage in the Maritime provinces and New England states. From there, they fly nonstop over the western Atlantic Ocean to their wintering grounds in South America.

songbirds by three or four hours after sunset, which encouraged them to sing in wintertime. Similar practices were used in the Netherlands — this time for less aesthetic reasons — to stimulate caged birds to sing in autumn to lure their migrating wild relatives into traps. Even now, poultry farmers illuminate their hens' enclosures to encourage winter laying.

In 1929, in perhaps the first scientific study of its kind, William Rowan of the University of Alberta subjected dark-eyed juncos (*Junco hyemalis*) to artificially lengthened days to stimulate sexual activity in caged birds during the subzero temperatures of midwinter. During the experiment he noticed a curious thing. Not only were the birds demonstrating changes associated with the onset of breeding condition, such as increased function of their sex organs, but they were also becoming progressively more restless as the "days" became longer. Rowan concluded that the longer days allowed the birds more time to exercise and that somehow this increased activity was stimulating their gonads into functionality. Unfortunately for Rowan, subsequent studies by other researchers failed to corroborate his hypothesis. They found that increased day length alone was responsible for the premature return of breeding condition. But what about the restlessness?

A decade and a half later, Albert Wolfson, then a young researcher at the University of California in Berkeley, again subjected dark-eyed juncos to experimentally manipulated changes in day length. Unlike Rowan, however, Wolfson focused his attention on two different junco populations, one that was migratory and one that was not. His results were conclusive: both populations could be brought into breeding condition early. However, despite identical experimental circumstances, only the migratory population became restless as the manipulated days became longer, and only they departed on their traditional migratory journey when the time was right. Wolfson had demonstrated that the urge to migrate is genetic, and the increased restlessness indicated the birds' innate desire to leave. Later studies with migratory blackcaps clearly established the potency of this genetic drive: it was reliably transmitted to hybrid offspring of migratory and nonmigratory populations in the first generation. And it was nature, not nurture, that stimulated migratory lesser black-backed gulls (*Larus fuscus*) raised by nonmigratory herring gulls to head south in autumn.

In experiments, migratory readiness in songbirds was observed to have two distinct manifestations: increased feeding and subsequent accumulation of fat reserves, and seemingly erratic hopping and fluttering during the evening hours—Rowan's "exercise." Eberhard Gwinner of the Max Planck Institute, a preeminent authority on bird migration, was likely the first to devise a term for this behavior: *Zugunruhe,* derived from the German *Zug* ("migration") and *Unruhe* ("restlessness"). In many experiments designed to understand its mysteries, *Zugunruhe* occurred in a distinct twice-yearly pattern. The caged bird would sleep after sunset for 15 to 120 minutes or so, then awaken to hop and flutter its wings with increasing vigor until just after midnight, when the activity would gradually subside.

Researchers eventually demonstrated similar nocturnal behavior in dozens of migratory species that were otherwise entirely diurnal in their activities. Moreover, the length of time the birds engaged in restless behavior correlated well with the length of their migratory route. Long-distance migrants developed considerable restlessness, short-distance birds smaller amounts, and medium-distance migrants somewhere in between. Peter Berthold and Ulrich Querner, also from the Max Planck Institute, took these observations one step further in their 1988 study using inexperienced young migratory birds. First they videotaped the birds' frenetic wing fluttering under infrared light to more carefully record the amplitude of their wingbeats. Then they multiplied the length of time during which this "whirring" occurred over subsequent nights by the average migratory flight speed for the particular species. The result would have placed each bird directly in the center of the rest area that marked the traditional end of its migratory route.

In other words, these young birds were genetically programmed to fly the appropriate number of nights for the length of time required to carry them to their ultimate destination, even though they had never been there.

An additional, and equally phenomenal, characteristic of these studies was that this nocturnal hopping and fluttering by the caged birds was oriented in the direction they would be traveling if they were actually migrating. Birds oriented in a southerly direction in late summer and fall and toward the north in spring. Also, their activities started and finished at about the same times as their wild relatives departed on their journey and subsequently arrived at their destination. This research was extended to include species such as great reed warblers (*Acrocephalus arundinaceus*), which migrate in two distinct legs: the first one taking them south of the Sahara Desert, where they molt and replenish their fat reserves, and the second continuing south to their final destination. Not surprisingly, *Zugunruhe* in caged members of this species accurately correlated with those movement periods, with an appropriate pause in between. Without question, all these birds were migrating, even if they were doing so only in their imaginations.

In spite of their delicate appearance, the feathered jewels that visit our backyards and bird feeders in summer are literally built for long-distance travel. They can fly high, fast and far with utmost fuel efficiency. Moreover, their endogenous programming urges them on to their alternative homes every year, and they are born with the basic knowledge of where to find them. But how does the tiny ruby-throated hummingbird return, year in and year out, to that same flowering vine in the vastness of the Amazonian forests?

European Birds of Prey
Habitat partitioning through the seasons

Being at the top of the food chain has inherent risks. Boom and bust years occur among most prey species, often with cyclical regularity, and predator populations must cope with the extremes of these fluctuations or perish.

Being at the top of the food chain has inherent risks. Most humans, of course, have not really experienced the trials of a predator's life since the advent of food plant cultivation and the domestication of animals. However, unlike us, other predators have little control over the resources available from farther down the trophic ladder. Boom and bust years occur among most prey species, often with cyclical regularity, and predator populations must cope with the extremes of these fluctuations or perish.

In northern Europe, a number of avian predators—hawks, owls, falcons, eagles and shrikes—depend largely on small mammals, including lemmings and several species of voles. Moreover, predators in Scandinavia must deal with enormous fluctuations in prey densities that occur in a three- to four-year cycle. Small rodents have an almost exponential reproductive capacity. Females can produce their first offspring at only a few weeks of age, after which they can give birth to litters of four to eight young about every three weeks; some species reproduce year-round. Consequently, burgeoning rodent populations can quickly outstrip local food resources; then

the resulting food shortages create huge die-offs and the prey population crashes. A contributing factor is the local predator population. Predators riding the upswing in food availability are able to feed more young, so their numbers also increase. However, as prey populations begin to decrease, the high pressure of predation on smaller prey numbers causes acceleration of the decline. The periodicity of the cycle is anchored to the rate at which the prey's food resources recover and the rate at which predator populations decline after the crash.

Fortunately for many avian predators, boom-and-bust prey cycles do not occur with the same periodicity everywhere; this provides them with a few options. One way in which predators cope with fluctuations in prey availability is by habitat partitioning. Studies of sympatric (living side by side) avian predators have uncovered some interesting facts. Basically, the food types available to a predator are determined to a large degree by its body size. Predators will take the largest prey that they can comfortably handle—according to availability, of course; most raptorial birds will choose prey no larger than about one-third to one-half of their body weight. Thus competition between sympatric species is reduced by vastly different body sizes among potential competitors.

Analyses of some predator communities in northern Europe have shown that sympatric species typically differ by a weight quotient of about two. For example, in open taiga (boreal forest), raptors that prey on mammals include the great grey, or northern, shrike (*Lanius excubitor*, 1.75 oz/50 g); the common kestrel (*Falco tinnunculus*, 7 oz/200 g); the hen, or northern, harrier (*Circus*

All birds of prey, including the common kestrel, must successfully weather catastrophic declines in their prey's populations.

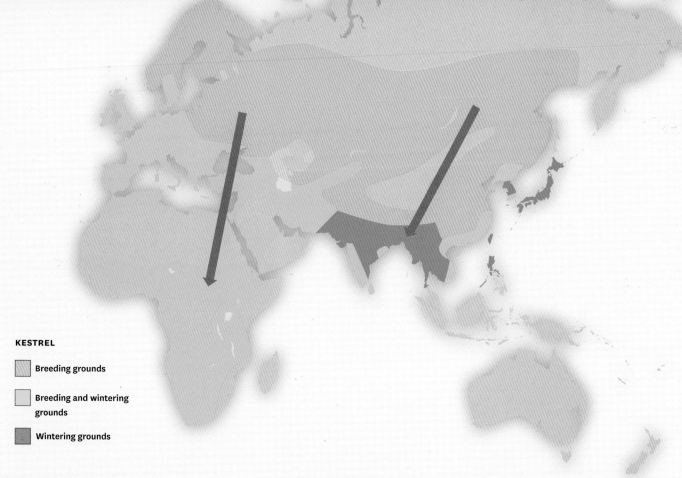

KESTREL

Breeding grounds

Breeding and wintering grounds

Wintering grounds

cyaneus, 17.5 oz/ 500 g); the common buzzard (*Buteo buteo,* 35 oz/1,000 g); and the golden eagle (*Aquila chrysaetos,* 140 oz/ 4,000 g). Ecologists are quick to note obvious gaps in some predator size classes, such as between the buzzard and golden eagle. It has been suggested that the gap may represent the absence of some prey to fill this particular niche, or perhaps an opening for another avian species such as the spotted eagle (*A. clanga,* 70 oz/2,000 g) to enter the arena.

Despite these built-in ecological safeguards, serious food shortages occur in some years, particularly in winter, when prey is more difficult to acquire. Here again local avian predators will exhibit different survival behaviors. Some species, including many owls, choose not to migrate. Owls are better equipped than hawks, eagles and falcons to find prey when the ground is snow covered; their acute hearing and asymmetrical ear placement allow them to detect the activities of

concealed rodents. Although prey may be scarcer in winter, these resident predators survive because predator densities are smaller than during summer, since some avian predators have left.

But even migration from the north varies considerably among avian predators. Some otherwise resident species are invasive migrants that leave only when food is exceedingly difficult to acquire. During those impoverished times, birders enjoy the thrill of seeing vast waves of predatory birds south of their normal distribution. In North America, for example, the great gray owl (*Strix nebulosa*) invasion of 2004–05 was the stuff of legend; countless individuals traveled hundreds of miles south to find food. In northern Europe, winter raptors need not travel too far; good feeding conditions are typically available by the time they reach southern Scandinavia, and only a small percentage of these invasive migrants travels as far as continental Europe.

Among the northern predators are also those that migrate consistently from year to year, such as buzzards, peregrine falcons (*Falco peregrinus*) and kestrels. Variation occurs among these species as well, with individuals from the most eastern and northeastern parts of their breeding distribution often migrating the farthest. For example, kestrels from southern Sweden migrate only as far as central Europe to escape the worst of winter; individuals from the north, on the other hand, cross the Sahara to winter in West Africa. Kestrels in western Europe are largely residents. It goes without saying that each of these avian groups must fit comfortably into the raptor community already in place wherever they spend their winter. Just as in summer, winter prey must be partitioned appropriately so that there is plenty for all. Living at the top of the food chain can be complicated. For winter raptors in Europe, the key to survival is flexibility— and not treading too hard on another bird's toes.

Yellow Warblers
The link between molt and migration

For migratory birds, the annual cycle of events is firmly rooted in the nesting season, which is in turn generally fixed by the availability of resources for provisioning their young.

The annual activities of birds must proceed like clockwork if they are to have enough time to complete everything prescribed by their species' life history and if their behaviors are to favor survivability. Wild things rarely live for today—they are invariably banking on tomorrow. For migratory birds, the annual cycle of events is firmly rooted in the nesting season, which is in turn generally fixed by the availability of resources for provisioning the young. After nesting, most birds begin replenishing their own energy stores in preparation for the autumn flight. This is a particularly critical time for females: producing one or more clutches of eggs, followed by incubating and nurturing the young to independence, requires considerable energy. A female bird must feed voraciously to fuel a successful journey to the wintering grounds.

Energy is required for other things in autumn as well. Part of an adult bird's annual cycle includes molting: the orderly replacement of feathers that occurs at least once each year. When fully grown, feathers are no longer supplied with nutrients the way other tissues and organs are. They must be replaced regularly before they become so tattered that they compromise flight or the bird's ability to thermoregulate. Most migratory species undergo a prebasic molt in late summer that typically replaces the flight feathers of the wings and tail and the contour feathers that cover the body. For birds that wear somber plumage when not breeding, such as most North American wood-warblers (family Parulidae), this is when they adopt their winter uniforms. A second molt in early spring, known as the prealternate molt, will restore their showy breeding costumes.

The timings of prebasic molt and autumn migration are intertwined, and limited to some degree by the two ends of a spectrum: breeding and wintering. Energy is required to grow feathers, and the feathers must be sufficiently grown before the migratory flight begins. Missing or half-grown wing feathers will affect the bird's power-to-weight ratio, diminishing the amount of lift generated by the wing's surface, which will increase the energy costs of traveling. Thus molt must begin when resources are plentiful but be more or less over before the time comes to leave the breeding grounds. Most birds pin their departure dates to when warm late-summer days are fading into crisp autumn mornings; some species, however, do something entirely different.

A remarkable case of opportunistic timing occurs among yellow warblers (*Dendroica petechia*). These bright yellow wood-warblers breed extensively across North America, where they favor wet deciduous thickets and willow groves for nesting habitat; they winter in semi-open tropical woodlands from southern Mexico through Central America and northern South America. Yellow warblers are among the first warblers to arrive on the

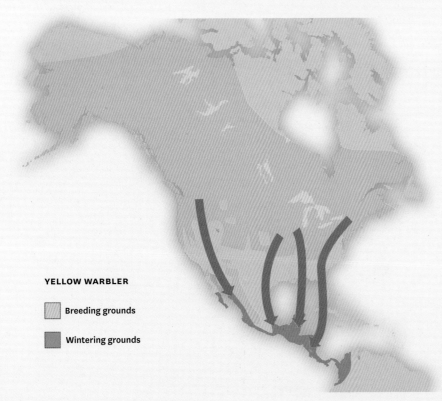

YELLOW WARBLER

Breeding grounds

Wintering grounds

breeding grounds in spring, particularly in the southern parts of their distribution; even in the north, some males are already advertising their territories by April. Nest building often begins shortly after the females arrive a week or so later, and by mid-May breeding is widespread across the species' range. Chicks grow rapidly: within eight or nine days of hatching, they have already made their first flight from the nest. Two weeks later they are taking their first steps toward complete independence from parental care.

By this time it is high summer on the breeding grounds. Insects and berries are plentiful, and many bird species are gearing up for their second clutch of young. Yellow warblers, however, are already turning their eyes south. Even with their young still hanging off their apron strings, the adults feed ravenously

to restock their energy and, of course, to replace their feathers. Studies have demonstrated that prebasic molt in yellow warblers begins while they are still tending to fledglings. Furthermore, the rate of feather replacement, which starts slowly with the growth of new body plumage, increases rapidly as the offspring become less demanding of their parents' time. At the northern extremes of their range, warblers anticipating departure exhibit the most extreme molt, sometimes simultaneously losing and regrowing as many as eight of their nine functional primary flight feathers. Enormous gaps left in their wings at this time render many of them virtually flightless. Within a month of its onset, molt has progressed sufficiently for fuel-efficient travel. And when the last two primaries are in their final stage of growth — usually by late July or early August — the yellow warblers fly south.

yellow warblers begin prebasic molt while they are still tending to their fledglings, thus facilitating a quick getaway from the breeding grounds once the young are sufficiently grown.

Some people might suggest that going against the grain presents insurmountable obstacles, but not so for yellow warblers. This species thrives because it chooses to pursue an alternative approach. Molting before food supplies wane in September allows for rapid allocation of energy to swift feather replacement, and summer departure from the north improves the likelihood of favorable weather en route. Moreover, early arrival on the wintering ground means less crowded conditions and the promise of a long rest before the frenetic cycle begins once again next spring.

CHAPTER 5

FINDING *the* WAY

In wilderness I sense the miracle of life, and behind it our
scientific accomplishments fade to trivia.

CHARLES LINDBERGH

I magine finding yourself on some unknown stretch of dirt
road in the Canadian wilderness far north of city streets. Your
car is idling on the gravel shoulder next to you. The fuel tank
is full, but each moment that you linger here expends precious
energy. A bag lunch and a Thermos of hot coffee sit on the front
seat, but there is no road map, nor are there any signs on the horizon to
aid you. A hawk cries overhead; the freshening breeze rustles the aspen
leaves in the nearby forest. You want to go home, but how will you get
there? Where is home from here? Where is *here*? These are the challenges met by every migratory bird, for seasonal travel from summer to
winter and back again requires each one to hone two impressive skills.
First, it needs to know where it is on the planet and where its destination
is located—this is orientation. In addition, it must be able to trace an efficient route between these two points—this is navigation.

It is fortunate that birds and other long-distance traveling animals
have an innate sense of site fidelity; if they have been there before,
they usually know how to get there again. In most avian species, the
strongest site fidelity shapes a desire to return to their birthplace. This

More than one million birds
stage in autumn on the Peace–
Athabasca Delta in Canada's
Wood Buffalo National Park.
One of the largest freshwater
deltas in the world, it measures
more than 1,475 square miles
(3,800 sq km).

behavior, known as natal philopatry, is extremely useful from an ecological point of view, because it returns the bird to a region where breeding—including its own—has occurred successfully in the past. Unless there has been significant habitat degradation in the bird's absence, conditions favorable to fruitful breeding, such as appropriate nesting and food resources, are likely to still be available. Thus, technically, migration requires only that you know where you are going that first autumn. Once there, site fidelity will lead you back to summer, then back to the wintering grounds again, to return to summer the following spring. Of course, things are never so simple.

Perhaps our first appreciation of avian site fidelity occurred when humans began keeping pigeons. The carrier pigeon (*Columba livia domestica*) is a domestic variety of rock dove that dates back several thousand years; the people of ancient Egypt, Rome and Crete initially learned to use this bird's natural homing behavior to deliver messages. Pigeons are strong, high-endurance fliers with cruising speeds of about 30 miles (50 km) per hour, capable of rapid bursts of more than 60 miles (100 km) per hour. When displaced from their home coop, pigeons will return reliably from distances of more than 1,600 miles (2,500 km), and if a lightweight message is tied to their leg, they will faithfully deliver it.

Carrier pigeons have been of greatest service to humankind during times of war and political unrest. They were employed regularly by Genghis Khan and Charlemagne. Rumor has it that a network of carrier pigeons delivered early word of Napoleon Bonaparte's defeat at Waterloo to interested parties in Britain, who used this ill-gotten information to manipulate stock prices to their own advantage. Paul Reuter, who later founded the Reuters press agency, routinely used four dozen birds to carry breaking news stories between major European cities in the mid-1800s. The pigeons were faster than horses or the mail train, and they served him well until they were replaced by a direct telegraph link in the 1850s. Where such technologically advanced means of communication were unavailable, carrier pigeons remained in use until well into the 20th century. Their wartime service included delivering 150,000 official and a million private messages into and out of Paris when it was under siege during the Franco-Prussian war of 1870–71. One memorable bird was even honored for its participation in the First World War Battle of the Argonne.

On October 4, 1918, Major Charles W. Whittlesey, commander of the American 77th Infantry Division, was holed up in small gully near Verdun, France. He was surrounded by a German unit that was engaged in a heavy artillery exchange with his countrymen, positioned some distance away. The shelling had been going on for two days, and Whittlesey's force had been reduced from more than 500 to only about 200. The American artillery knew that the 77th Division was out there somewhere, but they had been unable

Carrier pigeons have been used for centuries to transport messages. Fitted with harnesses and capsules, these birds were used to carry breaking news stories and photographs back to newspaper offices.

to determine its precise location; now, in an effort to provide protective cover for the men, they were raining "friendly fire" down on them. Major Whittlesey had one option left—a single carrier pigeon named Cher Ami ("dear friend" in French). He attached a hastily written note to the bird's left leg that read: "We are along the road parallel to 276.4. Our own artillery is dropping a barrage directly on us. For heaven's sake, stop it."

Whittlesey released the little bird above his head, only to have his hopes momentarily dashed as nearby German marksmen opened fire. But Cher Ami pressed on and, despite serious injury, flew 25 miles (40 km) in 25 minutes to deliver the crucial message to the American command post. The shelling stopped and the 77th Infantry Division was saved. Cher Ami almost died that day; gunshots blinded him in one eye, left a gaping hole in his chest and almost severed the leg that bore the precious note. Yet he completed his task, urged forward by his powerful innate desire to return home. Cher Ami's great courage was not overlooked by the people of France. The following year he was presented with the Croix de Guerre, one of the country's highest honors for distinguished acts of heroism during combat. This was no mean citation—Cher Ami shares this tribute with other worthy recipients, among them General George S. Patton, who led the U.S. Third Army during the liberation of France in the Second World War.

This miraculous ability to home is not restricted to pigeons. Hundreds of displacement experiments with dozens of avian species have demonstrated similar skills. In one such exercise, a Manx shearwater (*Puffinus puffinus*) returned to its nest burrow on the little Welsh island of Skokholm only

A Laysan albatross displaced to the west coast of the United States faithfully returned to its home breeding site on Midway Island in 10 days, a journey of about 5,200 miles (8,400 km).

12 days after it was released in Boston; the letter announcing its successful release arrived in Wales the day after the bird did. In similar transpositions, white-crowned sparrows (*Zonotrichia leucophrys*) displaced to Baton Rouge, Louisiana, and Laurel, Maryland, returned to their California wintering grounds in record time. Perhaps the longest displacement experiment occurred when a Laysan albatross (*Phoebastria immutabilis*) caught on Midway Island in the Pacific Ocean was released on the west coast of the United States, some 5,200 miles (8,400 km) from its island breeding site. The return journey required only 10 days to complete.

Despite our lengthy working relationship with homing pigeons, we are still unsure how the birds do it. We do know that, as a group, they have extremely well developed sensory systems, which evolved in tandem with their other requirements for flight, and that they likely use this instrumentation according to need and current conditions as they travel. Decades of research in this regard have demonstrated that birds' complementary navigation and orientation systems may use an assortment of tools—landmarks, odors, sounds, barometric pressure, gravity, polarized light from the setting sun, stellar and solar compasses and the earth's magnetic field—to map their global position and track the route between origin and destination. It has been suggested that navigating animals need this multifaceted approach to compensate for substantial variations in their environment, including changing weather conditions and topography, as well as differences in circadian and seasonal cycles, that are encountered as they travel.

Most early research work used homing pigeons as avian representatives because they are readily available through domestication, hardy by nature, easy to transport and relatively amenable to experimental manipulation. Although researchers caution against applying their conclusions more generally to other migratory birds, the startling results are difficult to sweep aside. Among the noteworthy experiments are those undertaken during the 1970s demonstrating that pigeons are capable of hearing low-frequency muffled sounds — also called infrasound — down to about 0.1 hertz (Hz, or frequency of vibrations per second). Moreover, they can detect minute variations in these infrasound frequencies; by comparison, humans can distinguish low-frequency sounds to only about 20 Hz. In a natural environment, infrasound is ever present, created by our planet's larger-scale phenomena such as earth tremors, thunderstorms, ocean waves, weather fronts and auroras (the northern and southern lights). Wind creates low-frequency sounds as it accelerates through mountain passes or around peaks and ranges. The jet stream, that fast-flowing river of air circulating in the upper atmosphere some 7 miles (11 km) over our heads, also generates infrasound that is audible to migratory birds. These long-wavelength sounds are capable of traveling a considerable distance, perhaps many thousands of miles, thus creating "landmarks" that are registered by the ears, not the eyes.

To use infrasound effectively for navigation, birds must not only detect and identify the distant source, they must also be able to specifically locate it. This can be done only by sensing differences in sound phase or intensity. Bilaterally symmetrical animals such as humans and other vertebrates, and most invertebrate species, use binaural (from the Latin for "two ears") differences in sounds to determine the direction of their origin. Test this for yourself: close your eyes and cover one ear and have a friend make a sound somewhere nearby. You will find it exceedingly difficult to work out where that sound is coming from without using your innate ability to evaluate the differences between the sound as registered independently by each ear. Just like binocular vision, binaural hearing provides "depth perception" that is critical for fixing location. Unfortunately for birds, phase differences in the long wavelengths characteristic of infrasound cannot be detected across the very short distance between their two ears. Consequently, they use another way to perceive differences in infrasound frequency: they fly in circles.

Homing pigeon studies from the early 1980s discovered that migratory birds use the so-called Doppler effect — shifts in frequency that occur when there is relative motion between the observer and the sound source — for sound localization. We notice the Doppler effect when we stand at a railroad crossing watching an oncoming train; the sound of the horn changes as the locomotive approaches, then passes. In order for flying birds to create a similar effect, they must listen to the infrasound as they fly toward it and away from it. And if a bird does not know the sound's precise location, the best way to find it is to fly in a circle while listening for frequency shifts. Experiments with pigeons have demonstrated that a bird flying in a circle at 20 meters per second (about 45 miles per hour) will encounter infrasound frequency differences of about 12 percent, which is well within its ability to discriminate aurally. No doubt infrasound also provides important clues about approaching weather systems that could affect a migratory bird's itinerary, as do changes in barometric pressure. Studies with pigeons determined that they are capable of detecting pressure differences in the order of 1 millibar — roughly equivalent to a 33-foot (10 m) change in altitude. No wonder birds are experts at predicting weather, and also capable of maintaining a constant flight altitude over long distances without needing a mechanical altimeter.

Researchers have also discovered that birds may be sensitive to small variations in gravity. Orientation experiments with pigeons showed peculiar corrections in their flight direction related to changes in the moon's position relative to that of the sun, regardless of whether or not the moon was visible. Interestingly, these corrections increased gradually through the month, but the flight path reverted back to its original direction with the coming of the full moon or the new moon, depending on the season. These perplexing observations may have resulted from the design of the experiment, which always ran at 12:00 noon local time. The solar day (about 24 hours long) differs in length from the lunar day (about 50 minutes longer), which accounts for why high tides — caused by the moon's gravitational influence on the earth's oceans — occur at different times each day. Somehow the pigeons were orienting using a lunar rhythm associated with the moon's gravitational pull; however, this required regular directional corrections because the experimental data were being collected according to a solar timetable. The ability to detect small gravitational effects may be of additional benefit to migratory birds in that earth's own gravity varies both temporally and spatially at the surface. For birds, these variations could paint an entirely different map of our planet.

Despite researchers' many fascinating discoveries, it is generally agreed that migratory birds rely most heavily on three fundamentally different compass systems — solar, stellar and geomagnetic — to plot their origin, stopover and destination positions and to follow a strict path between those points. Using more than one compass type (and a few additional backup devices) creates redundancy in the system that allows for verification and any necessary recalibration, and it also provides alternative ways to maintain a heading under changing environmental conditions. The earth's magnetic field is ever present; whether the bird uses a stellar or a solar compass depends almost entirely on whether it is a diurnal or nocturnal migrant.

Birds are influenced by the rhythms of both day and night, but the time of day that they travel is rooted heavily in their ecology and life history. A few species have flexibility in their agenda, primarily some waterfowl, waders and gulls, which may depart after noon and fly into the dark or lift off before dawn and travel into sunrise. Most migratory birds, however, are constrained to their characteristic pattern, as evolution has honed their navigational skills to function in tandem with it. Why some migratory species fly at night and others fly during the day has been a source of great debate, with a few exceptions. For example, it is obvious why migrants that soar on thermals, such as hawks, cranes and storks, are usually restricted to daytime movement—thermals form only when earth's surface is heated by the sun during the day. These diurnal migrants typically get underway several hours after sunrise and continue until sometime in the afternoon. Larger soaring birds usually depart somewhat later than smaller ones, because they require stronger thermal currents to carry them aloft. An interesting exception is a subset of white storks (*Ciconia ciconia*) that migrate across the deserts of Algeria at night. These resourceful birds take advantage of human-made thermals rising steadily over burning gas flames at oil-drilling installations and along pipelines. Apparently the storks can use this path to gain more ground on their journey, provided that the thermals occur predictably no more than about 3 miles (5 km) apart. Doubtless there is an added advantage in crossing the desert under the cool canopy of darkness.

However, some species of diurnally migratory land birds do not soar, including finches, buntings, swallows, crows, starlings and pigeons. Most are short-distance migrants, with the possible exception of swallows. Unlike soaring birds, which must wait for thermals to develop, these birds take off in the first moments of dawn, usually about 45 minutes before sunrise, and finish their day's journey by midday. They characteristically spend the last part of their daily trip searching for a suitable place to forage and spend the night. On occasion this avian group also migrates at night, but usually only when they must fly long stretches nonstop to cross barriers such as large bodies of water.

Many migratory birds, however, regularly travel at night. As might be expected, this group includes owls and nightjars, which are habitually nocturnal in their activities. However, it also comprises an immense number of small diurnal land bird species from a wide variety of taxonomic groups, including warblers, flycatchers, hummingbirds and thrushes. Across both North America and Europe, nocturnal migration begins with a bang after sunset, as thousands, perhaps millions of birds take to the air almost simultaneously over large areas. Radar tracking stations plot the speed of this great southbound mass at about 30 miles (50 km) per hour, and studies have shown that virtually all the migrants leave within 20 minutes of the first birds to depart. Nonetheless, these birds are not flocking. Although they move in large numbers, they migrate as individuals; even birds of the year (juveniles) typically travel at different times than their parents. The exodus seems to correlate with the end of twilight, when the sun is about 6 degrees below the horizon. This is the time when we humans can barely discern dark landmarks on the horizon and the first stars are appearing above our heads. Maybe these are the orientation and navigational cues that the small nocturnal migrants await. The evening's flight usually ends around midnight, but, like diurnal migrants, these nocturnal travelers will fly throughout the day when it is necessary to travel nonstop—often for two or three days without rest—to cross deserts and oceans.

Why do some small land birds travel at night and others during the day? It has been suggested that predator avoidance may be a factor. At least two diurnal European predators, the sooty falcon (*Falco concolor*) and Eleonora's falcon, breed in northern Africa and near the Mediterranean Sea respectively, at the same time as autumn migration so that their chicks will be well supplied with food in the form of exhausted migrants. Nocturnal migrants, on the other hand, must concern themselves with the falcons' nighttime predatory equivalents: owls. But there is little evidence to suggest that predation has a significant enough impact on migrant populations to warrant an evolutionary choice between night and day. It may be possible that nocturnal migration provides more opportunities to feed during daylight hours, but some ducks are known to forage regularly at night. Certainly nocturnal migration offers important energy-saving advantages. For one thing, it takes less energy to fly in cooler, denser night air. Winds are often more favorable after sunset because they generally diminish in intensity and become less variable in direction; thus, migrants are less likely to encounter headwinds and to drift off course because of crosswinds. There is also less vertical turbulence at night, and cooler temperatures decrease the likelihood of hyperthermia (overheating) and dehydration because of excessive water loss.

Thomas Alerstam of Lund University in Sweden believes that the distinction between nocturnal and diurnal migratory land birds arises from fundamental differences in their feeding ecology. Day migrants are typically dedicated to food resources that are unpredictable in availability and patchy

in distribution. For example, most are seed-eaters, relying on plants that may be heavily harvested by resident species or dependent on seasonally fluctuating growing conditions. Swallows are insect-eaters that must follow erratic irruptive swarms for sustenance. When diurnal migrants finish their day's passage, they must find a place that offers both sufficient food to augment their depleted reserves and a safe overnight roost. Birds arriving later in the day seek out members of their species that are already actively feeding and join them as they travel to the nighttime roost. Roosting locations often become enormous communal gatherings as flocking birds take their evening rest following the afternoon foraging expedition; they also provide an important source of community information for unsuccessful birds. The following morning, the migrants return to areas where food was found in plenty on the previous day to stock up before departure, and yesterday's nonstarters go with them. Several ecological studies have found similar links between flocking, communal roosting and patchy, unpredictable food sources. We have all seen colossal flocks of whistling, chattering starlings roosting on buildings and in city parks—now we know what they are talking about.

In contrast, night migrants forage alone, on food sources that are more or less evenly and predictably distributed in their environment. Many of these birds are insectivorous, feeding on small flying insects that do not swarm. Because their prey are not particularly abundant in any one place, foraging success would be hampered by flocking: imagine dozens or hundreds of like-minded birds descending on a single tree or shrub in order to find food.

Starlings are among those species that migrate during the day. They typically lift off about 45 minutes before sunrise and finish their day's journey about midday after finding a suitable site for foraging and roosting.

Defense of territory is a relatively rare phenomenon out of breeding season; however, some nocturnal migrants such as reed warblers (*Acrocephalus scirpaceus*) and pied flycatchers defend their ephemeral individual feeding territories during their migratory passage through the northern Mediterranean region. The advantage of flying at night, of course, is that it leaves the entire day to look for food, albeit with the occasional nap. Feeding usually begins with first light, and if these migrants happen to have made landfall in an impoverished food zone the previous night, it is simple to move a short distance in order to find something better.

When ornithologists began searching for a mechanism that migratory birds use to find their way, they first looked toward the sun as the most obvious celestial cue. As the earth rotates, the sun appears to rise in the east and set in the west, moving across the sky from sunrise to sunset at a rate of about 15 degrees per hour. If you know the time, a compass heading can be deduced from the sun's relative position. Assume a 6 a.m. sunrise somewhere in the Northern Hemisphere. As the sun breaks the horizon, due south is 90 degrees to your right. Two hours later, at 8 a.m., south will be only 60 degrees to the right, and by lunchtime the sun (and south) will be directly ahead of you. At teatime, around 4 p.m., look for the south about 60 degrees off your left shoulder. Using the sun to plot position and heading holds no mystery for humans. Sir Isaac Newton considered it thoroughly around 1700, but never published his findings. When they invented the first navigational sextant in 1759, naval officer John Campbell and astronomer John Bird demonstrated our enlightenment in a more practical fashion. Of course, birds may have navigated by a solar compass for many millions of years before we figured it out. We only had to be convinced that they could tell time.

Birds, like other earth entities (including humans), have an internal circadian rhythm with a period of approximately one day, usually 22 to 26 hours. Biorhythms set a time frame for daily activities and periods of sleep by establishing patterns of hormone secretion, body temperature and brain-wave function. Although the internal rhythms of some creatures may not be exactly one earth-day long, the light/dark cycles associated with living here more or less set the phases of each species' pursuits. In the absence of light, such as in an experimental manipulation, our biological clock—which has a period of about 25 hours—will spin freely, moving our sleep cycle forward about an hour each earth-day. Perhaps this is why jet lag seems worse when traveling from west to east, and the beginning of daylight saving time in spring seems more jarring than its end in the autumn. Both of these changes work against our ability to compensate quickly when our natural biorhythms

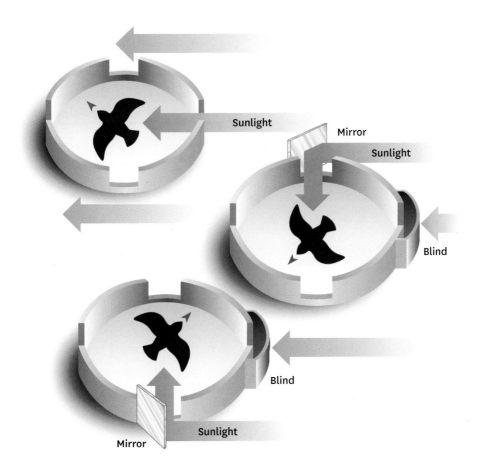

In the 1940s, German researchers determined that birds would orient their activities according to the sun's direction, even if that direction was altered experimentally through the use of mirrors.

are not entirely in sync with those of our planet. But does a bird's internal clock tick in such a way that it can tell time?

German ornithologist Gustav Kramer and his research team at the Max Planck Institute began experiments with this concept shortly after the Second World War. Kramer had noticed that European starlings kept in a circular cage with a good view of the sun oriented their daytime migratory restlessness in a compass direction that matched what free-living starlings were doing at the same time of year. He then used mirrors to change the sun's apparent direction by 90 degrees; not surprisingly, the birds changed the orientation of their activities accordingly. When he discovered that the birds would follow a powerful lamp in the absence of the real sun or its mirrored reflection, Kramer deceived the hapless birds by not moving the pseudo-sun at all throughout the day. Like clockwork, however, the starlings changed the orientation of their activities by gradually shifting them counter-clockwise 15 degrees per hour. The birds could indeed tell time and were maintaining their orientation to the northeast, precisely where they would be going if they were flying free with their compatriots.

Experiments with homing pigeons in the early 1950s found similar results, and later work demonstrated pigeons' sun-clocks to be accurate within

20 minutes. These studies also revealed something else: the built-in solar compass (at least in pigeons) is not innate—it is learned. The species does not even access this navigational tool until the birds are about 12 weeks old. Prior to that they use something else, perhaps the same system they employ on cloudy days. Likewise, there is clear evidence that other species, including starlings, do not implement their sun compass until their first spring migration, when they are about a year old. The autumn before, they found the way to their wintering grounds by some other mechanism, but more about this later.

Recent work has discovered that many birds, including penguins, waterfowl and songbirds, possess a solar compass as part of their standard navigational equipment. Even nocturnal migrants have them: experiments with European robins and savannah sparrows (*Passerculus sandwichensis*) showed that birds prevented from seeing the setting sun before departure oriented poorly when they switched to their stellar compass after twilight. What the migrants were detecting at sunset was polarized light, which occurs as sunlight penetrates the earth's atmosphere, causing a scattering effect. We typically see this as glare, which photographers block by using a polarizing filter to enhance the contrast between clouds and sky. For birds, the pattern of polarization provides reasonably accurate information about the sun's position, even if it is obscured by clouds or already setting behind mountains or forests.

Detection of polarized light is an ability that birds share with bees, many other invertebrate species and, to some degree, humans. Viking legend maintains that Nordic sailors used a "sun stone" to determine the sun's direction when it was otherwise not visible, such as during poor weather or when it was just below the horizon during the short northern winter days. When held up to a bright patch of sky and rotated, the crystalline stone would change from blue to yellow when oriented toward the obscured sun. Geologists confirm that many such crystalline stones can be found in northern Europe; Iceland is the source of optical calcite (Iceland spar), a mineral used in the production of modern high-performance polarizing filters. Today, flight navigation near the earth's magnetic poles, where a magnetic compass is unreliable, depends to some degree on the use of polarized light. It is thought that nocturnal migratory birds use a band of strongly polarized light, perpendicular (north/south) to the rays of the setting sun, to calibrate their other internal compasses just before their departure.

After the sun has dipped well below the horizon, migratory birds must employ yet another compass system. Ornithologists have known for more than 70 years that caged nocturnal migrants exhibit *Zugunruhe* at night that coincides with the daily and seasonal migratory patterns of their species. Furthermore, when the birds are placed in circular cages, they orient their activities toward the compass heading they would be following if they were actually migrating. Studies by Gustav Kramer and Franz Sauer with black-cap and garden warblers, lesser whitethroats (*Sylvia curruca*) and red-backed shrikes (*Lanius collurio*) in the 1950s found that the birds maintained this directional orientation as long as the brightest stars were visible in the sky, but their activities became random or ceased altogether under cloudy conditions. These results imply that they were fixing their direction by using an onboard stellar compass.

Franz Sauer and his wife, Eleonore, went one step further in 1957. They placed caged warblers in a planetarium where star patterns in the "sky" could be manipulated experimentally. When they duplicated autumn skies, the birds adopted a southeast or southwest bearing according to the habits of their species; for example, a blackcap under a spring sky oriented to the northeast, just as it would in the wild. Moreover, when the Sauers shifted the planetarium's star projector 180 degrees from stellar north, the birds readjusted their orientation to match the new sky pattern. But what cues were they using to calibrate their compasses? A logical answer was the North Star (also called the polestar or Polaris), a strikingly obvious celestial body in Northern Hemisphere skies. The North Star is the brightest star in the constellation Ursa Minor (Little Dipper), despite being 430 light-years away from earth; look for it at the end of the Little Dipper's handle. This star is aptly named: it is in direct line with the earth's rotational axis, thus appearing to us to stand motionless in the sky above the north pole; the other constellations nearby, such as Draco and Cepheus, seem to rotate around it in a counter-clockwise direction at about 15 degrees per hour. Human explorers and navigators through the ages—at least, those in the Northern Hemisphere, since it is not visible south of the equator—have used the North Star for directional finding and to determine their latitudinal position. Maybe birds do so as well.

In the 1960s, ornithologist Stephen Emlen of Cornell University took caged birds into a planetarium to further investigate star orientation. This time the birds were indigo buntings (*Passerina cyanea*), which breed in eastern North America and winter throughout Central America and the West Indies. For the experiment he developed an elegantly simple apparatus now known as the Emlen funnel. It was a small circular cage with sloping lower walls, covered with blotting paper, that funneled down to a wet inkpad at the bottom. When the buntings flapped and hopped inside their cages, the direction of their activities could be easily ascertained by looking at the patterns of their inky footprints.

Emlen's first experiments with the buntings mirrored the Sauers' results: the birds oriented north under a simulated spring sky and south when an autumn sky was projected. Likewise, they shifted their orientation when the

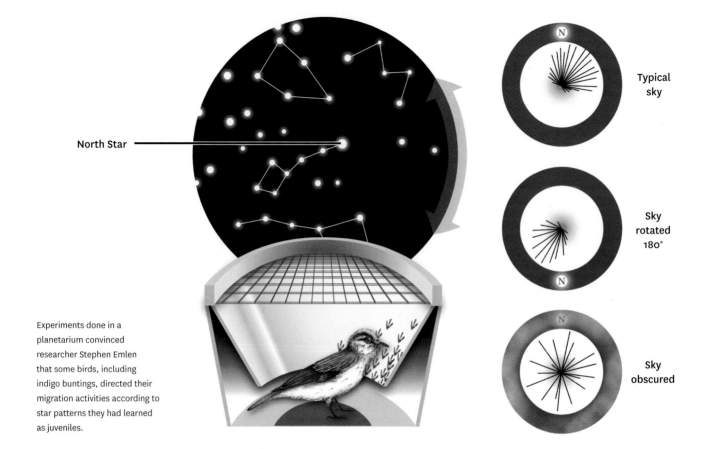

North Star

Typical sky

Sky rotated 180°

Sky obscured

Experiments done in a planetarium convinced researcher Stephen Emlen that some birds, including indigo buntings, directed their migration activities according to star patterns they had learned as juveniles.

stars' axes were reversed and generally became disoriented when the night sky was turned off. Emlen originally presumed that the birds were using the North Star to calibrate their compasses. To test this assumption, he switched off different sections of the night sky and observed the buntings' reactions. What he discovered was astonishing. The birds were navigating not by the North Star but by the stars and constellations rotating within 35 degrees around it. They knew the northern sky in great detail, including the constellations Ursa Major (Big Dipper, Great Bear or Plough), Ursa Minor (Little Dipper or Little Bear), Draco, Cepheus and Cassiopeia, and easily switched from using one to another when they were systematically blocked out. No doubt this knowledge, and the built-in redundancy inherent in the system, is highly useful in the real world when clouds obscure part of the night sky. One can only imagine the wealth of celestial information stored in the memories of such species as Arctic terns that travel under both Northern and Southern Hemisphere skies. But how was this knowledge acquired?

Once again, Stephen Emlen pushed the experimental envelope. He hand-raised three cohorts of baby indigo buntings in the laboratory. One group was never exposed to the planetarium's night sky; the second cohort (the control group) grew up with regular viewings of the normal northern sky; and the last cohort was exposed to an entirely alien sky, in which the star Betelgeuse—in the constellation Orion, normally found near the celestial equator—replaced the North Star as the point around which the sky rotated. When autumn migration was due to begin, Emlen observed the birds' nocturnal activities. When they were exposed to a typical northern sky, the cohort that had never seen stars failed to orient in any direction, and the control group, of course, oriented correctly, due south. Birds in the third group were equally decisive about their migratory trajectory: they were determined to travel directly away from Betelgeuse. Emlen concluded that buntings develop their stellar compass during the first month of life as they gaze sleepily skyward from the shelter of their parents' care. First they learn the night sky's axis of rotation, centered on the North Star, to provide a north/south point of reference; then they learn the constellations surrounding it. However, just like the sun, the stars are not always visible; when that is the case, birds must find another way to navigate.

Our earth is a great, spherical dipole magnet that generates a magnetic field from electrical currents in the outer, semi-molten region of its core. At present this magnetic field is directed downward in the Northern Hemisphere and upward in the Southern Hemisphere. The intensity of the field and its dip angle (inclination) change with latitude, providing a good map of horizontal space in much the same way that barometric pressure supplies data about vertical space. The suggestion that birds may use this reliable global map for orientation and navigation was first proposed in 1947 by Henry Yeagley, a professor of physics at Pennsylvania State College. In his experiments, Yeagley found that he could disrupt pigeons' ability to home by attaching small magnets to them; he concluded that the birds use the earth's magnetic field as part of their navigational toolkit. Unfortunately, his work garnered considerable skepticism, particularly because other researchers were unable to duplicate his results.

About 25 years later, neurobiologist William Keeton of Cornell University attempted a similar experiment, in which he attached magnetic or nonmagnetic bars to the base of the neck in two groups of homing pigeons. When the birds were displaced (trucked away from their home coop and released in an area unknown to them) on sunny days, they were able to find their way home. In cloudy weather, however, birds wearing magnets did not fare well. When drawing his conclusions, Keeton also determined why Yeagley's results had not been repeatable: he had failed to account for weather conditions in his experimental design. It was evident that the pigeons used a geomagnetic compass when navigating, but not necessarily all the time. When the sun was up, both groups preferentially steered by it, even if they were wearing the signal-disrupting magnets. However, the magnet-wearing group was doomed to get lost on cloudy days.

In 1974 the existence of a geomagnetic compass in birds was demonstrated in a compelling experiment that once again bent homing pigeons to ornithologists' scientific whims. Charles Walcott and Robert Green of the State University of New York at Stony Brook gave their birds little hats connected to battery-powered backpacks. Inside each diminutive fez were Helmholtz coils, which generate a magnetic field when an electrical current is passed through them; reversing the current reverses the direction of the magnetic field. On sunny days, all the birds homed well whether they were wearing normal or reverse-polarity hats, likely because they were able to lean more heavily on their solar compass. On cloudy days, however, the reverse-polarity birds did just what was expected of them: they flew in entirely the wrong direction. To rule out any possibility that the pigeons were using visual cues such as topographical landmarks to find their home coop, researchers then fitted them with tiny frosted contact lenses that made them extremely myopic (near-sighted): anything more than 10 feet (3 m) away dissolved into a blurry fog. The birds were subsequently displaced about 105 miles (170 km) from home and released. Within 10 hours or so they had returned. Some visually impaired individuals hovered over the roof of the coop, then landed safely like miniature helicopters; a few tentative birds crashed nearby. Nonetheless, they had found their way home; the ornithologists concluded that these birds likely relied heavily on their visual system only when they were within a short distance of their destination.

Throughout the 1970s, researchers in Europe worked to discover the precise means by which birds navigate using the earth's magnetic field. Wolfgang and Roswitha Wiltschko and their team at the University of Frankfurt observed European robins placed in circular cages surrounded by coils that could reproduce the earth's magnetic field and vary it experimentally. They found that the robins responded not so much to the north/south polarity of the earth's magnetic field as to its site-specific dip, or inclination. Currently the magnetic field points downward at the north magnetic pole and upward at the south magnetic pole (but watch for a reversal of polarity sometime in the next few thousand years) and is more or less horizontal—parallel to the earth's surface—at the magnetic equator. In between these points, the field at the earth's surface is angled up or down relative to the latitude. For example, the magnetic inclination in southern Canada is between +70 and +80 degrees; in Brisbane, Australia, it is about −56 degrees. The intensity of the field also varies with latitude, ranging from about 0.3 gauss at the equator to more than 0.6 gauss closer to the poles. Furthermore, the earth's "magnetic landscape" is painted with a myriad of anomalies because of the distribution of various magnetic minerals—quite a pretty picture for one able to see it.

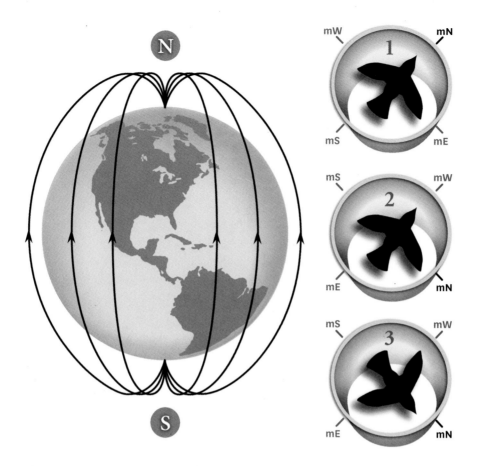

Caged robins surrounded by experimentally manipulated magnetic coils (right), which emulated the earth's magnetic field (left), oriented their activities according to the applied inclination. This research demonstrated that the robins were able to navigate using an innate magnetic compass.

The European studies implied something else: somewhere inside the birds there had to be a structure or substance that worked like a compass needle to align with the earth's magnetic field. This would explain why attaching a magnet or electric coil to a bird affects its ability to orient. Considerable searching finally found a magnetic material in pigeons' heads, on the front and rear of the head between the bones of the skull and the membranes covering the brain, as well as in the neck muscles. By 1980, within a year of this initial discovery, similar substances had been found in other birds, including white-crowned sparrows (*Zonotrichia leucophrys*), tree swallows (*Tachycineta bicolor*), western grebes (*Aechmophorus occidentalis*) and pintail ducks (*Anas acuta*). The material turned out to be tiny crystals of magnetite, a type of iron ore, each measuring about 1/10,000 of a millimeter; each bird possesses between 10 and 100 million of these crystals. Similar crystals have been found in the brains of bees and termites, possibly in whales and dolphins and, surprisingly, in sediment-dwelling bacteria that live in some oceans, lakes and salt marshes. In the Northern Hemisphere, the bacteria's magnetic crystals are aligned in a straight line parallel to the field direction, thus working like a north-seeking compass needle to direct the creatures downward (following the angle of inclination) to the bottom

Studies on bobolinks indicate that photopigments in the eye may be responsible for detecting "poleward" or "equatorward" inclinations in the earth's magnetic field.

sediment where they can find food. Equivalent bacteria have been found in Tasmania, other parts of Australia, and New Zealand; they are, of course, south-seeking.

Recent research has suggested that a photopigment in the eye, perhaps one called rhodopsin, is also part of birds' navigation toolkit. Photopigments are proteins in the retina that change in the presence of light and are then interpreted by the brain as visual perception. It appears that weak magnetic fields produce these neural responses in pigeons, suggesting that they may be able to "visualize" slight variations in the earth's magnetic field. More research into these mechanisms is needed before they can be fully understood; nonetheless, we know that birds carry their magnetic sensing devices at their front ends. Migratory birds in flight perform a curious scanning movement in which they swish their heads back and forth in order to detect the field direction. Where a typical magnetic plane is present, they scan and then move immediately into the proper migratory orientation. In the absence of a field, however, they increase their scanning rate threefold as they search for one. Not finding a magnetic field ultimately results in no obvious orientation pattern.

Perhaps birds possess two ways of viewing and processing the information provided by earth's magnetic field. Research on bobolinks (*Dolichonyx oryzivorus*)—small New World blackbirds that migrate about 12,500 miles (20,000 km) annually between breeding grounds in central North America and the pampas grasslands of Argentina—indicates that photopigments in the eye may be responsible for detecting "poleward" or "equatorward" inclinations in the field. Thus, birds do not really distinguish between north and south in the strictest sense but rather rely on their "inclination compass" relative to either pole. This is not unlike our model of the planet with lines of latitude that begin counting at the equator (0°) and progress north and south in equal measure, with the Tropic of Cancer and the Arctic Circle at approximately 23°N and 66°N latitude and the Tropic of Capricorn and Antarctic Circle at 23°S and 66°S. Studies also suggest that magnetite receptors in the visual branch of the trigeminal nerve (a sensory nerve in the head), which are sensitive to small changes in the field's intensity and topography, may provide specific "map" information relative to the bird's destination.

We cannot underestimate the importance of geomagnetism as the underlying system that birds, and perhaps many other animals, use to orient and navigate. Unlike landmarks, odors, infrasound and even the sun and stars, the earth's magnetic field is globally available both day and night, and it penetrates air, water and the earth itself. Nonetheless, at times it is subject to anomalies that make the information it provides somewhat unreliable. For example, there are regions just south of Moscow and in the mountains of Sweden where an abundance of magnetic materials, such as iron ore, causes substantial local intensification of field strength. Magnetic storms may also bring about fluctuations in geomagnetism; these phenomenon can result when a "shockwave" from solar flares strikes the earth's magnetic field. We see such anomalies as the breathtakingly beautiful polar auroras, the aurora borealis (northern lights) and aurora australis (southern lights), but birds see them as bad input data. Consequently, more than 2,000 experienced racing pigeons, worth as much as $250,000 each, were lost in two races in the eastern United States in October 2007. And those disappearances were not unprecedented; the previous July, 8,000 birds (almost 60 percent of those that started) failed to return home during a 700-mile (1,100 km) race from Portugal to the Netherlands. Both of these incidents, and many others like it, have been attributed to disturbances of the earth's magnetic field by the sun's activity.

But how do birds that are known to be geomagnetic navigators, such as the bobolink, complete their journey when they must cross the equator during the voyage? At the equator, the field lines run parallel to the earth's surface, thus providing no useful information. Obviously, to know where they are and to get where they are going, the birds must pool all available resources. They also have the ability to learn, and how they use information changes with experience. Every birdwatcher knows that "accidentals"—birds well outside their typical range—are frequently juveniles or young adults that have flown off course on their first migratory journey. These individuals are usually from species that do not have the added advantage of traveling in flocks with more experienced friends and relatives; they must rely on their own innate strengths.

A bird's navigation abilities derive partly from instinct and partly from learned behaviors, and each species' skills are based on both phylogeny (evolutionary history) and ecology. Unquestionably the most comprehensive study in this area was undertaken by a Dutch ornithologist at the Netherlands Institute of Ecology. Over a 10-year period, Albert C. Perdeck captured and banded more than 11,000 European starlings as they passed through The Hague during migration from northern Europe to their winter homes in southern England and France. The birds, both experienced adults and inexperienced juveniles, were then transported to Switzerland, about 370 miles (600 km) to the southwest, and released. For the most part, the adults corrected their orientation and flew northwest, back to their usual wintering grounds. The young birds, however, failed to realize that they were already well south of their usual winter quarters; following their instinctive compass, they continued to fly a course to the southwest. Interestingly, this occurred regardless of whether the juveniles were released together with a group of experienced adults.

The displacement experiments with starlings, and similar ones with different bird species, clearly demonstrated an obvious distinction between what are now known as navigational migration and orientation migration. The adults were using navigational migration; in other words, they were able to accurately determine their position relative to their destination and to correct their travel route accordingly in order to achieve their goal. Despite the counterintuitive nature of their input data, they knew upon release that their wintering grounds lay northwest, not southwest, of their current location. The young birds, on the other hand, were relying on orientation migration (also called compass migration or vector navigation), which is based on innate directional programming designed to guide them between summering and wintering grounds without prior knowledge of the route. Apparently these starlings used orientation migration only on their first voyage; the following spring, they reliably employed navigation migration to return to the breeding grounds where they were born.

Some of the young starlings traveled as far south as Portugal that autumn, well outside the species' typical nonbreeding distribution. They found its beautiful weather much to their liking, so they returned there the following year. Obviously they reached these new wintering grounds the second time by navigation migration, because the compass bearing between Portugal and their breeding grounds would not have been the same as from their release location the year before. Similar displacement experiments with other species, such as blackcaps and hooded crows (*Corvus cornix*), suggest that genetically encoded directions may persist beyond the first year; indeed, perhaps they are the basic equipment of the navigation toolkit that birds use throughout their lives.

Shining bronze-cuckoos are brood parasites that are reared by a nonmigratory host species. Nonetheless, young cuckoos faithfully migrate a difficult transoceanic route without the benefit of prior experience or another bird to show them the way.

A critical part of the toolkit is the innate time program. In order to arrive safely at a predetermined point without prior knowledge of its whereabouts, a bird must travel on a particular compass bearing at a known speed for a precise period of time. This is not unlike the navigational system used by aviator Charles Lindbergh on his historic nonstop solo voyage across the Atlantic in 1927. Studies of caged birds experiencing *Zugunruhe* clearly indicate both innate time and directional components to their activities. Serious doubters need look no further than New Zealand's shining bronze-cuckoo (*Chrysococcyx lucidus*) for the most convincing evidence.

Like 50-odd other cuckoo species, the shining bronze-cuckoo is a brood parasite that does not raise its own young. Rather, females lay their eggs in the nests of other bird species, leaving the hatching and feeding of these alien chicks to the foster parents. In New Zealand, the shining bronze-cuckoo most frequently parasitizes the grey warbler (*Gerygone igata*), a plain-plumaged nonmigratory songbird about a quarter its size. Brood-parasitic birds tend to select hosts much smaller than them so that their young have an advantage in size and strength over any host chicks that may hatch. Cuckoo chicks have additional behavioral strategies, such as ejecting host eggs and young from the nest, to ensure that they receive the undivided attention of their foster parents. Most host species actually prefer the young cuckoos to their own offspring, because bigger chicks send a strong message of increased likelihood of survival to the parents. Somehow they remain perpetually clueless about the cuckoo chicks' obviously anomalous appearance.

Grey warblers are doting parents, and when their healthy cuckoo chick achieves the age of independence, it migrates. This occurs about one month after the chick's real parents, unencumbered by domestic duties, have already departed for the wintering grounds. The young cuckoo takes flight and travels west about 1,200 miles (1,900 km) over open ocean to eastern Australia. It then veers north and continues its journey another 1,000 miles (1,600 km), making landfall on the Solomon or Bismarck islands — tiny oases of land amid an otherwise featureless ocean — where it joins its biological parents in their traditional wintering habitat. There can be no question that this species is born with innate knowledge of its migratory route and destination.

Sometimes a species that is not supposed to have prior knowledge of when and where to go can surprise us. The magnificent whooping crane (*Grus americana*) was once commonly seen migrating across the central grasslands of North America. Young whoopers learn to migrate by accompanying their parents on the journey during their first year of life; having done the trip once, they are then able to retrace their path between winter and summer every year afterward. Tragically, hunting and habitat loss drove this beautiful species to near extinction in the early 20th century.

In an effort to bolster the remaining wild cranes, conservation workers established two additional populations by reintroducing captive-bred individuals to sites in south-central Wisconsin and central Florida. The Wisconsin population was slated to be migratory. And since this project began in 2001, a host of dedicated people, including biologists and pilots from Operation Migration, have enjoyed resounding success as they carefully and painstakingly lead imprinted juvenile cranes to wintering grounds in Florida's Chassahowitzka National Wildlife Refuge behind ultralight aircraft that serve as surrogate parents. After an absence of more than a century, whooping cranes are now gracing North America's eastern flyways. On the other hand, no plans were made to teach the introduced Florida whooping cranes how to migrate. It had been decided that this population would remain where it had been established, to lollygag in the year-round abundance of those southerly latitudes.

One spring, however, two Florida birds got a different idea: they fattened up and flew north. By mid-May the pair (a female and a male) was seen feeding in corn and alfalfa fields near Sandusky, Michigan. They spent the summer in the area, singing and dancing and defending their territory from the local sandhill cranes (*Grus canadensis*). When the weather turned foul in late November, they flew south. The pair was tracked as they followed a strict compass bearing toward the Appalachian Mountains. Despite the loss of her partner along the way — perhaps in a storm they encountered over Lake Erie — the female continued her journey south. When she reached the mountains, she was observed spiraling upward and soaring in typical migratory crane fashion. She skillfully adjusted her heading and crossed the mountains without event, and then readjusted her course again toward her final destination. Eleven days after she had left Michigan, this so-called non-migratory crane touched down at her original release site in central Florida, having traveled an estimated 1,450 miles (2,300 km). Conservation workers were flummoxed, to say the least. Not only had these cranes somehow remembered a migratory legacy deemed lost for a score of generations, they had successfully flown the route without being shown how. Moreover, the complex course adjustments required to safely traverse the Appalachians clearly demonstrated the female's penchant for navigational migration. She was not flying aimlessly but knew precisely where she was going.

If innate migratory capabilities seem perplexing, navigational migration is even more so. Also called goal-oriented or true navigation, this skill requires a sense of direction and the ability to access point-coordinate data for both the destination and any position en route. If traditional stopover or staging locations dot the journey between winter and summer, coordinates for these critical sites must be filed for reference. Basically a migrating bird must have a map—or rather, maps—in its head, and the nature of these maps is frequently determined by the length of the journey.

Birds that make short, seasonal movements may rely more heavily on a map built from landmarks rather than one constructed, for instance, from variations in geomagnetic field intensity. Birds have good color vision, and their keen eyes are better than humans' at discerning fine details from a distance; the density of visual cells is very high over the entire retina, not just in its central region (the fovea), as in humans. Birds in flight get a good view of the landscape—in clear weather their vision is limited only by the earth's curvature. At an altitude of about 3,300 feet (1,000 m), a migrating bird can see ahead about 65 miles (100 km), and prominent features on the horizon, such as mountain ranges, can be distinguished even farther away than that. Hence, a bird flying at that altitude can see an area of approximately 11,500 square miles (30,000 sq km), roughly the size of Belgium or Massachusetts.

Some studies indicate that long-distance migrants near the end of their journey may use landmarks to home in on their final destination. Many young birds spend the weeks following fledging making short flights in the vicinity, acquiring extended knowledge of their natal environs that could be useful when returning the following spring. More prominent landmarks may also offer long-distance migrants an opportunity for simple in-flight course calibration, particularly when those features provide a checkpoint near stretches of inhospitable terrain. Perhaps this is one reason why large numbers of migrants pass over unmistakable topographical features near open-water crossings, such as Point Pelee and Thunder Cape on the Great

Migrating white storks (*Ciconia ciconia*) rest near the Strait of Gibraltar before continuing their journey south to their wintering grounds in Africa.

Lakes, and the straits of Gibraltar and Bosporus near the Mediterranean Sea. Huge kettles of hawks and vultures can also be observed seasonally, circling upward in the thermals over Panama City.

Do birds have the memory capacity to retain these visual images? Of course, some birds have extraordinary memories. Species that cache their excess food for later use by burying it or storing it in holes or under tree bark, such as Clark's nutcracker (*Nucifraga columbiana*), are able to relocate tens of thousands of such hidden sites several months later. Migratory birds may have significantly greater long-term memory capacity (particularly spatial memory over 12 months or more) than nonmigratory birds. The evidence is in the larger size of the hippocampus—a part of the forebrain that contributes to long-term memory processing—in juvenile migratory birds than in nonmigratory species. In addition, further hippocampal development occurs between a migratory bird's first and second year of life, while nonmigratory birds do not exhibit this phenomenon.

Local landmarks do not work on long legs of a journey, however, and this is where migratory birds employ their most useful global map: the one invisibly painted on the earth's surface by its endemic magnetic field. Magnetic mapping is not unlike plotting a position on a nautical chart. In theory, if an animal learns the alignment and inclination of magnetic gradients across its natal territory, the pattern of these values can be extrapolated into unfamiliar areas. By comparing data at the home site with the destination site, the bird can establish a linear map across the distance along which its position can be determined. If a second, nonparallel, line could be applied to the earth's surface — by either plotting an additional geomagnetic gradient or tuning into some other compass system — then the bird would be able to draw the map by taking a series of point samples with a known spatial relationship along the way. This is called bicoordinate position fixing.

Thus, true navigation requires knowing where you are, where you are going and where you would like to stop during the journey, and then following a compass course between those various places. How frequently a bird checks its position en route appears to vary with species. European robins, which are short-distance nocturnal migrants, use their magnetic map to adjust their stellar compass–based course only about every three days. On the other hand, garden warblers and whitethroats (*Sylvia communis*), which are long-distance nocturnal trans-Saharan migrants, check in every night during migration. The reasons for this discrepancy may be twofold. First, the short-distance migrants would undoubtedly have better knowledge of their "local" star systems, making them more reliable as navigational tools. Furthermore, long-distance migrants, given the distance they need to travel, could more easily miss their target if they were pushed slightly off course along the way — by wind drift, for example — and followed this incorrect bearing for some time. Checking in regularly keeps them on track.

Obviously, true navigation of this sort can be undertaken only by adult birds, because it requires traveling the route and using data collected along the way to establish the gradients. When data collection goes wrong, this is known as the "VW effect." Biologists have long suspected that pigeons displaced from their home coop expedite their return trip on the wing by assimilating map information on the outbound journey. Thus the home flight requires a simple reverse of direction to follow the traced points back to the coop. In one study, however, young pigeons showed an unusually poor ability to navigate anywhere when they were displaced. It was later determined that this failing had occurred because the birds were shipped in the backseat of a Volkswagen ("VW") that had its engine in the rear. Apparently the birds' readings of the earth's magnetic field were being scrambled by electrical fields produced by the engine. This was particularly problematic for inexperienced birds, which had no previously established map of the world to fall back on. Once established, however, this ingrained map is difficult to shake. Adult pigeons have brilliantly demonstrated their ability to home even after traveling in rapidly rotating barrels, sealed to shut out useful olfactory cues and surrounded by electric coils that changed polarity at random in eight different field directions. Upon arrival at the displacement site, the resolute birds shook off their motion sickness and plotted their course for home with the same precision as control-group pigeons that had been transported in the relative luxury of open cages with an unobstructed view of the scenery.

Birds that migrate in numbers
have the added advantage of
other flock members' opinions
when determining the correct
route to their destination.

Experiments with other short- and long-distance migratory species, including Australian silvereye birds (*Zosterops lateralis*), American alligators (*Alligator mississippiensis*), loggerhead sea turtles and eastern red-spotted newts (*Notophthalmus viridescens*), all support the existence of a magnetic map as part of the animals' navigation toolkit. And just like pigeons, robins, garden warblers and whitethroats, these species appear to collect their much-needed geomagnetic data through early experience. They then use it on their journeys to periodically check geographic location and calibrate their other navigational systems.

Of course, avian species that migrate in flocks or family groups, such as many waterfowl and waders, have the advantage of being able to collect geomagnetic data while being safely conveyed to the wintering grounds by more experienced individuals. Perhaps this is enough to explain why captive-bred whooping cranes need to be led to their winter homes only once to instill reliable migratory behavior. And group migration may have added benefits, even for adult birds. Navigation cues can be unreliable under certain situations. For example, geomagnetic fields work poorly near the equator; stellar rotational cues may be imprecise at the poles; and solar-based data vary with season and location. Add to this variability the effects of weather and wind drift, and you might wonder how they get there at all. Although we know little about how migratory birds communicate, we are aware that species traveling in groups have greater accuracy rates than those that go it alone. Even maladjusted pigeons released experimentally in a flock were able to come to a compromise about the right way to go.

So it appears that migratory birds use every means at their disposal — geomagnetism, stellar and solar compasses, geographic landmarks, barometric pressure, infrasound, olfactory cues, even the measured opinions of others — to correctly choose their course between winter and summer. However, the question remains as to whether these tools are sufficient explanation of so wondrous a phenomenon. Perhaps we have overlooked some other, fundamentally important mechanism. Ever since humans first witnessed the great seasonal movements of birds, avian migration has been labeled as one of nature's unsolved mysteries. But considering this remarkable behavior as somehow mysterious reveals more about our own lack of imagination than it does about the significance of these creatures, which are far more than tenuous reflections of ourselves. We humans tend to show the limits of our awareness by measuring the value of miracles only as far as we can understand them. Of course birds know how they do what they do — they are just not telling us.

Redwings and Fieldfares
Colonizing thrushes

Out-of-place-or-time birds are typically called vagrants or accidentals, which is not to imply that they could not adapt to new locations. When birds live and breed successfully in an atypical locale, it is called colonization.

The distribution of bird species in winter and summer and the routes that they fly between the seasons have a considerable component of tradition. In other words, generations of birds migrate the same corridor for millennia, adhering strictly to time and place. They are guided along their path by innate and learned navigation and orientation systems designed with overlapping failsafe programs. They are physiologically invested as well, with a hormonal complement that urges them to travel when the time is right. Occasionally, however, migratory birds go astray. They may be blown off course by foul weather or strong winds. Sometimes inexperienced birds, often juveniles on their first migratory journey, simply go in the wrong direction.

Common navigation errors include mirror-image migration, when birds travel at an angle to the proper direction, and reverse-direction migration, which occurs when they fly in the opposite direction from where they should be going at that time of year—in autumn these birds fly north rather than south. On rare occasions it is our technological influence that interferes. At least one migratory species, the house crow (*Corvus splendens*), a showy, raucous, highly opportunistic South Asian member of the crow family (Corvidae), has traveled around the world—East Africa, Iran, Australia, even the Netherlands—by stowing away on ships. Its fearless nature and pedestrian food preferences may have helped. And sometimes migratory birds simply decide not to migrate but rather to explore local opportunities throughout the seasons.

No matter how it got there, all birders know that seeing a bird outside its normal distribution at the wrong time of year is a rare treat, and definitely one to be noted on one's "life list." These off-course, out-of-place-or-time birds are typically called vagrants or accidentals. The name *vagrant* seems to imply that the bird is doomed to a life of despair and solitude, but this need not be the case. A bird may be somewhere it does not usually occur, but that does not mean it could not live there successfully if the opportunity presented itself. And when that happens—provided that at least one male and one female are present—it is called colonization.

Some bird groups are better colonizers than others; for example, egrets and white-eyes are renowned for their ability to establish novel breeding distributions. In Great Britain, thrushes appear to do quite well. The traditional nesting

Until recently, fieldfares were seen in Great Britain only during the winter and when migrating; however, they are now rare but regular breeders in scattered locations throughout England and Scotland.

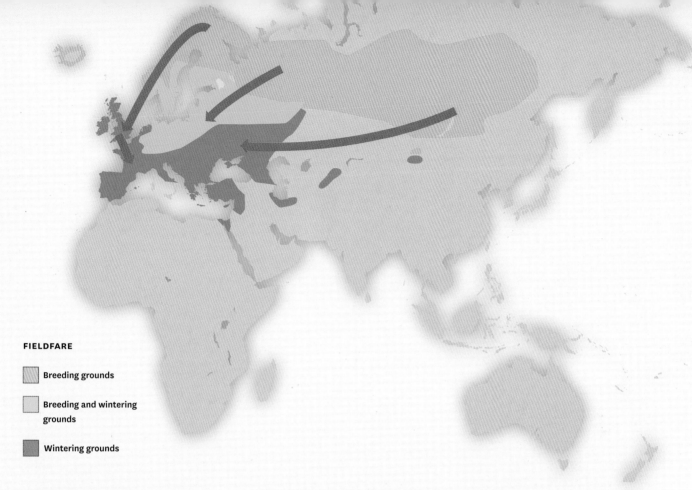

avifauna of Britain includes about 10 thrushes, most of which are migratory, and about 26 additional species that occur rarely, as vagrants. In addition, two otherwise migratory thrush species have recently decided to stay the summer: the fieldfare (*Turdus pilaris*) and the redwing (*T. iliacus*). Breeding redwings are native to taiga forests of northern Europe and western Asia from Scandinavia through eastern Russia; they winter farther south in Europe, northwest Africa and east to Iran. Until recently they were seen only during winter in Great Britain, where about 600,000-plus individuals would spend the off-season. Fieldfares occupy much the same breeding distribution as redwings, except that they do not occur quite so far east in Asia. They also spend their winters in central and southern Europe, south to the Mediterranean and northern Africa and east to Israel. An estimated 700,000 fieldfares occur in Great Britain during winter; they are regularly seen there as birds of passage destined for more southerly climes.

In the summer of 1932, Major A.H. Daukes discovered a redwing pair nesting in the shrubbery in Moray, Scotland. Since that time the species has continued to nest in northern Scotland, having been observed in Sunderland, Ross-shire, northern Perthshire and the northwestern Highlands. Some accounts suggest that as many as 200 pairs make northern Scotland their place of year-round residence; other ornithologists believe the number may be considerably smaller. Despite the six decades since their colonization, however, redwings have strayed little from their original Scottish breeding distribution. Fieldfares, on the other hand, appear to be more adventurous. This species was first recorded as breeding in Orkney, northeast of the Scottish mainland, as recently as 1967. Unlike redwings, fieldfares have expanded their breeding distribution southward to the county of Kent, in the extreme southeast of England. Although they are still rare (but regular) breeders in scattered locations in England and

Scotland, this rapid range expansion seems to suggest that fieldfares have an innate talent for colonization.

Colonizing species must be dependable breeders, with some degree of flexibility in their ecological needs and ability to interact favorably with the environment. Maybe redwings and fieldfares differ somewhat in this regard. Although these closely related species breed alongside one another throughout much of their continental range, the redwing has been unable to accomplish this in Great Britain. Competition between the two species for limited local resources may be playing a hand. On some scale, the current distributions of many migratory bird species can be explained by a myriad of small historical colonization events and their subsequent interactions with other species living there. When it comes to redwings and fieldfares in Great Britain, perhaps we are witnessing an early snapshot of a colonization work in progress.

Bohemian Waxwings
Expert irruptive migrants

Some birds choose to exploit habitats or food choices that offer great abundance in some places during some years but not in others. The seasonal movements of these irruptive migrants are as ephemeral as the resources they seek.

Bird migration is typically viewed as an event that occurs with cyclical regularity: fly south in autumn, fly north in spring. This is the evolutionary hallmark of species that have developed in tandem with relatively predictable resources; in other words, nest sites or wintering food resources will be available upon arrival every year. Some birds, however, choose to exploit habitats or food choices that are not so predictable—that offer great abundance in some places during some years but not in others. The seasonal movements of these species, sometimes called irruptive migrants, are as ephemeral as the resources they seek. They may be present in vast numbers in a particular location one year, but virtually absent the next.

Some ecological niches lend themselves to unpredictability better than others. In the Northern Hemisphere, the trees of the boreal forest that produce seed cones and fruit offer perhaps the greatest feast-or-famine opportunities. Known as taiga in the Old World, the boreal forest is the world's largest biome. It cloaks an estimated 6.5 million square miles (17 million sq km) of our planet just south of the tundra and steppes of Russia, Scandinavia, Canada and Alaska. This region boasts the harshest climate on earth (with the exception of more polar latitudes), which results in slow decay of the leaf litter and woody debris on the forest floor. Boreal soils are characteristically nutrient-poor, bereft of the lush organic material that is typical of more southerly deciduous forests. Consequently, boreal trees such as Norway spruce (*Picea abies*), larch (*Larix* species), birch (*Betula* species) and mountain ash or rowan (*Sorbus aucuparia*) may need more than one growing season to accumulate sufficient stores of nutrients to produce a crop. Weather is also a factor: unless the preceding autumn is warm, fruit buds will not form; if the spring is too cool, flowers will not develop. When conditions are favorable, however, the bounty for seed- and fruit-eating birds is almost immeasurable. Flexibility is the key—these birds must be on site when the table is set.

Among the best known and most welcome irruptive migrants of the boreal forest are Bohemian waxwings (*Bombycilla garrulus*), which are known simply as waxwings in Europe and Great Britain. These lovely songbirds are typified by handsome grayish plumage elegantly accessorized with a silky crest, black facial mask, yellow-banded tail and bright sealing-wax-red wing tips that give this group its

When sugary fruits and ripe berries are in short supply in the north, large nomadic flocks of Bohemian waxwings move south in search of food.

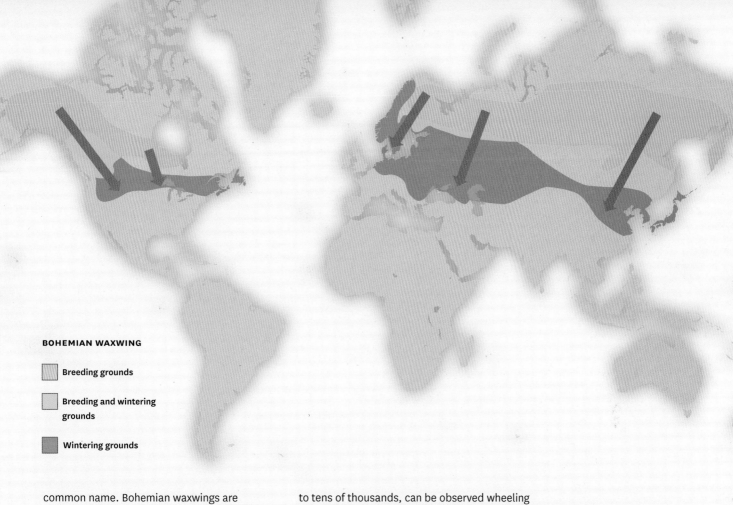

BOHEMIAN WAXWING

Breeding grounds

Breeding and wintering grounds

Wintering grounds

common name. Bohemian waxwings are distributed through an extensive circumglobal range lying just south of the tundra latitudes, where seasonal resources may be fleeting and unpredictable. Unlike most songbirds, waxwing pairs do not defend a breeding territory, nor do they exhibit any form of true song. Both behaviors are unnecessary in an environment where resources are not present in the same place from year to year: why defend a space that may be unprofitable in the future?

Bohemian waxwings favor the fruit of the mountain ash (rowan) tree but will also regularly eat other sugary fruits such as the berries of hawthorn (*Crataegus* species), cedar (*Juniperus* species), cotoneaster (*Cotoneaster* species) and mulberry (*Morus* species). Their appetites are voracious: one study estimated that each 2-ounce (57 g) waxwing gulps down about 6 ounces (170 g) of ripe berries per day. And when the fruit crop in the north fails, particularly in late autumn, Bohemian waxwings move south, seeking more berry-laden shrubs and trees. During these erratic irregular irruptions, flocks of gregarious waxwings, numbering in the hundreds

to tens of thousands, can be observed wheeling in acrobatic turns as they scan the horizon in search of food. Their ability to find even isolated patches of fruit is remarkable. Huge flocks have been reported making brief feeding stopovers in otherwise arid communities where irrigated shrubs and trees are planted around homes and other buildings. Once the vegetation is stripped of berries, the birds depart as quickly as they came.

Despite their northern boreal distribution, roving flocks of Bohemian waxwings can be seen during winter as far south as southern England, through central Europe and west across Eurasia to Japan. In North America they may occur throughout southern Canada and the U.S. Midwest, even as far south as central Texas in particularly poor years. People living within the potential winter range of Bohemian waxwings can try to entice these remarkable birds to their backyards by planting shrubs and trees that retain their fruits through winter. But do not expect to see them for long. Just like the ephemeral resources on which they depend, waxwings are here today and gone tomorrow.

CHAPTER 6

MIGRATORY BIRDS *in* PERIL

The beauty and genius of a work of art may be reconceived, though its first material expression be destroyed; a vanished harmony may yet again inspire the composer; but when the last individual of a race of living things breathes no more, another heaven and another earth must pass before such a one can be again.

CHARLES WILLIAM BEEBE

L ife on our blue planet is in a state of decline, and although we may debate the gravity of each cause, the end result remains undisputable. Plant and animal species are disappearing at a rate that echoes the greatest historical mass extinctions, those that ended the Ordovician, Devonian, Permian, Triassic and Cretaceous periods, where as much as 95 percent of all life on earth disappeared in a blink of geological time. Unfortunately, birds are now suffering along with the rest. The World Conservation Union—an international organization that promotes biodiversity conservation and sustainable resource use—lists 16,928 animals at risk of extinction in the near future, and the list includes 1,222 bird species. The ecological processes involved in the 21st-century collapse of global biodiversity may be complex, but the ultimate explanation is very simple. This time, the mass extinction is being caused entirely by humans.

Humans have had a direct effect on avian species since our very origins. Birds and their by-products have always fed us, clothed us and helped us win wars. In the past two centuries alone, more than a hundred

The peregrine falcon (*Falco peregrinus*) was once endangered as a result of reproductive failure caused by pesticide residues in its environment. Thanks to conservation measures, however, populations are now recovering.

Wood thrush populations are declining precipitously from the synergistic effects of forest fragmentation, including loss of habitat, brood parasitism, predation and other deleterious changes to the environment.

bird species are known to have disappeared because of single human-caused factors. The feathers of Hawaiian honeycreepers (Drepanidinae) adorned the robes of kings and queens; the giant moa (*Dinornis robustus*) was eaten to extinction; the great auk (*Pinguinus impennis*) was clubbed to death for sport; and the passenger pigeon (*Ectopistes migratorius*) was driven into oblivion for financial gain. From a conservation point of view, such causes are relatively easy to remedy if intervention is timely. For example, the recovery of the peregrine falcon—a recent conservation success story—was reversed because their decline was due almost entirely to reproductive failure caused by DDT pesticide residues in the environment. Removal of the offending substance allowed conservation workers to gain some advantage and the falcon's downward spiral was arrested.

What complicates bird conservation now, however, are the insidious effects of indirect human-caused factors, such as habitat loss, global climate change and uncontrolled population growth. Early ripples are already being observed as species distributions decline and shift and populations falter. Without a commitment to reform, we shall soon see not just destruction of single species, but failure of entire communities, ecosystems and biomes. And among the biodiversity most likely to succumb are migratory birds—their very existence requires a degree of environmental stasis that spans geographic and political boundaries. Five case studies follow, each describing migrants whose recent declines have been induced by human hands. These species may not yet be extinct, and some are not yet even endangered, but their impending demise provides a springboard for contemplation. We stand on the brink of a great chasm. Will we jump or will we fall?

The Wood Thrush

*Our remnants of wilderness will yield bigger values to the nation's character
and health than they will to its pocketbook, and to destroy them will be to
admit that the latter are the only values that interest us.*

ALDO LEOPOLD

An American folk legend claims that when the first colonists arrived in the New World, the virgin forests were so dense and expansive that a squirrel could travel from the Atlantic Ocean to the Mississippi River without ever touching the ground. While it is unlikely that such an industrious rodent ever existed, those forests certainly did. Biologists have estimated that 400 years ago, forests covered about 46 percent of the land in the United States and 54 percent in Canada—all told, about 3.5 million square miles (9 million sq km).

Trees have always fallen to humans for fuel wood or the creation of useful items, but it was when the first settlers turned the soil that the epidemic of deforestation began in North America. Since that time the eastern deciduous forests have been decimated to only 20 percent of their original extent in Canada, and an alarming 7 percent in the United States. And although forests in North America are rarely being lost nowadays to agricultural expansion, they still are elsewhere in the world. Moreover, they are being reduced at a frightening pace, thanks to the efficiency of modern commercial forestry practices and the expansion of cities and suburbs because of unbridled population growth. Between 1990 and 2005, our planet lost an average of 32 million acres (13 million hectares) of forest per year—an area the size of two small countries—with little hope of deceleration in the foreseeable future.

Although these statistics clearly demonstrate the rapid decline in global forested areas, they fail to reveal a second, equally devastating aspect of deforestation: forest fragmentation. Many plant and animal species are adapted to thrive deep in the forest interior, where the stability of the ecological system is reflected in minimum overall disturbance. Change occurs only rarely in large tracts of mature forest, and when it does, it happens gradually. Typically, most of the action takes place along the margins, where attributes of the forest collide with those of the adjacent habitat type. Ecologists call this the edge effect. Edges usually have their own biodiversity complement, including species such as white-tailed deer (*Odocoileus virginianus*) and wild turkeys, that benefits from access to both habitats for food and shelter. Not so for the wood thrush (*Hylocichla mustelina*), one of many neotropical migratory songbirds that depend entirely on mature forest interior for reproductive success and survival.

Forests must be relatively large to have an interior, and this is the primary problem with fragmentation. Imagine a forest doughnut in which the cake part is the edge and the hole is the interior. The larger the hole, the greater the number of breeding pairs it can support. However, if you incrementally reduce the overall dimensions of the doughnut without sacrificing the cake part, you gradually diminish the size of the hole, ultimately losing it altogether. In many of today's forests, particularly in North America's eastern deciduous forests, there is plenty of cake but not too many holes. These forest fragments, lacking the sanctuary of a sufficiently large interior, are unable to provide adequate breeding territory for multiple pairs. What is more, they allow dangerous things from the outside—such as predators that can comfortably cross the open edge habitat—into these once-safe refugia.

The wood thrush is not likely to win any awards for its appearance, although its bright-eyed, inquisitive nature is certainly endearing to admirers of little brown birds. This thrush's special appeal lies in the clear, flute-like notes of its song, which lilt through the forest canopy at dawn and dusk with such breathtaking virtuosity that they put other songbirds to shame. Wood thrushes nest in moist, shady deciduous and mixed forest from southern Canada to the Florida panhandle, using the same breeding territory every year. They feed primarily on the ground, picking among decaying leaf litter for insects, millipedes and wood lice. They sometimes eat berries and other small fruits, and are known to become tipsy on occasion from devouring fermenting fruits that have clung too long to the branch.

Like many neotropical migrants, wood thrushes leave their northern summer home in August en route to their wintering grounds in Central America. They migrate at night, and in flight they utter a distinctive call, used by them to insure flock cohesion but used by us to census the size of their migrating populations. By October the thrushes are settling into their winter quarters amid the understory of primary forest or old secondary-growth forest in southern Mexico and south to Panama.

Not long ago, wood thrushes were considered one of the most common avian species in North America's eastern forests. Then, almost overnight, they became a symbol of vanishing neotropical migratory songbirds. What began slowly in the 1960s steamrolled into a steady, significant decay in numbers across virtually all of their summer and winter distribution. In the north, populations declined by nearly half, and a 1985 census of wintering birds in Veracruz, Mexico, revealed a 70 percent reduction in abundance from only 25 years earlier. Obviously, what was happening to the wood thrush was occurring on both fronts. Biologists soon discovered that our insatiable urge to chop up forests into isolated patches of edge habitat, either for wood products or to make land available for other purposes, was depriving wood thrushes and countless other birds of their forest-interior sanctuaries. As a consequence of habitat fragmentation and loss, breeding populations were being ravaged by increased brood parasitism and predation, as well as the secondary effects of acid rain. In winter they were dying from exposure and starvation when they were forced to occupy open, resource-deprived marginal forests. Wood thrushes had few places left to go.

One major problem for the thrushes was the brown-headed cowbird (*Molothrus ater*), a North American avian brood parasite (although it, too, was the result of indirect human meddling with the environment). Cowbirds, like cuckoos, lay their eggs in the nests of other bird species, leaving the child-rearing entirely to foster parents. Cowbird chicks are robust and rowdy and typically out-compete hosts' chicks for food and nest space. Needless to say, parasitized nests rarely fledge anything other than cowbirds.

Before the European settlement of North America, cowbirds were found only on the grasslands of the Great Plains. Being open-country birds, their range was restricted to the east by the great deciduous forest that stretched south from Ontario to Texas. They had evolved in concert with the American bison (*Bison bison*), whose immense herds—some 60 million strong—trampled the prairie grasses, stirring up the insects and seeds that cowbirds favor. Other grassland birds were familiar with their alternative breeding habits, so cowbirds got away with their behavior only enough to comfortably maintain their population numbers. This was a stable ecosystem, but the peace could not last forever. By the 1800s, newly arrived settlers were clearing great tracts of virgin forest for growing crops and grazing livestock. The remaining forests were carved into fragments small enough to render them primarily edge habitat, with very little interior. Female cowbirds can easily penetrate open edges, and what they found was a virtual smorgasbord of new habitat filled with inexperienced hosts.

Brown-headed cowbird females can lay up to 40 eggs in a single breeding season, and the naïve wood thrushes were frequently used as hosts, particularly in the Midwest. One study found that every thrush nest contained at least one cowbird egg, while some had as many as eight. Wood thrushes are characterized as "acceptor species" because they are both tolerant of adult cowbirds and unaware that their nest has been parasitized. Larger "rejector species" such as gray catbirds can distinguish between cowbird eggs and their own, and will destroy the offending eggs by pecking holes in them. Some smaller rejector species, including American goldfinches (*Carduelis tristis*), bury cowbird eggs in thick layers of nest-lining material so that they receive too little parental warmth for successful incubation. Rejector species can live quite comfortably amid increasing cowbird populations without suffering too many ill effects.

Localized wood thrush populations, on the other hand, began to decline considerably as the cowbirds expanded into their realm and east to the Atlantic coast by the 1950s. Ornithologists soon determined that wood

In one study in the Midwestern United States, every wood thrush nest in sampled forest fragments contained at least one brown speckled cowbird egg among the blue thrush eggs.

thrush reproductive success—based on the number of chicks that fledge from the nest—could be predicted according to the size of the forest patch where they nested. In continuous forests, wood thrushes enjoyed success rates exceeding 85 percent; in patches smaller than 200 acres (80 hectares), however, less than half of their nests fledged young. These numbers were certainly not viable in the long term, particularly when other factors were added into the equation.

Of course, cowbirds were not the only threats easily able to cross plowed fields and forest edges. Wood thrushes, particularly young birds and roosting adults, were also falling prey to the increased predation inherent in forest fragments. Common predators included not only raccoons (*Procyon lotor*), black rat snakes (*Elaphe obsoleta*) and American crows (*Corvus brachyrhynchos*), but also the beloved house cat. Domestic cats (*Felis catus*) descended from *Felis silvestris,* a Near Eastern species of desert wildcat, about 10,000 years ago. They were first domesticated in Egypt around 2000 BCE for their effective skills as predators, and keeping cats to rid houses and yards of vermin subsequently spread across Eurasia. When colonists arrived in North America in the 1600s, they brought their cats with them. Native wild predators such as bobcats (*Lynx rufus*) and red foxes (*Vulpes vulpes*), being in tune with their local environment, are limited in numbers by disease and resource availability. Introduced species, however, typically lack such innate system controls. Ecological disaster usually follows the introduction of exotic predators; the most notable cases occur on islands such as Guam, where brown tree snakes (*Boiga irregularis*) devoured virtually every native bird in a few decades. Likewise, the introduced domestic cat had not evolved as part of the North American food chain.

Domestic cats also enjoy the benefits of human attention: food, shelter and veterinary care. Research has demonstrated that these advantages do not make them less likely to take wild prey; on the contrary, they are better able to catch it. Their lifestyle also encourages population growth. Ecologists Stanley Temple, a professor at the University of Wisconsin, and John Coleman, of the Great Lakes Indian Fish and Wildlife Commission, have studied the population ecology of domestic cats and their effects on native birds and mammals. They estimate the combined total of pets and free-ranging cats in the United States at more than 100 million individuals; Wisconsin alone has about 114 cats per square mile (44 per sq km), many times higher than native predator densities. Moreover, their most reasonable appraisals suggest that the domestic cats of Wisconsin kill approximately 40 million birds per year. Across North America, cat predation rates may exceed 2 million birds per day, more than deaths due to oil spills, pesticides, motor vehicles and communication towers combined. The solution is relatively simple: domestic cats should be kept inside, where they pose no danger to local

wildlife. Responsible cat owners reap additional benefits, as indoor cats live three to five times longer than those allowed to roam freely. They also have fewer opportunities to contribute to the feline population explosion — all good reasons to enjoy our pets at home.

Although it was evident that wood thrushes were declining throughout their range, indirectly because of human modifications to their forest habitat — including increased predation and brood parasitism — researchers at the Cornell Lab of Ornithology only recently discovered a growing paradox in localized patterns of decline. Areas where thrushes were historically most abundant — such as along the Appalachian slopes from the Adirondacks and White Mountains south to the Smoky Mountains — were precisely where the steepest declines were being observed. Interestingly, these areas were also subject to some of the highest acid rain levels on the continent. Acid rain is formed when atmospheric water combines with air pollution, primarily sulfur and nitrogen oxides from burning coal, oil and gasoline. When acid rain falls on a forest ecosystem, it affects the trees most obviously, with incremental loss of needles and leaves. Ultimately, tree die-off leads to openings in the forest canopy. This was problematic, of course, but likely not enough to explain the wood thrushes' dilemma. When researchers looked further, however, they found that acid rain falling on fragile forest soils caused calcium to be leached from the upper layers, making it unsuitable for the resident plant and animal species.

Female wood thrushes, like all birds, require large amounts of calcium during breeding season — 10 to 15 times more than mammals of equivalent size — in order to produce calcium carbonate for their eggshells. During this time of year they supplement their diet with calcium-rich foods such as snail shells. Lack of nutritional calcium results in thin eggshells, which break during incubation or allow too much moisture to be lost through the porous shell; in either case, the eggs fail to hatch. In heavily polluted regions of the Netherlands, where highly acidic rain was the status quo, complete reproductive failure was occurring among some forest birds, resulting in enormous declines in biodiversity. These areas were also found to be entirely devoid of snails.

It was no surprise when North American studies demonstrated a similar decline in calcium-rich food sources in acidified forests. What was not expected, however, was that the negative effects of acid rain were magnified in fragmented forests — an example of ecological synergy. Perhaps the fragments were already too small to provide an adequate resource base; maybe they were too isolated from one another to allow for emigration, should suitable breeding territories become available. Whatever the explanation, multiple factors acting on an already modified playing field were driving nesting wood thrushes and other forest interior birds rapidly toward the brink.

Things are no rosier for wood thrushes in winter. Deforestation and fragmentation are rampant in Central and South America as land is being cleared for exotic tropical wood products and conversion to cropland and pasture. An estimated 11.1 million acres (4.5 million hectares) of mature forest is destroyed for these purposes in the neotropics every year. Unfortunately, the needs of the wood thrush differ little from season to season: as forest-interior birds, they seek out old-growth forest for food and shelter during the nonbreeding season as well.

Northern migrants are faced with a difficult choice if their traditional wintering grounds are fragmented, destroyed or otherwise compromised. Some resort to poorer-quality habitat where food may be limited and shelter from inclement weather is inadequate. Others may crowd into the remaining preferred habitat only to find that competition from other birds reduces their access to essential resources. Both scenarios led to greater mortality on the wintering grounds. Furthermore, birds surviving winter under these conditions may be ill-prepared to face the trials of spring migration and the uncertainty of habitat quality at their northern breeding grounds.

The wood thrush currently figures prominently on North America's watch lists and consistently scores in the top 10 percent of neotropical migrants of management concern. Conservation plans recommend protection of large tracts of old-growth broadleaf tropical forests on the wintering grounds, plus preservation of appropriate deciduous forest patches of more than 250 acres (100 hectares) throughout their breeding distribution. Partners in Flight, a cooperative venture among government, philanthropic, industrial, academic and professional organizations, has suggested that a key component to ensuring the species' survival is preservation of at least 6.2 million acres (2.5 million hectares) of mature deciduous forest in the Ohio Hills — one of the few regions where wood thrush populations are stable — in order to maintain a minimum core breeding population of 725,000 pairs.

However, such seemingly straightforward measures may not be so easily achieved. Canada and the United States continue to be major consumers and exporters of wood products, most of which are still acquired through clearcutting primary and old-growth secondary forests. Furthermore, exploration and extraction of energy and mineral resources, plus urban expansion, undermine efforts to avoid forest loss and fragmentation. Less than 15 percent of North America's eastern forests currently enjoy any public or private protection, and land stewardship practice in Central and South America is even more appalling. Regardless, it is imperative that the habitat of forest birds be safeguarded in summer, in winter and along the migratory route between the seasons. The wood thrush's ethereal voice is synonymous with forests in springtime. What a dismal shame should it be forever silenced.

The Red Knot

If all mankind were to disappear, the world would regenerate back to the rich state of equilibrium that existed ten thousand years ago. If insects were to vanish, the environment would collapse into chaos.

E.O. WILSON

Ever since humans became sentient beings, they have undoubtedly had an extravagant view of their own importance. We can now be considered the most ecologically influential species on the planet, but this honor is dubious at best. Under more equitable conditions, ecologically influential species serve to support the persistence of plants and animals living around them, not to undermine it. These critical players are typically neither the largest nor the most ostentatious members of their community. Sometimes they are so unobtrusive we do not even know they are there—until the effects of their removal become devastatingly apparent. Ecologists often classify these quiet heroes under the moniker "keystone species." In Delaware Bay, the keystone is shaped like a horseshoe.

Horseshoe crabs have existed in the world's oceans since the Cambrian period, at least 500 million years ago. They have survived countless background extinction events as coastlines were shaped by cyclical ice ages and shifting continents, and they lived through the asteroid impact that marked the end of the dinosaurs. In fact, *Limulus polyphemus,* the species that still graces the North American Atlantic coast, has remained unchanged both anatomically and ecologically for 225 million years. Why this particular horseshoe crab has persisted over the millennia remains an enigma; perhaps it is perfectly designed for its ecological role, but more likely it was just a beneficiary of good luck and happenstance. Whatever the reason, *Limulus* was there long before most of the species that now depend upon it, which perhaps explains its pivotal role in the community.

Despite their name, horseshoe crabs are not crabs at all, but relatives of spiders and scorpions. They are most closely allied with the eurypterids—extinct giant predatory sea scorpions—that terrorized ancient jawless fishes, the very first vertebrates. Like most of their chelicerate (spiderlike) cousins, horseshoe crabs are protected by a tough exoskeleton. Their underside sports two pairs of appendages for manipulating food, four pairs of walking legs and five pairs of plate-like gills. They have a long spiny tail, or telson, which the animal uses to flip itself over if its vulnerable belly is exposed by wave action. Horseshoe crabs are elegantly suited to their shallow-water existence, which is where they remain until spawning season.

Red knots (*Calidris canutus*) have one of the longest migratory routes in the world, corridors that are beset with deteriorating resources at critical stopover sites. This juvenile red knot faces an uncertain future.

In late spring, horseshoe crabs congregate in intertidal areas near sheltered beaches; then, under the full or new moon they come ashore at high tide to mate. The female digs a shallow burrow into which she sheds her eggs. Her smaller consort, clinging tenaciously to her carapace, quickly fertilizes the nest before she covers it with sand. Each burrow may contain 4,000 eggs that, warmed by the sun, develop without parental care. The larvae, miniature replicas of their parents, hatch after 14 days and return to the seas with another high tide. In a single breeding season a female will produce about 80,000 eggs, coming ashore repeatedly during successive tides to deposit four or five clutches at a time. Despite this apparent fecundity, however, fewer than 10 eggs per female per breeding season survive to adulthood, and these few individuals require another decade to reach sexual maturity.

Ironically, it is among the non-survivors that we find one component of the horseshoe crab's ecological importance. Not all nest locations are appropriately selected, and those lying too close to the tide line are frequently disrupted by wave action, bringing billions of eggs to the surface. In Delaware Bay, between Delaware and New Jersey on North America's Atlantic coast, these unearthed eggs are an essential food source for at least 11 species of travel-weary migratory shorebirds. Among the estimated one million shorebirds that converge on the bay each spring are rusty-plumaged "peeps" called red knots (*Calidris canutus*).

Red knots have one of the longest migratory routes in the world. *Calidris canutus rufa,* the New World subspecies, breeds inland on the high, barren tundra of Greenland and the Canadian Arctic. The birds spend their winter some 10,000 miles (16,000 km) distant on the rich tidal flats and sheltered beaches at the southern tip of South America. Red knots make few stops along their migratory route; most individuals undertake the journey in two or three long legs, pausing only briefly en route to restock their fat reserves. Some staging areas are critically important to this bird's survival: an estimated 90 percent of the entire North American subspecies—about 15,000 individuals—may be present on the beaches of Delaware Bay on any single day during spring migration. Without a doubt, the red knots are there because horseshoe crabs are there.

Most knots seen feeding voraciously on horseshoe crab eggs along the tide line have just flown nonstop from South America. Their high-speed wings are not built for soaring, so they must flap constantly in order to stay aloft. Fat reserves accumulated prior to departure have been depleted, and many birds arrive at the staging area emaciated. Despite the distance they have already covered, these shorebirds still have several thousand more miles to travel before they reach their tundra breeding grounds. During the next two or three weeks, the red knots feed almost constantly during

daylight hours. Horseshoe crab eggs are undoubtedly their preferred food source—simple to procure and easily metabolized into stored fat and muscle protein. Most individuals increase their body weight by 2 to 3 percent per day, almost doubling in size before their departure. Ornithologists have estimated that 100,000 shorebirds stopping at Delaware Bay in spring would consume more than 250 tons (225 tonnes) of horseshoe crab eggs and gain a total of 5.7 tons (5.2 tonnes) of fat. And being prepared is a necessity not only for the coming flight. Many red knots arrive on breeding grounds still covered with snow, long before insects and other invertebrates become active. Some birds resort to eating poor-quality plant foods at this time, but knots that do not arrive on the breeding grounds in good condition will likely perish from starvation before the short arctic summer begins.

Not long ago it seemed that something was going dreadfully wrong with red knots. Aerial surveys along Delaware Bay over a 30-year period indicated a drastic decline in their abundance. Bird counts in South America from the mid-1980s to 2003 discovered only half the knots that traditionally used these wintering grounds. Furthermore, adult annual survival, estimated to be about 85 percent in the mid-1990s, had plummeted to 50 percent by 2005. At this rate of decline, population models predicted that North American red knots would be extinct within 10 years. The U.S. Shorebird Conservation Plan of August 2004 confirmed the bad news: the red knot was listed among seven "highly imperiled" species. But what was causing these disastrous declines? Yet another study provided the clue. It revealed a 60 percent decline in red knots leaving Delaware Bay in good physical condition—and, of course, lower-weight birds are known to have lower survival rates. Consequently, conservation workers shifted their gaze to the horseshoe crab, in particular, the horseshoe crab fishing industry. Perhaps the recent increases in harvests were taking their toll.

Commercial fishing of horseshoe crabs on the U.S. Atlantic coast began in earnest during the late 1800s. Horseshoe crabs were ripe for exploitation because they congregate in large numbers in shallow inshore waters or on beaches at predictable times. Thus spawning crabs were harvested by the millions to be processed into fertilizer or animal feed. Populations declined steadily until the 1950s, when the burgeoning chemical industry made horseshoe crab products obsolete. Unfortunately, the reprieve was short-lived; by the 1980s another reason to fish the crabs had materialized. Emerging markets for exotic seafood in the Far East and Europe were becoming increasingly enticing to East Coast fishermen. Horseshoe crabs, particularly females bearing eggs, made perfect bait for catching American eels (*Anguilla rostrata*), channeled whelks (*Busycotypus canaliculatus*) and knobbed whelks (*Busycon carica*).

Conservative estimates suggest that between 2.3 and 4.5 million horseshoe crabs occur on the U.S. Atlantic coast from New Jersey south to Virginia. These populations can safely tolerate about 10 percent annual adult mortality from natural causes such as beach strandings, predation and disease. However, commercial fishery harvests grossly exceed these sustainable factors. In 1996, for example, eel and whelk fishermen landed an estimated two million horseshoe crabs, with a distinct bias toward breeding females. Compounding the horseshoe crab's plight is limulus amebocyte lysate (LAL), a component of its blood useful to the biomedical industry for detecting bacterial contamination of drugs and intravenous devices. Although the industry claims humane live-release protocols—following removal of a third of the crab's blood—records show that 10 to 15 percent of the animals do not survive the procedure. In light of these and other contributing factors—including shoreline development, beach erosion, pesticide use and periodic toxic red tide blooms—doom seemed inevitable for horseshoe crabs and the many species of shorebirds that depend upon them.

In 1997, in response to rapidly declining shorebird populations, the Audubon Society spearheaded an initiative to stop exploitation of horseshoe crabs and to impose sustainable practices on the fisheries. In some states, restrictions have been adopted that ban the horseshoe crab harvest altogether during the spawning season, or limit the catches to males only. But although commercial landings have declined dramatically—from 726,660 individuals in Delaware and New Jersey in 1999 to 173,777 in 2004 — we are not out of the woods yet. Horseshoe crabs take 10 years to reach breeding age. Even with restricted harvesting, it might be decades before we see any changes reflected in rebounding shorebird numbers.

So why fish horseshoe crabs at all? Economic arguments certainly do not support the fishery's continuance. In 1996, a boom year for crab fishermen, the commercial harvest of horseshoe crabs was estimated to be worth $1.5 million. The worldwide market for crab products for biomedical purposes stands at about $50 million annually. Also in 1996, however, ecotourism — which features shorebird migration prominently among its must-see attractions — poured $399 million into household incomes in New Jersey and Delaware, through tourist spending and the creation of 15,127 jobs. Perhaps the "highest and best use" for horseshoe crabs is simply to leave them alone.

And what of the red knots? In 2005 the Audubon Society and allied conservation groups, such as the Defenders of Wildlife and the American Bird Conservancy, petitioned the U.S. Fish and Wildlife Service (FWS) to have the red knot declared an endangered species, which would provide a means to address threats to the birds' survival under the Endangered Species Act. The disappointment resounded in the summer of 2007 when the FWS failed to comply. Although it recognized the need to protect faltering red knot populations, it passed over the birds in favor of other species at greater risk. The service cited factors affecting red knots that were occurring beyond their jurisdiction, such as hunting in northern South America and habitat degradation in the wintering grounds and southern staging areas. It is true that many birds are arriving at the Atlantic coast stopovers in poor condition because of events happening elsewhere. However, if successful arrival on the breeding grounds is to be encouraged, it would seem all the more sensible to optimize feeding opportunities in Delaware Bay.

As for any threatened species, the survival of the red knot will depend upon the trajectories of a myriad of causal factors, plus a bit of good fortune. Recovery-plan initiatives include designation of reserve sites for wintering and migrating birds, careful monitoring of population numbers and breeding status, and reduction of feeding competition with other bird species during stopovers. None of these measures, however, will contribute to their survival as significantly as recovery of the horseshoe crab. This is the nature of a keystone species: in its absence the system collapses, despite other efforts to maintain equilibrium. Thus the ecological equation is simple. For the price of saving horseshoe crabs, you will receive in return the safety of sea turtles, sponges, snails, leeches, mussels, shrimps, kingfish, bass, perch, flounders, eels, dowitchers, sandpipers, turnstones, sanderlings, plovers — and the ever-tireless red knot.

The Eskimo Curlew

Hunters would drive out from Omaha and shoot the birds without mercy until they had literally slaughtered a wagonload of them, the wagons being actually filled, and often with the sideboards on at that. Sometimes when the flight was unusually heavy and the hunters were well supplied with ammunition their wagons were too quickly and easily filled, so whole loads of the birds would be dumped on the prairie, their bodies forming piles as large as a couple of tons of coal, where they would be allowed to rot while the hunters proceeded to refill their wagons with fresh victims.

MYRON H. SWENK

It is an irrefutable human weakness that we frequently fail to appreciate the value of something—or even notice its existence—until it is lost to us forever. Such is often our way with first sweethearts, estranged relatives and the misplaced innocence of childhood. The folly is enhanced when the object of our apathy was once a common thing; after the fact, we are left wondering why intercession came so late, if it came at all. This is certainly the case with extinct species.

Within the annals of extinctions, the "once common, now gone" animals figure prominently, and species such as the passenger pigeon and the great auk (*Pinguinus impennis*) are prominent examples. The passenger pigeon, once numbering in the many billions, is said to have comprised almost 40 percent of the total avifauna in colonial America. Amateur naturalist Cotton Mather (1663–1728)—better known for his reprehensible involvement in the Salem witch trials—described a migrating flock that measured a mile wide and took several hours to pass overhead. Yet by the close of the 19th century this astonishingly ubiquitous species had vanished. Even such an immense biomass was no match for the ambitions of greedy hunters.

By their very nature, many migratory bird species, even one as abundant as the passenger pigeon, are prone to annihilation by humans. Their life history dictates traveling in flocks, which is intended to ensure greater survivability en route. Flock members enjoy the benefit of increased vigilance: each gets an opportunity to feed or doze without interruption while a fellow bird scans the horizon. Moreover, large flocks on stopover can easily swamp local predator populations, and the few kills that result will have little effect on the resilience of the flock as a whole. Migratory birds are also slaves to the predictability of changing seasons; they can reliably be found at a certain time in a particular place year after year. For example, we have all heard of the return of the cliff swallows (*Petrochelidon pyrrhonota*) to California's San Juan Capistrano mission, which reportedly occurs on March 19 every year.

Esquimaux Curlew. NUMENIUS BOREALIS. Lin. Male 1. Female 2.

Eskimo curlews were easy for market hunters to kill, particularly when disturbed flocks lingered around the body of a fallen companion.

Unfortunately, the attributes designed to mitigate the dangers of migration only increase the risk when humans become predators. So it was with the passenger pigeon—and, likewise, with the Eskimo curlew—when hunters came out in droves to meet the migrating flocks.

The Eskimo curlew (*Numenius borealis*) was the smallest New World curlew. Being shorter than a whimbrel (*N. phaeopus*) but taller than an upland sandpiper (*Bartramia longicauda*), it most closely resembled the palearctic little curlew (*N. minutus*), which breeds in eastern Siberia. To 19th-century hunters the Eskimo curlew was better known as the "dough bird," presumably because of the thick layer of fat stored beneath the migrating bird's skin. And migrate they did, in a veritable river of birds that darkened the sky along their 9,300-mile (15,000 km) route from the tundra meadows near the Arctic Circle, south across the Atlantic Ocean east of Bermuda, to the pampas grasslands of Patagonia. This annual phenomenon may have played an integral, almost ironic role in world history, and ultimately in the fate of the bird itself.

More than five centuries ago, three small ships found themselves at a critical juncture. They were 31 days out of their home port with no land in sight, and the patience of the crew was slipping toward mutiny. Then, without warning, on October 7, 1492, they sailed into the slipstream of a flock of migrating birds traveling quickly southward through the night. The mariners noticed that the birds did not alight on the water, and those that stopped briefly to rest upon the ships' decks had the distinctive shape of land birds. The crew's spirits lifted when Captain Christopher Columbus gave orders to turn the little fleet and follow the birds to shore. Four days later he discovered the New World, and among the birds that had steered this chapter of North American history was the Eskimo curlew.

No one knows how many Eskimo curlews existed in the sanctuary of pre-Columbian North America. Their flocks certainly figured in the hundreds of thousands to tens of millions, estimates based in part on the number known to have been destroyed by market hunters during the 1880s and '90s. In autumn the curlews staged in great multitudes in coastal Newfoundland and Labrador and the New England states, where they fed on crowberry shrubs (*Empetrum* species) with such gusto that their breast feathers were stained purple by the rich juice. In springtime the birds gathered in the tallgrass and eastern mixed-grass prairies of Oklahoma, Missouri, Kansas and Nebraska, lingering there until May before beginning their northward journey's last long leg to their tundra nesting grounds. Their abundance and seasonal predictability—and their sweet-tasting flesh—proved irresistible to humans.

In the last quarter of the 19th century, market hunters began seeking new quarry. The legendary flocks of passenger pigeons were declining as the massacres of previous decades began to take effect. Hunters soon found that Eskimo curlews lacked an innate fear of humans and could be readily decoyed. Their gregarious nature made it simple to kill them in plenty, particularly as disturbed flocks would assemble in great numbers around the body of a fallen companion. A single shot could easily bring down three dozen curlews in flight. Thousands more exhausted birds were pummeled to death with sticks as they roosted on darkened beaches. The flight of 1872 was typical: two Nantucket market hunters killed $300 worth at a time, and in those days Eskimo curlews fetched about six cents each. Prized for the table and simple to hunt, they were shipped by the barrelful (300 curlews per barrel) to restaurants and shops in Halifax, Montreal, Chicago, New York and Philadelphia. In the mid-1800s there appeared to be enough for everyone, but by 1900 a sighting was considered a rare event.

The Eskimo curlew and hundreds of other North American bird species gained protection when the ratification of the Migratory Birds Convention of 1916 made it illegal (in principle) to harm North American nongame birds. By this time market hunting of Eskimo curlews had slowed to a standstill, primarily because their rarity had rendered it impractical. Theoretically, what remained of the fragmented curlew population might have enjoyed some degree of recovery, but it did not. During the years of slaughter, other factors were making themselves felt. The vast stretches of pristine interior grasslands favored by Eskimo curlews for stopovers had all but disappeared as they were converted to cropland and pastures. As the habitat was destroyed, so were species that depended on it. One of these species, of special importance to the Eskimo curlew, was the Rocky Mountain locust (*Melanoplus spretus*), which came to a particularly mysterious end.

Eskimo curlews and other migratory upland birds rely on emerging insect swarms for sustenance during spring stopovers, and the Rocky Mountain locust was present in force. This species was once considered the most formidable agricultural pest in North America; one 1874 swarm was estimated to be 198,000 square miles (513,000 sq km) in size, an area larger than California. They devoured axe handles, saddles and clean laundry hanging on the line; some farmers claimed they ate the wool right off their sheep. Between 1873 and 1877 these grasshoppers caused $200 million (roughly $30 billion today) in crop damage in Colorado and neighboring states. However, less than 30 years later the species was extinct.

For many years, the cause of the insects' abrupt disappearance remained a mystery; it is now thought that aspects of their annual cycle may have determined their fate. After swarming, the grasshoppers would retreat to sandy riverbeds to breed. But as conversion of grasslands for agricultural purposes accelerated in the late 19th century, this critical breeding habitat was destroyed by plowing and irrigation, and plummeting grasshopper populations drove the last nail into the Eskimo curlew's coffin. It goes without saying that the Rocky Mountain locust was underappreciated at its peak. Despite swarms numbering over 12 trillion individuals, fewer than 300 museum specimens exist—no one thought that anything so plentiful could ever become extinct.

The Eskimo curlew clings tenuously to its critically endangered status under the Endangered Species Act of 1966, but it has not been seen reliably for about 40 years, since one was brought down by a gun in Barbados. Occasional unconfirmed sightings in Texas and Saskatchewan give us some hope that a small breeding population may exist somewhere, but extensive surveys of historic breeding grounds throughout the 1970s, '80s and '90s failed to reveal any concrete evidence. In all likelihood the Eskimo curlew is extinct. Maybe this species' demise should foster some timely introspection. Is hunting really sustainable in today's rapidly changing global environment? Do we know enough about wild species to anticipate their ability to weather multiple human-induced impacts on their survival? More than 100 million ducks, geese, swans, doves, shorebirds, grouse, rails, cranes and other birds are legally hunted each year. Perhaps we should learn to appreciate these species more while we still have the chance.

Studies made at Canadian lighthouses over a century ago were among the first to demonstrate clearly that a great many migratory birds were killed each year when they collided with human-built structures.

An Indiscriminate Killer

What's the use of a fine house if you haven't got a tolerable planet to put it on?

HENRY DAVID THOREAU

There was a time in the not-so-distant past when migratory birds shared the skies with no one and nothing, and the route between the seasons presented only natural hazards. Those were the days before telecommunications, electric power generation and glass-curtain buildings. But as humans progressed through the 20th century, we made the journey more perilous without even trying. And unlike hunting, environmental toxins, brood parasites and exotic predators, the modern menace we have created strikes down thousands of birds indiscriminately both day and night — or rather, they strike it.

Daniel Klem Jr., a professor of ornithology and conservation biology at Muhlenberg College in Allentown, Pennsylvania, has studied this threat for more than two decades. His conclusion? Collisions with human-built structures kill more birds than any other single factor. Evaluating the magnitude of this problem is not without difficulty; predators and scavengers ensure that the victims' bodies rarely last more than a few hours. Certainly all calculations tend to underestimate the death toll, Nonetheless, Klem's work suggests that, in the United States alone, as many as 976 million birds die annually from striking windows. This figure may represent at least 10 percent of annual bird mortality from all causes, including natural ones, and includes one in four North American bird species.

Furthermore, U.S. Fish and Wildlife Service records indicate that more than 170 million birds die each year after colliding with power-transmission lines, and 50 million more perish from hitting communication towers. In total, these figures represent more than 10,000 times as many birds as are killed annually by wind turbines, which proponents of fossil fuel consumption claim are major destroyers of avian life. European statistics on birds colliding with structures are less well known, but the tragedy is still pervasive. In the Netherlands, for example, an estimated 300,000 blackbirds (*Turdus merula*) are killed annually by window strikes. Italian studies suggest that 15 birds die of electrocution each year for every 100 poles supporting overhead wires.

When they collide with structures, migratory birds die primarily from cranial contusions and hemorrhages in the body cavity; sometimes they perish from blood loss when limbs are severed by guy wires and transmission lines. The degree of injury depends entirely on the bird's momentum at impact. Not all collisions are immediately fatal, but stunned birds are usually taken by predators while attempting to shake free from their confusion. The victims are not misguided or misled, nor are they weak or diseased—this is not natural selection in action. These birds are healthy and fat and otherwise entirely capable of reaching their destination. Such is the heartbreak of the situation.

The earliest official report of avian mortality from collision with human-made structures was made by the venerable American ornithologist Elliot Coues in 1876. He was traveling by horseback from Denver, Colorado, to Cheyenne, Wyoming—about 110 miles (177 km)—when he observed 100 bird carcasses beneath a 3-mile (5 km) stretch of newly erected telegraph lines. Even then he estimated that many hundreds of thousands of birds were likely being killed that way every year. His words were echoed by Californian ornithologist W. Otto Emerson in 1904, as he summarized the "infinity of birds" that perished when they struck lighthouses along the Pacific coast. Two decades later, the Canadian Commissioner of Dominion Parks sent questionnaires to 453 lighthouse keepers on both seaboards. Of the 197 returns received, 45 reported many dead and injured birds near lighthouse bases in the morning. The lighthouse keepers were surprised to discover that the victims were for the most part small land birds, not resident seabirds.

They also noted that most of the deaths took place in rain and fog, although one stupendous kill occurred in 1908 at Cape Anguille, Newfoundland, when 1,000 birds met their demise on a "clear dark night." More recent reports differ little from these accounts, except in the nature of the fatal instrument—now communication towers, skyscrapers, ceilometers (cloud-measuring devices), chimney stacks and cooling towers, overhead wires, windows, even NASA's vehicle assembly building at the Kennedy Space Center—and the concomitant severity of the problem.

The appalling statistics reveal that most collisions occur at night during fall migration. Autumn storms may bring cloudy, rainy or snowy skies, and they also pack strong winds from the north that produce favorable tailwinds for southbound birds. At night birds are attracted to illuminated buildings and other structures, which may affect their ability to navigate. Rain heightens the confusion because lights are refracted or reflected by falling water droplets. Bright lights may also cause temporary blindness; this effect, called flash blindness, occurs when retinal pigments are "bleached" by an intense blast of light. The consequences are usually temporary, but it may take from a few minutes to several hours for the eyes to return to normal. Flash blindness is more devastating at night because the eyes' dark-adapted pupils are open wide to improve night vision.

Attraction to bright lights is usually higher in fog or under overcast skies, and the potential for collision is increased because the migrants will circle the light source repeatedly. Sometimes, rather than colliding with the object, they flutter around it until they succumb to exhaustion. Birds also fly at lower elevations during bad weather, which increases their likelihood of striking something. Studies show that most nighttime collisions occur under 80 to 100 percent cloud cover, with reduced visibility and a ceiling of 400 to 1,600 feet (120–485 m). These night kills are usually small insectivorous birds; in many areas, disproportionate numbers of birds such as common yellowthroats (*Geothlypis trichas*) and ovenbirds (*Seiurus aurocapilla*) may comprise 20 percent or more of recorded kills. Night passages are characteristic of these species because they can then feed during the day, when their preferred food is active.

Collisions with communication towers at night may account for as many as 50 million bird fatalities in the United States each year, and some towers are legendary. In the late 1950s, the city of Eau Claire, Wisconsin, replaced a 500-foot (150 m) television tower with a new one twice as tall. Almost immediately, dead birds were being found at the tower's base. A health officer was brought in, who suggested that the birds were diseased, and ordered them buried. However, on the evening of September 19, 1963, local physician and surgeon Charles Kemper received a call from a fellow birdwatcher—an unusually large flight of migrants was passing over that night under overcast skies. Kemper had suspected that birds were dying from colliding with the tower, not from some unknown sickness. He drove out to the tower the following morning to find lawns, fields, roads, even rooftops within 100 yards (90 m) of the tower littered with the bodies of dead songbirds. The cloudy weather persisted through the following day, and Kemper took another trip to the tower, this time just after sunset. He was horrified by what he heard: an almost continuous *peep-peep-peep* of birds flying overhead, mingled with rhythmic thuds as their lifeless bodies hit the ground. It was raining birds. On those two September nights, 30,000 birds were killed in Eau Claire.

Studies reveal that bird-killing towers often share characteristics: they are typically taller than 200 feet (60 m); they are spatially isolated, often on a prominent topographic feature, such as a bluff, that migrants use for landmark navigation; and they are lit by floodlights or other fixed light sources. In the United States in 2002, at least 100,000 communication towers fitted this general description, and 10,000 or more were scheduled to be built each year following. Some say that the increasing demands of cellphones and digital television may require construction of as many as 500,000 towers in the next decade. This would spell disaster for fall migrants.

Spring losses are generally lower than autumn kills—often about 10 percent—because favorable southerly winds are usually associated with clear weather. Typically, spring kills occur when birds strike unlit objects such as power-transmission lines, barbed-wire fences and guy wires securing communication towers and chimney stacks. Many of these collisions occur during daylight hours; birds in flight simply do not see the thin wires until it is too late—the horizon rises to meet you very quickly at cruising speeds of 30 to 60 miles (50–100 km) per hour. Studies in the Netherlands revealed an astonishing death toll of about 260 birds per mile (418 per km) of wire each year, with kill rates near river crossings approaching 500 birds per mile (800 per km). Transmission lines pose the additional threat of electrocution. Unlike classic night kills, this type of collision usually affects larger birds such as cranes, bustards, storks, waterfowl and birds of prey. Nationwide totals of death due to electrocution are generally unavailable, but mortality records from utility workers, wildlife rehabilitators and falconers suggest that it measures many, many thousands annually, perhaps more.

The greatest killer, however, is glass windows in private homes and highrise residential and office buildings. Many of us have experienced the dull thump as a bird in flight crashes against a living-room window. The magnitude of this tragedy has grown in recent decades in concert with modern architectural preferences: large windows offer pleasing views of the outside world and bathe interior spaces with ample light. Unfortunately, most birds are unable to distinguish between the real sky and its image reflected in plate glass. Nearby trees and shrubs are also mirrored in the window, suggesting more habitat ahead. Some forest species, including Swainson's thrush, use patches of sunlight to navigate through dense understory vegetation; to them a bright reflection looks like a way through.

At night, illuminated windows pose even greater dangers; they stand out like beacons against the dark sky, particularly in poor weather. Why are so many hundreds of millions of nocturnal migrant birds drawn to their death on city streets? It is likely that a 54-story office building with every light burning is simply missing from the visual cues passed down to migratory birds through evolutionary time. We can only assume that, under poor flying conditions such as rain or fog, a patch of brighter light in the visual field represents clearer air. The logical action? Fly toward it. We also know that birds have both innate and learned abilities to navigate using fixed points of light. Before human technology superseded them, stars were the only lights at night. Perhaps migratory birds lost amid the light pollution of the modern era simply do not know which way to turn.

In recent years conservation organizations have stepped forward to educate those with their fingers on the light switches of North America about the decimation of birdlife by glass windows. Among the most noteworthy proponents are the Fatal Light Awareness Program (FLAP) in Toronto, the Audubon Society's Project Safe Flight in New York City, Lights Out initiatives sponsored by the Field Museum and the Chicago Audubon Society, and Project BirdSafe in Minneapolis–St. Paul and Project Safe Passage Great Lakes in Detroit, both also spearheaded by local chapters of the Audubon Society. Their message is simple: just turn off the lights between midnight and dawn during spring and fall migration periods. Fortunately these voices are starting to be heard and have met with resounding success. At McCormick Place in Chicago's downtown core, a single initiative to darken nighttime windows by switching off lights or drawing light-blocking curtains reduced the number of dead birds from 1,297 to 192 during the study period—a statistically significant reduction of 83 percent. One can only wonder what effect these simple practices would have on migratory bird populations if implemented globally. The secondary benefits, of course, are many billions of dollars saved annually in electrical energy consumption, not to mention the costs of environmental damage created by its production.

Migratory birds are declining worldwide. In the spirit of the Migratory Bird Treaty Act of 1918, we must not let them perish from the secondary effects of our day-to-day existence. The problem is not so difficult to eliminate: consider translucent (frosted) glass; reevaluate foundation plantings; mark transmission lines; replace white floodlights with red or blue ones; illuminate structures by using revolving or intermittent lights. And above all, just turn off the lights.

The Adélie Penguin

More than any other time in history, mankind faces a crossroads. One path leads to despair and utter hopelessness. The other, to total extinction. Let us pray we have the wisdom to choose correctly.

WOODY ALLEN

Historically, conservation biology often took a single-species approach. Many captive-breeding programs adopted this simplistic regime: the animal population declines, so you make more animals and put them back into the wild. The primary problem with this approach, of course, is that unless the factors that imperiled the species in the first place are resolved, the new recruits will have little chance of survival. Later on, biologists began to pursue a habitat-level approach: if the integrity of the community or the ecosystem can be safeguarded, then everything that resides in it will benefit. Although it is not always easy to preserve or restore habitat—particularly given the influence of private enterprise and the whims of local politicians—there have been numerous success stories, usually involving a great many dollars and the sweat and tears of dedicated conservation workers.

Unfortunately we now teeter on the edge of an ecological calamity that cannot be repaired by backfilling populations or cordoning off small fragments of habitat. It will descend upon us on such a massive scale that we may be unable to juggle all the required components. Imagine a runaway train hurtling across a rickety trestle; imagine a jet aircraft spinning wildly toward a patchwork landscape; imagine your worst nightmare—this is global climate change.

Humans began to create this environmental disaster about 200 years ago, during the Industrial Revolution. In the name of progress we began burning increasingly large quantities of fossil fuels—coal, oil and natural gas derived from dead ancient plants that had accumulated in primeval sea sediments—to power factories and transportation systems and to provide our homes with creature comforts. A by-product of fossil fuel combustion is carbon dioxide. When excessive amounts of this gas accumulate in the atmosphere, it creates a shield around our planet that prevents heat built up at the surface from escaping into space. Consequently the global temperature rises—and the word *global* must not be swept under the rug in this case. Although the United States produces more carbon dioxide per capita than any other country—22 tons (19.8 tonnes) per person, compared to 6.7 tons (6 tonnes) in Sweden—the atmosphere knows no borders. This is a problem that no nation can deny.

The daily news already resounds with predictions about how global climate change will affect us. We can anticipate a reduction in agricultural yields due to drought and an increase in heat-related deaths. Anomalous severe weather will be widespread, including more violent hurricanes and typhoons. Freshwater resources will be compromised, particularly those fed by glacial runoff. In addition, heating of the oceans and melting of the polar ice caps will cause sea level to rise as much as 20 feet (6 m)—if you are fond of Florida, it might be advisable to visit soon.

Global climate change will not only affect the daily lives of all humanity but will also have a devastating impact on biodiversity, particularly among plants and animals that lack the genetic programming for versatility. Thus global climate change will instigate higher extinction rates than does habitat loss, which is now considered the greatest general threat to biodiversity. Early estimates suggested that severe losses will begin with a 3.6°F (2°C) increase in global temperature; a 1.5°F (0.8°C) rise had already occurred by 2007. No doubt birds will be among the species lost, as they are highly sensitive to changes in temperature, precipitation and relative humidity. And although most birds demonstrate considerable mobility, they rely for food and shelter on other species that do not. Predicted avian extinction rates are horrific: 75 percent of Australia's tropical birds will disappear, South Africa should experience a 40 percent decline in avian diversity, and Europe will lose about 170 of its 426 breeding bird species. All told, 84 percent of all migratory birds are threatened by global climate change because of alteration to their breeding, nonbreeding and stopover territories. And among the migratory species at risk are seemingly unlikely candidates that dress in formal wear—penguins.

There are 17 species of penguins on the planet, and already 13 have appeared on the World Conservation Union Red List: four species are endangered, seven are threatened, and two more are considered to be near threatened. Penguins are astoundingly well adapted to survive in the severe cold of Antarctica, but that icy continent is warming up rapidly. One of the misconceptions about global climate change is that every part of the planet will be affected equally; however, this is not the case. The Western Antarctic Peninsula has already registered average temperature increases of about 10.8°F (6°C), the highest on the planet. Elevated sea temperatures, first noted in the 1940s, coincided with the greatest decline in Antarctic bird species, which began a decade later. Not so gradually, the cold, dry ecosystem of the South Pole is being replaced by a warm maritime climate, and with this conversion we are seeing the melting of sea and continental ice, changes in ocean salinity and the total collapse of Antarctic food chains. One of the casualties will be the Adélie penguin (*Pygoscelis adeliae*).

The Adélie penguin is one of many Antarctic bird species that will disappear forever as the southern continent heats up.

No other birds breed farther south than the Adélie penguin. Named after the wife of 19th-century French explorer Jules Dumont d'Urville, this gregarious species stands 2.5 feet (80 cm) tall and weighs about 8 pounds (3.6 kg). From October to February, the birds nest in colonies of a few dozen to many thousands of breeding pairs on the shores of continental Antarctica and on southern islands surrounding the mainland. Their nests are merely shallow depressions lined with small stones, which are in high demand because they keep meltwater away from the eggs. In particularly crowded colonies, fanatical mothers have been known to pilfer stones from their neighbors.

Adélie penguins are migratory—although they travel by swimming rather than flying—but little is known about their movements after they leave the breeding grounds in autumn. Satellite telemetry indicates that adults travel north to feed about 370 miles (600 km) from the Ross Sea. Juvenile birds venture farther; they have been reported as far away as the island of South Georgia, the Falkland Islands, Tasmania and New Zealand. The penguins do not return to the southern continent until just before breeding season the following spring.

Adélie penguins are now suffering from both direct and indirect effects of global warming: populations are faltering because of starvation, loss of nesting habitat and other physical changes to their environment. Censuses demonstrate an overall decline in their numbers of 35 to 40 percent since the late 1980s, and some populations, such those on Anvers Island, have decreased by 70 percent. Biologists suggest that Adélie penguins are among those inflexible species that are incapable of modifying the "hardwired" legacy of their evolutionary past. Despite rapidly deteriorating conditions, they continue to return to traditional nesting and feeding grounds. This is disastrous, because global climate change will inevitably cause failure of Antarctica's food supplies.

Many species, including Adélies, are highly dependent on krill (especially Antarctic krill, *Euphausia superba*), small shrimplike crustaceans that comprise immense schools of zooplankton in all the world's oceans. Krill are keystone species; they feed primarily on plantlike phytoplankton at the bottom of the food chain, making these nutrients available to larger animals higher up on the chain. Antarctic krill have a biomass roughly twice that of humans—more than 500 million tons (453 tonnes)—which nourishes vast numbers of whales, seals, fish and penguins in the southern oceans. Unfortunately, krill populations are rapidly diminishing. In winter, krill eat plankton and algae stored in sea ice. However, warmer temperatures since the 1970s have caused contraction of the winter sea ice around Antarctica, and krill are starving on their spawning grounds. Moreover, warmer ocean

temperatures favor the proliferation of salps—pelagic jellylike organisms that share a common ancestor with vertebrates—which are unpalatable to most krill-eating animals.

Penguins are starving in other ways as well. Melting associated with global warming is causing huge icebergs to calve off continental ice shelves. In December 2004, McMurdo Sound, which opens north to the Ross Sea, was blocked by the largest iceberg in recorded history. Measuring about 1,200 square miles (3,100 sq km) and containing enough water to supply the Nile River complex for 80 years, the iceberg blocked shipping routes and impeded wind and water currents that normally break up ice floes in the sound. Newspapers made much of three stranded research stations (even though they routinely stock a year's supply of food), but few reports even mentioned the 10,000 Adélie penguin chicks at Cape Royds that starved to death that spring. The iceberg had trapped the birds inland, and some adults were obliged to walk 112 miles (180 km) to the ocean to find food. These

Adélie penguins (*Pygoscelis adeliae*) are suffering catastrophic declines in their numbers because they are "programmed" to return to traditional feeding and nesting grounds, even if these areas no longer provide the resources they require.

flightless birds can barely manage 1 mile (1.6 km) per hour over ground; in order to survive, many of the adults were forced to eat the food they were carrying back to their young. And this was not an isolated case. Each summer, across the continent, Adélie colonies face multiple impediments to their reproductive success. The 2007 breeding season at Cape Bird reflects what may soon become the status quo: only 10 percent of the breeding pairs successfully raised a chick.

The global population of Adélie penguins currently stands at about two million breeding pairs. Although this seems sufficiently plentiful to withstand declining reproductive rates, it is not. What we are witnessing is only the beginning of this species' demise. Other penguin species, including the vulnerable rockhopper (*Eudyptes chrysocome*), are farther down the road toward extinction than Adélies. Rockhoppers on sub-Antarctic Campbell Island declined from 1.6 million strong to only 100,000 individuals in just four decades, and many of their traditional breeding grounds now stand vacant. Likewise, some emperor penguin (*Aptenodytes forsteri*) colonies have diminished by 50 percent since the 1970s because of increased adult mortality; abnormally warm temperatures and reduced sea ice have been blamed for this rapid deterioration.

The repercussions of global climate change are not restricted to the Southern Hemisphere. Birds of the Northern Hemisphere are also suffering as its onset affects their spatial and temporal distribution; many species already demonstrate anomalous changes to their annual cycle. Birds by design have evolved to schedule their breeding in concert with periods of plentiful food. Unlike mammals, which can convert stored fat reserves into milk, most birds must use the resources currently available to them on their breeding grounds. Many northern breeders rely on massive swarms of insects that emerge in spring. But global warming is causing these insect "blooms" to occur earlier, often before the birds have arrived on their breeding grounds.

In the Netherlands, pied flycatchers have declined by 90 percent in two decades because their traditional nesting period, which has not changed considerably, is no longer synchronous with food availability. The increased mortality is twofold: chicks perish because they have insufficient food and parents die because they are overtaxed by trying to provision their young from an empty larder. Other species are suffering the same fate: blue tits (*Cyanistes caeruleus*), great tits (*Parus major*), American robins (*Turdus migratorius*) and red-winged blackbirds (*Agelaius phoeniceus*), to name just a few. Even species that are able to store food for later use, such as gray jays (*Perisoreus canadensis*), are being compromised as warmer winters become typical. Many jay populations, particularly those along the southern borders of their boreal forest distribution, have declined as much as 60 percent because the berries, beetles and bits of meat they cached under bark and among tree branches in autumn have spoiled by spring.

Birds will also be affected by global climate change during the nonbreeding season. Europe's Mediterranean wetlands—critical stopover habitat for many species of palearctic migrants—will be gone in less than 75 years. A 4.5°F (2.5°C) increase in global temperature will reduce the amount of prairie pothole habitat—essential for stopover and breeding for 80 percent of North American's waterfowl species—by at least two-thirds. Wetlands are among our most endangered habitats, and many of the world's wetland birds must rely on patches that have been protected by law. Climate change could easily produce distributional shifts in these species so that their range falls outside of refuge boundaries, making them vulnerable to hunting. Even wintering birds will find no sanctuary from global climate change. Declines in dozens of long-distance Afro-palearctic migrant species have already been linked to widespread desertification and habitat degradation caused by reduced rainfall in North Africa's Sahel region.

Birds have always been useful indicators of environmental health because they are highly sensitive to changes that may elude us. It was for this reason that 19th-century miners took caged canaries down into the coal pits as early-warning detectors of deadly gases in the mine shafts. Even now birds may be foreshadowing the trials that we will face in the future, and it would be sheer hubris to suggest that those trials will be any easier for us than for other animals. Perhaps it is timely that humans recently passed a disturbing milestone: the people of Vanuatu—a small island in the South Pacific—became the first official refugees of climate change, when rising sea levels caused loss of their own habitat. Humans are notoriously xenophobic, so let us hope that the 200 million or more people rendered homeless in the coming decades will be able find safe haven on higher ground.

We cannot arrest global climate change, nor can we ban the activities that created it. We might slow the warming process if we begin to adopt the energy-responsible customs we should have practiced in the first place, but ultimately all humanity must learn to live with the fate we have dealt ourselves. And just as for the plants and animals with which we share the planet, this will be our species' greatest test of versatility and compromise. Are we up to the challenge? We will know soon enough.

GLOSSARY

Accidental A vagrant or stray individual observed beyond the boundaries of its typical species' distribution.

Allopatric speciation Speciation that occurs in populations that are geographically separated by a barrier such as a mountain range or body of water.

Altitudinal migration Seasonal movements that occur vertically between lower and higher elevations.

Alula The feather group attached to the first digit (thumb) of a bird's wing that reduces air turbulence over the wing.

Anterior The head end.

Assortative mating Mating that occurs when organisms tend to select individuals from the population that are similar to themselves.

Austral migrants Birds breeding in the Southern Hemisphere that migrate northward to their nonbreeding distributions.

Avifauna Bird life.

Barb The side branches in a feather's structure that extend from the central main axis, or rachis.

Barbules Branches that extend from barbs, which interlock to provide the feather with rigidity.

Bicoordinate position fixing The process through which global position can be determined using two gradients running in different directions.

Biomass The total weight of living organisms or a species' population in a given area.

Biome The largest ecological unit that comprises communities of plants and animals (e.g., tundra, tropical rainforest, desert).

Bronchi The branches of the trachea (windpipe) that enter the lungs.

Carrying capacity The maximum population size of a species that can be supported by available environmental resources.

Chord The distance from the leading edge to the trailing edge of a wing.

Circadian rhythm The patterns of bodily activities and functions that comprise the daily cycle of an animal.

Contour feathers The outermost vaned body feathers that form the bird's outline.

Coverts Small feathers that cover the bases of flight feathers.

Cursorial Specialized for running.

Dimorphic Existing in two distinct forms, such as variation in size or plumage coloration.

Diurnal Active during daylight hours.

Dorsal Back or upper side.

Ectothermic Having a variable body temperature through which body heat is derived from the external environment.

Edge effect The result of changes in ecological diversity which occur along the boundary between contrasting natural habitats.

Endothermic Having a constant high body temperature, where body heat is derived from internal metabolic processes.

Estuarine Relating to an estuary, where the sea extends inland to meet the mouth of a river.

Flash blindness Temporary impairment of vision resulting from an intense flash of light.

Frugivorous Fruit-eating.

Furcula The fused clavicles of a bird; the wishbone.

Genome The total of an organism's genetic material.

Habitat partitioning An ecological concept where similar species living in the same habitat use somewhat different subsets of resources to avoid competition with one another.

Hippocampus The part of the forebrain that plays a role in memory and spatial navigation.

Humerus The long bone in the upper forelimb that extends from shoulder to elbow.

Hyperphagia The act of eating to excess.

Hyperthermia Elevated body temperature.

Hypothalamus The lower part of the forebrain that regulates body temperature, biorhythms and other autonomic activities.

Hypothermia Low body temperature.

Infrasound Sound with a long-ranging frequency that is too low to be heard by the human ear; it emanates from natural phenomena such as severe weather, earthquakes and ocean waves.

Insectivorous Insect-eating.

Irruptive Involving massive irregular immigration of individuals to a particular region.

Latitudinal migration Seasonal movements of animals generally north and south.

Lipogenesis The conversion of consumed food into fat for storage.

Longitudinal migration Seasonal movements of animals generally east and west.

Manus The hand; in birds, the fused bones comprising the wingtip, where primary flight feathers are attached.

Melanin A naturally occurring pigment responsible for producing black and dark-brown coloration.

Molting The predictable and seasonal replacement of feathers.

Morphology The form and structure of an organism.

Neotropical Pertaining to the tropical regions of the Western Hemisphere, including Central America, South America and the West Indies.

Nucleotide A basic building block of DNA or RNA.

Ovoviviparous Producing eggs that are retained and hatched within the mother's body.

Paleoecology An ecological discipline that studies the interactions between ancient organisms and their environment.

Paleornithology The scientific study of fossil birds and avian evolution.

Parabronchi Tiny air tubules in the lungs of birds where gas exchange between blood and air occur.

Partial migration A situation where some birds from a breeding population migrate elsewhere for the nonbreeding season, while others remain on the breeding grounds year-round.

Pectoral girdle Bones of the shoulder that attach the forelimbs to the body.

Pectoralis major The largest flight muscle in birds, which powers the downstroke of the wing; it extends between the sternum and humerus.

Pelagic Pertaining to the open ocean.

Phenology The study of seasonal timing of biological events, such as flowering or breeding, and its relationship to climatic conditions.

Philopatry (natal) The tendency of an individual to return to its birthplace.

Photoperiod The daylight period of the daily cycle of day and night.

Phylogeny The evolutionary history of the origin and diversification of a group of organisms; it is typically depicted as a branching tree.

Phylum The second-largest standard category of taxonomic classification (after kingdom); it includes organisms sharing a fundamental pattern of organization (e.g., arthropods, mollusks, chordates).

Physiology The branch of science that deals with the biological functions of a living organism and its bodily parts.

Pineal gland An endocrine gland located in the brain; it produces melanin.

Plate tectonics The geological theory that explains large-scale movements of the earth's crustal plates; it encompasses the concepts of continental drift and sea-floor spreading.

Polyandry The mating system in which one female pairs with more than one male within a breeding season.

Polymorphic Occurring in several distinct forms within a population or species.

Posterior The hind end.

Prealternate molt Molt that occurs just prior to breeding in some bird species and which results in breeding plumage.

Prebasic molt Molt that typically replaces all or most of a bird's feathers, usually occurring annually after the breeding season.

Primaries Flight feathers attached to the manus of a bird; they generate forward thrust during the powered downstroke.

Pygostyle The fused caudal vertebrae (tailbone) of a bird to which the tail feathers attach.

Rachis The central supporting structure of a feather.

Radius The thinner of the two bones in the forelimb that extend from elbow to wrist.

Refugium An area where climate and vegetation remain unchanged historically although surrounding areas have varied considerably.

Remiges The flight feathers of the wing.

Retina The light-sensitive region at the back of the eyeball.

Rhodopsin A photopigment of the retina that may be sensitive to magnetic fields.

Riparian The area of interface between land and a river or stream where a distinctive community of plants and animals occurs.

Schleifenzug (**loop migration**) A migration route that is markedly different on outbound and return legs.

Secondaries The flight feathers attached to the ulna of a bird which generate lift.

Slotting Spaces between flight feathers of the wing that confer additional lift when opened.

STR (**short tandem repeat**) The fragment of DNA in which the nucleotide pattern exhibits short, repeated sequences.

Subduction A geological process in which the edge of one crustal plate is forced below an adjacent one.

Supracoracoideus The smaller flight muscle lying beneath the pectoralis that operates the recovery stroke of the wing.

Sympatric Living within the same local area.

Taiga Boreal forest; northern biome characterized by coniferous forest and nutrient-poor soils.

Tertials The feather group attached to the humerus that fills the space between the secondaries and the body.

Thermal A rising column of warm air used by soaring birds to gain elevation.

Theropod The lineage of bipedal, primarily carnivorous dinosaurs that gave rise to birds; it included tyrannosaurids and dromaeosaurids.

Torpor The temporary, energy-saving state of dormancy characterized by reduced body temperature and metabolic function.

Triosseal canal The bony structure in the pectoral girdle through which the supracoracoideus tendon passes. The triosseal canal allows the wing's recovery stroke (upstroke) to be effected by a muscle located on the bird's underside.

Tundra The northern, treeless biome characterized by permanently frozen soil (permafrost).

Ulna The thicker of the two bones in the forelimb that extend from elbow to wrist.

Vagrant A stray individual observed beyond the boundaries of its typical species' distribution.

Ventral The belly or underside.

Volant Capable of flying.

Wing flip The rapid recovery stroke of the wing during take off.

Zugunruhe Migratory restlessness; the state of elevated activity that indicates a bird's readiness to migrate.

FURTHER READING

Able, K.P. (ed.). 1999. *Gathering of Angels: Migrating Birds and Their Ecology.* Cornell University Press. Ithaca, NY. 193 pp.

Alerstam, T. 1990. *Bird Migration.* Cambridge University Press. Cambridge, UK. 420 pp.

Allen, E.G. 1951. *The History of American Ornithology before Audubon.* American Philosophical Society. Philadelphia, PA. 207 pp.

Aristotle. *History of Animals (Historia animalium),* books 7–10. Reprint, 1991. D.M. Balme, ed. Loeb Classical Library, Harvard University Press. Cambridge, MA. 605 pp.

Audubon, J.J. 1999. *John James Audubon: Writings and Drawings.* C. Irmscher, ed. Library of America. New York, NY. 928 pp.

Berthold, P. 1996. *Control of Bird Migration.* Springer-Verlag. New York, NY. 368 pp.

———. 2001. *Bird Migration: A General Survey.* Oxford University Press. Oxford, UK. 253 pp.

Berthold, P., E. Gwinner and E. Sonnenschein (eds.). 2003. *Avian Migration.* Springer-Verlag. New York, NY. 610 pp.

Bodsworth, F. 1998. *Last of the Curlews.* Counterpoint. Berkeley, CA. 192 pp.

Chiappe, L.M. 2007. *Glorified Dinosaurs: The Origin and Early Evolution of Birds.* John Wiley & Sons. Hoboken, NJ. 262 pp.

Cho, M. 2006. *Songbird Journeys: Four Seasons in the Lives of Migratory Birds.* Walker & Company. New York, NY. 224 pp.

Dingle, H. 1996. *Migration: The Biology of Life on the Move.* Oxford University Press. New York, NY. 480 pp.

Elphick, J. (ed.). 2007. *Atlas of Bird Migration: Tracing the Great Journeys of the World's Birds.* Firefly Books. Buffalo, NY. 176 pp.

Faaborg, J. 2002. *Saving Migrant Birds: Developing Strategies for the Future.* University of Texas Press. Austin, TX. 226 pp.

Frederick II Hohenstaufen. *On the Art of Hunting with Birds (De arte venandi cum avibus).* Reprint, 1943, as *The Art of Falconry.* Stanford University Press. Palo Alto, CA. 748 pp.

Gill, F.B. 2006. *Ornithology.* W.H. Freeman. New York, NY. 758 pp.

Greenberg, R., and P.P. Marra. 2005. *Birds of Two Worlds: The Ecology and Evolution of Migration.* Johns Hopkins University Press. Baltimore, MD. 466 pp.

Gwinner, E. (ed.). 1990. *Bird Migration: Physiology and Ecophysiology.* Springer-Verlag. New York, NY. 435 pp.

McGowan, C. 1999. *A Practical Guide to Vertebrate Mechanics.* Cambridge University Press. New York, NY. 301 pp.

Mead, C. 1983. *Bird Migration.* Facts on File. New York, NY. 224 pp.

Moller, A.P., W. Fiedler and P. Berthold. 2004. *Birds and Climate Change.* Elsevier. Amsterdam, Netherlands. 251 pp.

Newton, I. 2003. *The Speciation and Biogeography of Birds.* Academic Press. London, UK. 668 pp.

———. 2007. *The Migration Ecology of Birds.* Academic Press. London, UK. 984 pp.

Perrins, C.M., and T.R. Birkhead. 1983. *Avian Ecology.* Blackie & Sons. Glasgow, Scotland. 221 pp.

Pliny the Elder. *Natural History (Historia naturalis),* vol. 3, books 8–11. Reprint, 1962. W.H.S. Jones, trans. D.M. Balme, ed. Loeb Classical Library, Harvard University Press. Cambridge, MA. 368 pp.

Rappole, J.H. 1995. *The Ecology of Migrant Birds: A Neotropical Perspective.* Smithsonian Institution Press. Washington, DC. 288 pp.

Sibley, D.A. 2001. *The Sibley Guide to Bird Life and Behavior.* Alfred A. Knopf. New York, NY. 608 pp.

Stresemann, E. 1975. *Ornithology: From Aristotle to the Present.* Harvard University Press. Cambridge, MA. 432 pp.

Stutchbury, B. 2007. *Silence of the Songbirds.* HarperCollins. Toronto, ON. 256 pp.

Sutherland, W.J., I. Newton and R.E. Green. 2004. *Bird Ecology and Conservation: A Handbook of Techniques.* Oxford University Press. Oxford, UK. 386 pp.

Terborgh, J. 1989. *Where Have All the Birds Gone?: Essays on the Biology and Conservation of Birds That Migrate to the American Tropics.* Princeton University Press. Princeton, NJ. 224 pp.

Videler, J.J. 2005. *Avian Flight.* Oxford University Press. Oxford, UK. 258 pp.

Weidensaul, S. 1999. *Living on the Wind: Across the Hemisphere with Migratory Birds.* North Point Press. New York, NY. 420 pp.

Welty, J.C., and L.F. Baptista. 1988. *The Life of Birds.* Harcourt Brace. Orlando, FL. 768 pp.

PHOTO CREDITS

GENERAL INDEX

Page references in **bold** type indicate photographs.

SPECIES INDEX

Page references in **bold** type indicate photographs.